DIAGNOSTIC
PROBLEM
SOLVING

DIAGNOSTIC PROBLEM SOLVING

COMBINING HEURISTIC, APPROXIMATE AND CAUSAL REASONING

PIETRO TORASSO
AND
LUCA CONSOLE

VNR VAN NOSTRAND REINHOLD
_____ New York

First published in 1989 by North Oxford Academic
Publishers Ltd, a subsidiary of Kogan Page Ltd,
120 Pentonville Road, London N1 9JN

Published in the United States of America by
Van Nostrand Reinhold
115 Fifth Avenue, New York, NY 10003, USA

Distributed in Canada by
Macmillan of Canada
Division of Canada Publishing Corporation
164 Commander Boulevard
Agincourt, Ontario M1S 3C7, Canada

16 15 14 13 12 11 10 9 8 7 6 5 4 3 2 1

Library of Congress Number 88 - 33867
ISBN 0 - 442 - 23798 - 7

Printed and bound in Great Britain

Preface

This book is devoted to an analysis of diagnostic problem solving and to describing a set of Artificial Intelligence techniques that have been proposed to develop knowledge-based systems that can imitate (to some extent) the capabilities of a human expert exposed to a diagnostic problem.

Over the last decade, diagnosis has emerged as one of the most interesting tasks for Artificial Intelligence, both from a theoretical and a practical point of view. In this book we will review recent advances in diagnostic problem solving by describing some innovative approaches involving both "heuristic" and "deep" forms of reasoning, and by discussing the results of some in-depth analyses which have been carried out to determine the main characteristics of diagnostic problem solving in a variety of domains (medicine, digital circuits, troubleshooting, etc.).

In this book we aim to show that diagnostic problem solving is generally such a complex task that the use of a single form of representing knowledge and a single reasoning mechanism is not the most appropriate way to approach and solve the problem. We claim that a combination of different approaches (in particular a combination of "heuristic", "approximate" and "causal" reasoning) is technically possible, and that the resulting strategy resembles, to some extent, the way human experts approach and solve a diagnostic problem.

Therefore, the book concentrates on the description and analysis of the architecture of CHECK, a knowledge-based system developed at Dipartimento di Informatica dell'Universita` di Torino that is able to combine heuristic and causal reasoning in a diagnostic task. The CHECK project dates back to late 1985, but its architecture has been strongly influenced (especially regarding the organization of "heuristic" knowledge, the mechanism of "approximate" reasoning and the control strategy at the "heuristic" level) by the results obtained in the LITO project, developed between 1979 and 1985.

Most of the early work on approximate reasoning and knowledge-based systems carried out at the Dipartimento di Informatica dell'Universita` di Torino was co-authored with Prof. Leonardo Lesmo and Prof. Lorenza Saitta, while the adoption of Logic Programming techniques for implementing knowledge-based systems was proposed by Prof. Alberto Martelli and Dr. Gianfranco Rossi. The resulting architecture of a diagnostic system has evolved over time: the authors have benefited from discussions with many colleagues of the Artificial Intelligence group and with domain experts of different applications (electrical engineers, computer technicians, expert physicians).

The authors are deeply indebted to Prof. Gianpaolo Molino (Department of Biomedicine-Universita` di Torino) and to Dr. Cesare Cravetto (Ospedale San Giovanni-Torino) for their efforts in analyzing medical diagnostic problem solving, their willingness to make available their medical expertise and their patience in validating and revising knowledge sources. Other useful insights in the field of medical decision making, particularly concerning the requirements of man-machine interface design are thanks to Prof. A. Rocha and his group at the Universidad Estadual de Campinas-Campinas (Brazil).

Many students cooperated in the implementation of the CHECK prototype; among them, the authors are especially indebted to Mauro Fossa, Anna Furno, Roberta Pavia, Luigi Portinale, Marco Signorello and Daniele Theseider.

Finally, many thanks to Dr. Ladislav Kohout for encouraging us to write this book and for his helpful suggestions and many thanks to the editorial staff of Kogan Page for their patient work in improving the readability of the book.

However, responsibility for the final shape and content of the book lies entirely with the authors.

The research described herein has been supported by many organizations, most particularly the C.N.R (National Research Council) via the Strategic Projects on "Expert Systems", "Expert Systems in Medicine" and "Medical Informatics", the Ministero della Pubblica Istruzione via the ASSI project, and the Regione Piemonte via Progetto Finalizzato Sanita'.

Pietro Torasso, Luca Console
Dipartimento di Informatica
Universita` di Torino

CONTENTS

CONTENTS

1

INTRODUCTION

Interest in automatic problem solving techniques has grown considerably since the first seminal works presented in the late 50's and early 60's [Newell et al. 59]. Much research has been carried out on subjects such as "representing" the problem to be solved, defining strategies for searching for solutions and defining heuristics to guide these strategies (for an overview of the most interesting results of such research see [Nilsson 71]). The problems faced by the first "problem solving systems" were very simple ones (for example "puzzles"), so the techniques used to represent the problem to be solved in a computer program were very primitive.

When researchers tried to apply such problem solving techniques to real-world problems, they discovered that the techniques were too limited. In particular, the schemes of representation designed for simple problems were not adequate, since "knowledge" is needed to solve complex (real-world) problems. Rather complex forms of heuristics, similar to those commonly used by human problem solvers, are needed.

Such observations led to new trends in research. Special interest was paid to the design of "knowledge-based problem solving systems" and, among them, of expert systems. These were systems that were supposed to mimic the behavior and performance of human experts in solving problems in limited domains, and they have held a prominent position since the early 70's.

Different types of tasks performed by human experts were considered and techniques for solving them using a computer program were studied (an interesting overview of expert problem solving tasks is reported in [Stefik et al. 82] and then, in a more extended form, in [Hayes-Roth et al. 84], in which the major problems associated with each task are discussed). Among the major tasks "data interpretation", "monitoring and interpretation of signals", "planning", "design and configuration" and "classification and diagnosis" have received much attention in the past few years.

Diagnosis, in particular, has been one of the major subjects of research in Artificial Intelligence and in the expert systems community since the early 70's. Adopting the "operational" definition given in [Stefik et al. 82] (page 137): "Diagnosis is the process of fault-finding in a system (or determination of a disease state in a living system) based on the interpretation of potentially noisy data". Diagnostic problems were considered in many different domains, from troubleshooting in electronic (or electric) appliances and circuits (or, more generally, in simple artifacts), to diagnosis of complex mechanical or physical systems, to medical diagnosis. Although apparently very different, all the diagnostic domains have many aspects in common and roughly the same problems have to be solved:

- Single-fault versus multiple-fault diagnosis. Searching for single-fault solutions is simpler but can be too limited in many cases, so techniques for multiple-fault diagnosis have to be devised (taking into account problems such as the interaction between faults and their effects on the external manifestations that can be observed in a system).
- Interpretation and abstraction of data, i.e. of the manifestations observed in the system to be diagnosed. In many cases, in fact, observed data must be abstracted in a form that can be directly used by the program.
- Observed data are often noisy and uncertain.
- Very often measurements in the system to be diagnosed that could directly confirm a diagnostic hypothesis are very dangerous and expensive.

Many diagnostic expert systems have been developed since the early 70's and have been operating in different domains. Each one of the systems which has been developed is based on a particular formalism for knowledge representation and a particular scheme for inference, but from the conceptual aspect most of them are based on a "classification scheme" [Clancey 85][Bylander & Mittal 86]. As has been recently recognized by Clancey in his analysis of knowledge-based systems and problem solving [Clancey 85], the task faced by these systems can be redirected to a unifying scheme: the "Heuristic Classification" scheme.

Almost all the systems developed during the 70's were based only on the representation of heuristic knowledge, that is heuristic relationships between findings of the system to be diagnosed and possible diagnoses. This approach proved very useful and led to the development of systems with good diagnostic performances, in limited domains. On the other hand, these systems exhibited severe limitations in many demanding tasks [Steels 85][Partridge 87], such as explanation capabilities or knowledge acquisition, which prompted, starting from the late 70's and early 80's, the development of a new generation of expert systems (Second Generation Expert Systems [Hart 82][Clancey 85] [Steels 85]). The aim of these expert systems is to reason on representations of the physical system to be diagnosed which are at a deeper level than those used in heuristic systems. More specifically, causal models of the behavior of the system and/or models of its structure and function are generally used. With these types of systems many of the problems arising in systems based only on heuristic classification are solved, but other problems arise (inefficiency for example). For this reason, many researchers argue nowadays that the building of systems that combine heuristic and deep reasoning is an interesting possibility. This combination should include most of the advantages of both pure heuristic and deep systems.

In this book, after a brief introduction on the scheme of heuristic classification and on the major proposals for deep modelling and reasoning, we shall have a detailed description of CHECK (Combining HEuristic and Causal Knowledge), a two-level diagnostic architecture combining heuristic and causal reasoning we have developed over the last few years [Molino et al. 86][Torasso & Console 87] [Console & Torasso 88c][Console & Torasso 88e][Console & Torasso 89].

1.1 DIAGNOSTIC EXPERT SYSTEMS

In a recent deep analysis of the task performed by expert systems, Clancey [Clancey 83][Clancey 85] has recognized that in many cases they solve problems using a *classification* approach. Certainly diagnostic systems belong to such a class of systems - that is, in general, they are able to produce diagnoses relating data to a pre-enumerated set of possible solutions through a process that can be more or less sophisticated or complex.

More specifically, a particular form of classification is adopted by expert systems, based on heuristic forms of match between data and solutions, i.e. they use heuristic reasoning in their inference process. Moreover, it is important to point out that the main characteristic which distinguish expert systems from other types of programs (e.g. statistical classification programs) is that with expert systems there is an explicit representation of knowledge about their domain of competence, so the classification process is based on forms of reasoning on such knowledge bases.

Three different steps can be recognized in the process of heuristic classification:

-   *Data abstraction.* In this phase data provided to the system are abstracted in a form which can be directly used by the system itself. Different types of abstractions can be made: for example, quantitative descriptions may be transformed into qualitative ones, or definitions may be applied to abstract concepts from data. Usually "factual" or "definitional" knowledge is used in the data abstraction process and no uncertainty is introduced.

-   *Heuristic match.* This is the step which strongly characterizes heuristic classification with respect to "simple classification". In the latter case, in fact, the process of classification is immediate, that is, given an unknown object and a set of classes of known objects (of which, for example, a stereotypical description is given), the problem is to recognize to which class the unknown object belongs (using parametric, e.g. measurement of features or non-parametric, e.g. distance criteria, approaches [Hunt 75]). The peculiarity of heuristic classification is that, generally, the classes in the classification hierarchy represent objects which are not of the same type as those built during the data abstraction process. For example, to clarify the point, consider the case of medical diagnosis: data abstraction produces models of the patient, while the classification hierarchy is constituted of descriptions of diseases. This means that a direct match is not possible and complex relationships between data and solutions have to be represented (domain knowledge) and forms of reasoning on *domain knowledge* are needed. It is the representation of such relationships (heuristic knowledge) and the need for reasoning strategies which characterize the heuristic classification method. It is worth noting that heuristic relationships are often uncertain since they are only able to capture the stereotypical and most common characteristics exhibited by the objects of a given class. As a consequence, some form of approximate reasoning has to be adopted to deal with them.

-   *Refinement.* Usually the diagnostic hypotheses considered by a system can be described at different levels of abstraction. This means that, in general, a "generalization/specialization" relationship holds among the "classes" used to interpret (classify) a given case. For example, in a medical application one can define a class "liver diseases" and a class "hepatitis", which is clearly a specialization of the class "liver diseases". The aim of the "match phase" of the heuristic classification process is to find a class which describes the case under examination. On the other hand, the aim of the "refinement phase" is to specialize the hypothesized class to find a more accurate interpretation. In other words, the refinement process allows precise solutions to be reached from the abstraction generated in the heuristic match phase: it consists mainly of reasoning on the classification hierarchy.

Some points concerning the scheme of heuristic classification are worth making. This scheme is, in a certain sense, misleading since it suggests that the whole heuristic classification process is a sequential one in which, first, data abstraction is performed, followed by heuristic match and refinement in a rigid order. Moreover, it suggests that the process is always data-driven, which is certainly not true. A rigid sequential heuristic classification scheme can be very limited (although it has been applied in some early systems): in many cases it is necessary to apply more complex inference strategies in which forward (data-driven) and backward (goal-driven) steps are combined. In particular, "*hypothesize and test*" approaches have often been used in which the stages of the generation of (diagnostic) hypotheses from data and of the testing of such hypotheses (which involves further reasoning on data) are interleaved [Erman et al. 80]. This means that heuristic classification is far more complex than the scheme discussed above. In particular, complex inference and control strategies to deal with data and with the generation and testing of hypotheses are needed, especially to solve interesting real-world problems.

It is important to point out once again that not all the problems faced by expert systems can be matched to the heuristic classification scheme. In fact there are other categories of problems which cannot be solved using this approach - for example, planning, monitoring and design [Stefik et al. 82][Hayes-Roth et al. 84]. Moreover, although diagnosis is classically solved through classification, there are cases in which this approach is too limited to produce good results [Szolovits 85]: an example is when it is not possible to enumerate all the possible combinations of diseases that have to be considered to produce a multiple diagnosis (a more detailed discussion of the limitations of the heuristic classification approach will appear in the next section).

As noted earlier, Clancey's analysis is a very general and conceptual one. It abstracts completely from the specific techniques that can be adopted to put heuristic classification into practice. Many different approaches have been used (and are used) to solve this problem, and these are based on different schemes for knowledge representation and reasoning. Clancey [Clancey 85] surveys some systems and analyzes the specific problems they solve in terms of the general scheme of heuristic classification.

A different analysis of the tasks performed by "Knowledge Based Systems" has recently been presented by Chandrasekaran [Chandrasekaran 83] [Chandrasekaran 87]. Chandrasekaran's analysis is more general than

Clancey's since it concerns knowledge based systems and problem solving in general, whilst Clancey's is mainly concerned with the classification task (nevertheless great attention is paid in Chandrasekaran's works to the diagnostic task).

The starting point of Chandrasekaran's analysis is that the abstraction level of most knowledge representation languages (such as rules, frames and semantic networks) is inadequate to describe knowledge and strategies for complex problem solving. He proposes a more conceptual level of analysis at which different "tasks" (the so-called "Generic Tasks" [Chandrasekaran 87]), involving different types of knowledge representation formalisms and reasoning strategies, can be recognized and defined. More specifically, each task is characterized primarily by its "function", its formalism for organizing and representing knowledge and its inference strategy. In this way a complex system is formed by a collection of co-operating tasks (functional units).

This general approach has been specialized by Chandrasekaran and his colleagues on diagnostic problem solving. In [Chandrasekaran 87] [Josephson et al. 87] the general structure of a diagnostic system based on the interaction of different tasks is outlined. More specifically, a scheme of *hierarchical classification* (based on the establish-refine cycle [Chandrasekaran & Mittal 83a]) is proposed. In such a scheme different tasks co-operate to generate diagnostic hypotheses - in particular, a "structure matcher task" is responsible for the verification of each diagnostic hypothesis, a "data-base management task" is responsible for the inferences on data (e.g. data abstraction) and an "abductive assembler task" is responsible for generating diagnostic hypotheses (multiple-fault diagnoses) by taking into account the different types of relationships between them. This conceptual analysis has been put into practice in the design of two specific systems: MDX [Chandrasekaran & Mittal 83a] and RED [Josephson et al. 87]. Moreover, the "Generic tasks" approach has led to the design of different tools and languages for describing knowledge within each task and problem solving activity. As far as diagnosis is concerned this has led to the design of CSRL [Bylander & Mittal 86], a conceptual language for hierarchical classification problem solving.

Other interesting analyses of knowledge based systems can be found in [Stefik et al. 82] [Hayes-Roth et al. 84][Johnson & Keravnou 85] [Kohout & Bandler 86]; more specific descriptions of the diagnostic systems developed during the 70's in medical domains have been recently published in the survey books edited by Szolovits [Szolovits 82], Clancey and Shortliffe [Clancey & Shortliffe 84] and Buchanan and Shortliffe [Buchanan & Shortliffe 84].

In the following, we shall give a brief overview of the main techniques and approaches that have been adopted in building diagnostic expert systems, mentioning the most significant examples of systems. Before overviewing such different approaches, it is worth considering the fact that the choice of a particular knowledge representation formalism and inference strategy in a particular application depends on many different factors such as the type of problem, the type of knowledge elicitation method used and the type of use of the system [Wielinga & Breuker 86], thus the ideas we shall put forward are very general (this means that a real and meaningful comparison between different approaches should be made considering the problems and needs of each specific application).

The simpler and one of the more widely adopted schemes for knowledge representation in diagnostic systems is that based on the use of *production rules* [Davis & King 77]. Starting from MYCIN [Shortliffe 76], many other systems have been built based on this approach, in which heuristic relationships between data and diagnostic hypotheses (classes in the classification hierarchy) are represented by means of **IF ... THEN ...** structures. Within this scheme different types of inference strategies can be defined - for example, goal-driven (backward) and data-driven (forward) ones.

At first glance, production rules seem to be a very natural and easy to use scheme of knowledge representation:

- they are modular, so they are (or are supposed to be) easily modifiable;
- they represent "normative knowledge" in a very natural way;
- it is easy to build mechanisms for uncertain reasoning and for generating explanations.

On the other hand, a deeper analysis of the formalism indicates that many problems arise in their use [Aikins 83]; for example:

- the formalism is very flat and a great number of rules are needed to model real-world domains;
- they do not permit the natural representation of "descriptive knowledge";
- in many cases it is necessary to insert predicates implicitly to represent control information in the premise part of a rule so the rules which result are very difficult to understand and modify.

A more complex and interesting formalism for knowledge representation that is widely used in diagnostic expert systems is the "*frame*" formalism, originally proposed by Minsky [Minsky 75]. The very general idea of the formalism is to represent prototypical knowledge - that is, each frame can be used to represent a diagnostic hypothesis in the classification hierarchy in a stereotypical way. It follows that a hierarchy of frames can be used to represent the classification hierarchy of diagnostic hypotheses, and heuristic reasoning corresponds to searching in the frame system for a frame (or for more than one frame) which can be instantiated (successfully matched) to actual data (data abstractions). Obviously different approaches and strategies can be adopted both for searching in the frame system and for matching prototypical descriptions against data.

Frame structures are particularly suitable for diagnostic applications; in particular:

-    they permit prototypical descriptions of diagnostic hypotheses in a very modular way;

-    they can be easily modified in an independent way;

-    they allow a good representation of "descriptive knowledge" which is very important with such problems (but they are lacking in the representation of "normative knowledge").

Conversely, the main problem is that of giving a precise and formal definition of the reasoning process to be used in a frame system, especially as regards the operation of heuristic (and approximate) match of prototypical descriptions and data is concerned (some attempt towards such a formalization has been recently made - see, for example, [Reggia et al. 83][Peng & Reggia 87]).

Analysis of the problems deriving from the use of production rules and frames suggested, around the end of the 70's, the possibility of investigating combining the two formalisms into a more powerful hybrid formalism. The combination can be obtained in different ways (e.g. using frames to partition sets of rules, or introducing rules in prototypical descriptions) and it enables the exploitation of the advantages of both formalisms. The approach was first proposed by Aikins in the CENTAUR system [Aikins 83] and by Engelman in the KNOBS system [Engelman & Stanton 84]. Since then, hybrid knowledge representation formalisms have been widely studied and adopted in many systems. Moreover, almost all the evolved and powerful tools for developing expert systems which have been recently proposed are based on hybrid formalisms for knowledge representation (see, for example, KEE [Fikes & Kehler 85]).

The description we have given is a very brief (and certainly incomplete) one. However, this only shows that very different approaches have been adopted for the design of heuristic diagnostic expert systems, approaches that can be recognized as special cases of the general scheme of "heuristic classification". In the following sections we shall discuss the limitations of the heuristic approach which have led to the development of new models for diagnostic expert systems (so called "*deep models*" [Hart 82]).

1.2 APPROXIMATE REASONING

Many decisions taken by a human expert are not "certain"; in other words, there are very often cases where no single choice is possible but the expertise of the human expert, his/her knowledge of previous similar situations, his/her ability to balance the evidence coming from different kinds of findings, are of paramount importance in choosing the correct line of behavior. In complex problems, a variety of factors makes categorical reasoning often inapplicable:

- The uncertainty inherent in the knowledge itself (in many cases the domain cannot be modelled via causal relations relating a situation to a given state, so the relationships are associational in nature and derived from experience).

- The noise and the lack of accuracy affecting the data. In fact, in many cases the user cannot be absolutely precise in providing the system with data describing the particular case under examination. This is especially true in medicine since some of the clinical data are elicited just by questioning the patient, while others can be obtained by means of a physical examination and are, therefore, (at least partly) subjective.

- The stochastic uncertainty due to noise and intrinsic variability.

- The fuzziness arising from using the same linguistic terms for describing slightly different situations.

- The different relevance of various pieces of information in arriving at a final decision.

In order to deal with these different aspects of "uncertainty" different models have been proposed and investigated: they range from pure heuristic methods (where "heuristic" is used to denote rather *ad hoc* methods) to very formalized ones. We believe that in order to explain the choices we have used in developing approximate reasoning techniques, we have to compare merits and defects along different parameters:

- Mathematical basis; that is, the possibility of defining a precise semantic from a logical and mathematical point of view. The formal definition should help the user in estimating the final result (that is, the global evidence degree), given the evidence degrees of the single components of the system to.be modelled.

- An intuitive semantics; since in most cases the diagnostic expert system and the human user have to co-operate in reaching a solution, the

formalism adopted in the diagnostic system should be easily understandable by the human user.

-   The robustness. Again, in real cases no one can provide perfect esti-
    mates of the model's various types of parameters that represent the
    uncertainty, noise and fuzziness in the system. Therefore, the diagnos-
    tic expert system should reach the same conclusion even in cases where
    the values of the parameters have to be slightly changed; in other
    words, the behavior of the system should not be too sensitive to the
    values of the parameters.

The problem of dealing with uncertainty in expert systems has generated
a lot of attention in the past few years. Apart from the non-numeric methods
(typical examples are Truth Maintenance Systems [Doyle 79][de Kleer 86]
and the Theory of Endorsement [Cohen 86]; a more detailed discussion on
these methods takes place in the following pages), there are at least three
classes of approaches that have been adopted to model the uncertainty associated with many human activities:

-   probabilistic approaches;

-   approaches based on Dempster-Shafer's theory of evidence;

-   approaches based on fuzzy logic.

Probability theory is the most classical theory to use to model uncertainty. But is probability theory psychologically plausible? It has very strong
mathematical limitations; its results are only valid in cases where there are
strict constraints on data independence and perfect knowledge about the
hypothesis space (that is, the hypotheses should be mutually exclusive and the
set of hypotheses has to be exhaustive). Another common point concerns the
difficulty of providing (either via statistical inference from a large sample or
via human experience) the large amount of parameter values that are necessary for Bayesian classification (see [Szolovits & Pauker 78] and [Halpern &
Rabin 87] for an in-depth discussion). Moreover, the assignment of values to
parameters may be critical, since small errors in the "local" evaluations may
result in very large errors in the final result. Although probability theory is
suitable for modelling the stochastic uncertainty, it does not lend itself to
representing approximate data that are usually characterized by linguistic
terms like "high", "normal", etc. These are not reasons for rejecting probability theory in toto, but they must be considered carefully before accepting it as
a practically viable model (remember again that the model must meet the
behavior of a human; if its constraints are too strong to be met by human
behavior, this is a serious defect of the model itself). For a discussion of probabilistic approaches see, for instance, [Charniak 83] [Spiegelhalter & Knill-
Jones 84] [Cheeseman 85] [Nilsson 86].

As regards Dempster-Shafer's theory of evidence [Shafer 76], this tries, starting from probability, to model uncertainty in a more sophisticated way while offering mathematical soundness. In fact, the main contribution of this theory concerns the different treatment of lack of knowledge (that is, "ignorance") with respect to balanced evidence. For example, if we have two possible different hypotheses, H_1 and H_2, which are mutually exclusive and have the same a priori probability, then they are assigned the probability value 0.5. If, after a number of measurements, we get equal evidence for both of them then their probability remains unchanged. On the contrary, evidence theory introduces a third element, i.e. the set including both hypotheses, and associates with it a value representing "ignorance" about the problem, which decreases when more data are available. Correspondingly, the evidences of the two hypotheses increase but maintain equal values.

Another important characteristic of the theory of evidence regards its ability to avoid the restriction (valid in the Bayesian approach) that commitment of belief to a hypothesis implies commitment of the residual part of belief not attributed to H to the negation of H. This is particularly important in diagnostic reasoning since in many cases the observation of an event strongly supports a hypothesis H, whilst the absence of observation does not stand against that hypothesis.

Although the theory of evidence has many nice features, there are severe problems attached to its actual use. Apart from some problems arising from the formula used for combining evidence (see [Zadeh 86] for further discussion), the theory of evidence requires (in the same way as the Bayesian approach) the hypotheses to be exhaustive and mutually exclusive. This prevents its application in some cases since this assumption cannot be verified in some domains. However, the major drawback of this approach regards its computational complexity that makes it intractable to computers. It must, however, be noted that some attempts to reduce this complexity have been made [Barnett 81], but the simplifications that have been introduced have some drawbacks with respect to completeness and perspicuity; other researchers (see, for example, [Gordon & Shortliffe 85]) have introduced a hierarchical organization to impose more structure on the domain and to limit the problem (see [Glymour 85] and [Pearl 86] for an alternative view based on probability theory).

The last approach we will discuss is based on fuzzy logic [Zadeh 78] [Zadeh 83]. The main advantage of this approach is its intuitive semantics (which does not rule out the possibility of providing a rather precise semantic). The ability of fuzzy logic to deal with various sources of uncertainty in a homogeneous way, the clear and sound representation of imprecise data and the possibility of defining linguistic variables suggest that it should be adopted as a basic tool for modelling approximate reasoning (see [Negoita 85] for a survey of the application of fuzzy logic to expert systems). Some problems may arise in selecting the precise mathematical formula used for representing the semantics of fuzzy logical connectives. In fact, different definitions may lead to different numerical results; this does not matter from a theoretical point of view, but may have a strong impact on the user who may find some results surprising. For example, the usual semantics of the logical connectives AND and OR is given in terms of "Min" and "Max" respectively. Let us suppose that we have various sources of evidence confirming a given hypothesis with various degrees of certainty. Then, it is possible to select the source giving the maximum evidence and to disregard all other data (since the maximum would not change). This seems counter-intuitive in the sense that the existence of more supporting evidence should always positively contribute to the total evidence to be associated with a given hypothesis. Obviously this is not a drawback of the approach in fact, it is sufficient to select another definition in order to avoid the problems mentioned above (see [Lesmo, Saitta, Torasso 85] for a possible solution or [Weber 83] for an in-depth analysis), but it highlights the necessity of an accurate analysis of the domain requirements in order to select an appropriate definition. Notice, however, that an experimental study investigating how people evaluate complex formulae involving logical connectives showed a significant discrepancy with respect to fuzzy logic, at least as regards the AND connective [Greco & Rocha 87].

It is worth noting that the approaches introduced above have not always been adopted in their pure form in the implementation of expert systems. Many systems have adopted a mixed approach - that is to say, some of the underlying mechanisms have been substituted by heuristic methods. A notable example is provided by "Subjective Bayesian Probabilities" [Duda, Hart, Nilsson 76] (adopted in the PROSPECTOR system [Duda 80]), where the human expert has to provide the system with a large number of a priori and conditional probabilities that are used to obtain the a posteriori probability of a hypothesis on the basis of some relevant observations. Even further from the three approaches previously described is the "Confirmation Theory" [Shortliffe & Buchanan 75] used in the MYCIN expert system [Shortliffe 76]; although some changes were made to the basic tools for combining evidences [Buchanan & Shortliffe 84], "Confirmation Theory" still remains a classic example of a "heuristic" method, i.e. a method having a more intuitive than theoretical basis. Its lack of soundness is acknowledged by its inventors, who are studying alternative methods [Gordon & Shortliffe 85].

The presentation above has necessarily been very concise; the interested reader may refer to [Szolovits & Pauker 78] [Adlassnig 82] [Charniak 83] [Prade 85] [Bonissone & Tong 85] [Lesmo, Saitta, Torasso 85] [Weber 83] in order to get more details on methods of combining evidence.

A final comment concerns the approach based on "endorsements" [Cohen 86], in which the uncertainty is not modelled by numeric values but by a set of justifications of the conclusions; the work of Cohen provides a rich set of arguments against the use of probability theory (as well as of other "numerical approaches") in expert systems. This work can be seen as an intermediate solution between the approaches aimed at modelling real problems at a heuristic level (therefore taking into account phenomena such as noise, uncertainty, etc.) and the ones which try to model complex (but in some cases artificial) domains in a deep fashion. In the latter case the researchers have to face the problem that additional information may contradict previous conclusions, so some mechanism of revision of belief is necessary. Various sorts of non-monotonic logics have been proposed [Bobrow 80] [Genesereth and Nilsson 87]: none of them makes use of numeric values for modelling the evidence degree.

Particularly interesting, with respect to approximate reasoning, are the non-monotonic logic approaches to reasoning about "likelihood" (see, for example, [Halpern & Rabin 87] in which a modal operator L, representing the "likelihood" of a formula, has been introduced and in which it is possible to reason about "different levels of likelihood" represented through the iteration of the operator L, that is $L^2,...,L^n$).

Even if the approaches based on non-monotonic logic may appear quite different from the ones used for approximate reasoning, there has recently been a growing interest in analyzing their relationships. Interesting results have been obtained by Yager [Yager 87] who shows how a mechanism derived from fuzzy logic can solve the problem of default-reasoning, and by Ruspini [Ruspini 87] who has proposed a logical foundation of probability theory by means of non-standard logics. The last remark concerns the difference of assumption between the two approaches: usually the non-numeric formalisms can be applied just in cases in which a deep model is available, that is a complete formalization of the system in term of axioms is available.

1.3 SECOND GENERATION EXPERT SYSTEMS

Diagnostic expert systems based on the paradigm of Heuristic Classification have proven to have interesting diagnostic performances in limited domains (see, for example, [Buchanan & Shortliffe 84] for a discussion of the accuracy of MYCIN advice, or [Miller et al. 82] for a discussion of the performances of INTERNIST), but they did show severe limitations in some demanding tasks.

The major problem with these systems concerns their explanation capabilities, since they cannot provide the user with more than very simple explanations (e.g. the display of their discovery path or of some instantiated prototypical structure). This limitation is inherent in the scheme of heuristic classification, i.e. it does not depend on the adoption of a particular approach to knowledge representation (e.g. production rules or frames or hybrid structures) or a particular problem solving strategy (e.g. data-driven or goal-driven or "hypothesize and test").

Heuristic classification corresponds to the behavior of a domain expert who can solve most of the problems that he/she faces simply by using the experience (that is, "heuristic rules") gained in solving similar cases. When he/she has to explain his/her choices, he/she must use different forms of knowledge, i.e. deep, precise models of the structure, function and behavior of the system he/she is concerned with. To be more precise, consider a simple example: suppose your car breaks down on a motorway on a hot day and will not start, and suppose, in a previous case, in a similar situation, you had solved the problem by pouring cold water on the oil-pump; your experience would heuristically suggest to you that you should do this again, but it cannot explain to another person the mechanical reasons why pouring cold water makes the engine start again (or even if there are other cases in which the same solution can be applied to a non starting car). These explanations derive from different sources of knowledge, e.g. a model of the structure and behavior (function) of an engine. Similarly, in more complex domains experience plays a very important role. Consider, for example, an expert physician: when he/she is analyzing a new case, he/she is often able to provide a diagnosis by considering the analogies with previous cases he/she has solved. But suppose now he/she needs to provide an explanation to a non-expert physician: certainly he/she cannot limit the explanation to a list of rules from experience. In such a case the listener would be unlikely to be convinced about the correctness of the diagnosis or even to understand the reasons for the advice and, consequently could tend to reject it. Moreover, he/she can learn nothing from the expert, i.e. he/she certainly does not improve his/her ability. For such reasons expert physicians provide different kinds of explanations, in terms of deeper knowledge, involving the pathophysiological status of the patient.

The consequences of such limited explanations, based only on heuristic models borrowed from experience, can be dramatic in a knowledge based system. In fact, users who are provided with a system which gives advice without explaining it appropriately tend to refuse to use the system itself. It is necessary for users to understand the (deep) motivations of the advice and to follow the line of reasoning of the system in terms of deep comprehension of the status of the diagnosed system. In this way they can rationally compare themselves with the system and accept it as a consultant. The problem is even greater when a diagnostic system is used for tutoring purposes [Richer & Clancey 85] and very deep and clear explanations are needed to enable a student to actually verify his/her comprehension of a domain (problem) and acquire new expertise.

The inability to produce effective explanations is certainly the major limitation of heuristic systems, but it is not the only one. Another problem directly concerns their diagnostic behavior (or, in other words, their diagnostic performances). We noted before that heuristic classification corresponds to diagnosing through experience, i.e. by analyzing the analogies in the set of "data-diagnoses" relationships between the new case and previously encountered ones. There are some cases in which experience does not work, either suggesting no idea for a particular case under examination or producing too many plausible different diagnoses. This typically happens when unusual or "difficult" cases are presented to a system - that is heuristic systems often have very good performances on "typical cases" but their ability rapidly decreases when different cases are considered. A typical example of such a situation is when a system produces several answers to a given problem with similar confidence (probability) degrees (low or high), and thus the user cannot get any help or guidance. Again, the limitation is not directly addressable to the choice of a particular knowledge representation formalism or to the adoption of particular functions for evidence combination. In this case, as in the previous one, the analysis of human experts' behavior suggests that deep knowledge can be used to solve the problem. This means that when their experience fails to produce a diagnosis, human experts start to consider the problem they are concerned with in a different and deeper way. Physicians, for example, start to analyze the deep status of the patient and to reason in terms of causal/temporal relationships between pathophysiological states.

A further problem of heuristic expert systems concerns the phase of knowledge acquisition. The schemes of knowledge representation used in these systems are not natural for domain experts to express their expertise. Moreover, in such models domain knowledge has to be intermixed with spurious information (e.g. to guide or influence control as in the case of production rules). This often makes the process of designing, maintaining and modifying a knowledge based system difficult. On the contrary, the design of deep models based on causal/temporal or functional/behavioral relationships is simpler and more natural for domain experts, since such forms of knowledge are closer to their traditional cultural and reasoning background. This has further important consequences: (1) domain experts other than those who directly developed a system can more easily comprehend the knowledge model adopted (this is often quite difficult when heuristic models are used) [Steels 85]; (2) there is greater agreement on the "soundness" and "correctness" of the model itself. In a certain sense, whilst a heuristic model is subjective, since it derives from the specific experiences of the human expert who designed it and combines both domain knowledge and information about its effective use, deep models are objective, in the sense that they are models of the structure and behavior (function) of the physical (physiological) system to be diagnosed.

It should be clear from this brief discussion that diagnostic expert systems need to rely on other forms of knowledge than mere heuristics to improve both their diagnostic performances and their acceptability in application environments. This need has been felt since the beginning of the eighties and several efforts have been made towards the design of schemes of representation and reasoning for such forms of knowledge. The presentation that follows is not strictly chronological in the sense that we will first outline some of the major proposals for dealing with various kinds of deep knowledge, then we will sketch the effective applications in the field of expert systems design.

1.3.1 CAUSAL AND DEEP MODELS

One of the most interesting forms of knowledge for "Second Generation Expert Systems" is *causal knowledge*. Causal/temporal relationships can be effectively used to describe the behavior of the modelled system in a very precise way. Before starting to consider the main approaches proposed so far to represent causal knowledge in "Second generation Expert Systems", a comment is needed to clarify the following description.

In many cases in the literature the terms "deep models" and "causal models" are used as synonyms, creating some misunderstanding. The point is that in almost all cases the deep models that have been used (particularly in diagnostic systems) are causal ones, in the sense that they are based on the representation of causal relationships. It is important to consider, however, that a causal model (or a causal relationship) is not necessarily a deep one. As an example, consider the problem of building a causal model for a medical diagnostic expert system. The relationship:

$$\text{hepatitis} \rightarrow \text{liver pain}$$

is a typical causal relationship, but it is not a deep one (rather, it can be considered as a heuristic one).

The idea is that a deep (causal) model should involve not only relationships between diagnostic hypotheses and observable data, but that it should describe the actual behavior of the modelled system as well [Hart 82]. It should be clear that this requirement is a very general one and that deep models to describe the behavior of a given physical or physiological system can be built at different levels of abstraction.

Causal models have been used in the last few years in the design of some diagnostic expert systems. One of the most interesting examples of the use of causal (but not deep) models in diagnostic problem solving is that proposed by Reggia [Reggia et al. 83][Peng & Reggia 87]. In this approach, knowledge is represented by means of causal relationships between observations (findings) and diagnostic hypotheses. The aim of the control strategy is to determine the minimal set of diagnostic hypotheses which covers the data observed in a particular case under examination ("parsimonious covering set" approach [Reggia et al. 83]). The approach is certainly very interesting (in particular since it proposes a solution to the multiple-diagnoses problem in a rather formal way), but it still suffers from most of the limitations typical of the heuristic systems.

More interesting for the purpose of "Second Generation Expert Systems" is the problem of representing and dealing with *deep causal knowledge*. By using such a form of knowledge, one can describe the behavior of a particular system in a very precise way. In particular, the interest is generally in representing faulty behavior, since the model of correct behavior is often too complex (e.g. consider the case of a medical domain). From a very abstract point of view, a causal model[1] consists of the representation of the possible states of a system (mechanical, physical or physiological) and of the relationships between these states. The kinds of relationships can be different depending on the particular domain of application; among them, cause-effect relationships, correlations between states and their external manifestations (observable effects), states and diagnostic hypotheses and states and their external perturbation causes play an important role. Moreover, it is often necessary to represent the temporal information about the relationships, e.g. the delay between the arising of a state and that of its consequences.

Different forms of reasoning can be performed on causal models. A simple possibility is that of analyzing the consequences of an (external) perturbation on a system under specific conditions or, conversely, that of searching for the possible causes of some particular state.

---

[1] In the rest of the paragraph we will use the terms "deep models" and "causal models" in an interchangeable way, to mean "deep causal model".

Let us consider now, from a very abstract and general point of view, how a causal model can be used in a diagnostic system. We have noted earlier that one can build a model of correct or of faulty behavior: this obviously has a great impact on how diagnosis can be performed. In the former case, in fact, the reasoning component has to search out which states in the system under examination differ from the expected behavior and then has to find the causes of such anomalies. As an example, consider the (simple) model of a mechanical system reported in figure 1.1. If it is discovered that a particular engine does not work regularly, one can deduce that this could have been caused by the abnormality of one of the states "lubricating_oil_temperature regular", "water_temperature regular", "oil present", since these states are

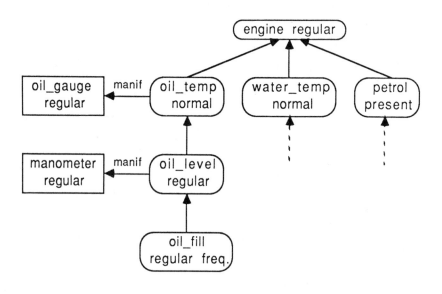

Figure 1.1 - A causal model of the correct behavior of a mechanical system.

normal in a correctly functioning engine. The original cause of the malfunction can be discovered by analyzing which of these states is, in fact, not regular (by considering their causing states or by a direct observation, if they are observable). For an example of a diagnostic approach based on this method see [Steels & Van de Velde 85] [Van de Velde 86].

A second possibility is that of representing the faulty behavior of a physical (mechanical, physiological) system, that is, representing the causes and consequences of its possible malfunctions. In this case the reasoning process consists of an operation of "matching" the status of the particular system under examination with such a model in order to diagnose which one is malfunctioning and to discover what are the possible ultimate causes. As an example, consider a mechanical system; a very simple network for the diagnosis of engine problems is the one in figure 1.2. A "hypothesize and test" method can be adopted to establish a particular diagnostic hypothesis, i.e. one can hypothesize the presence of a malfunction (diagnostic hypothesis) and then test the correctness of the hypothesis by searching for a causal path from an initial perturbation to the state defining the presence of the malfunction. The presence of the manifestations of the states can be used to confirm the presence of the states themselves. It is worth noting that the abstract models used in the last examples are very simple. In practical applications states are complex structures and the relationships between them have to involve a wide set of parameters (conditions and/or restrictions, e.g. temporal).

Let us now briefly discuss which are the major practical approaches proposed in recent years to represent causal knowledge. One of the first examples of causal models is that proposed by Weiss and Kulikowski in the CASNET expert system [Weiss et al. 78], in which simple relations between pathophysiological states are represented (CASNET operates in the medical domain of glaucoma disease). The system cannot be considered a deep-based one since heuristic correlations between states, findings and hypotheses are still the most important components to produce diagnoses, but it is certainly the grandparent of second generation systems.

More recently, systems based only on causal knowledge have been developed. In ABEL [Patil 81], knowledge is represented by means of causal networks at different levels of abstraction. At the higher level, very general states are connected, whilst at the lower one more specific states and relations are represented. Reasoning is performed on the causal network at a specific level of abstraction and by means of elaboration of general nodes in more precise descriptions and abstraction of low level groups of states in more general ones. More specifically in ABEL three levels of knowledge representation have been introduced in the system, namely the "pathophysiological", "intermediate" and "clinical" ones. Actually the third level (i.e. the clinical

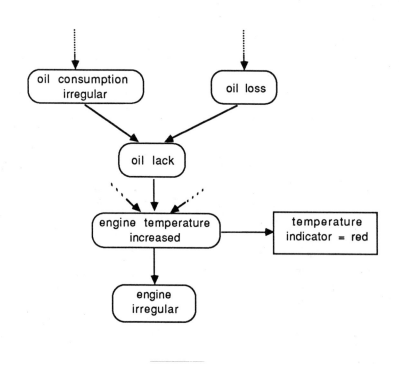

Figure 1.2 - The causal model of a faulty behavior of a mechanical system.

one) is a sort of heuristic level, so that ABEL can be considered a system combining deep and heuristic knowledge, see next paragraph for an in-depth discussion.

Shortly after this, Long [Long 83a,b] proposed a model in which temporal attributes of the causal relationships play an important role in the causal reasoning in a system for the treatment of heart failure. In Long's system a physiological model in which parameters of the state of the patient are qualitatively (and in part quantitatively) correlated is used for different forms of causal reasoning: for interpreting patient's data, for producing diagnoses and for reasoning about possible therapies. Two aspects of this system are particularly interesting and innovative. First, a "*consistency maintaining system*" approach is used in order to maintain the consistency in the network of parameters: when perturbations occur (that is, the value of some parameter is modified), changes are propagated into the network considering the relationships between parameters until a consistent state is reached; secondly some interesting studies of the representation of *time* in cause-effect relationships have been made [Long 83a,b]. Moreover, the combination of different forms of causal reasoning in a unique knowledge model is very interesting [Long 87].

Simple uses of causal knowledge can be found also in [Thompson & Clancey 86]; in MDX [Chandrasekaran & Mittal 83a], in which deep relationships are compiled in a higher level problem solving strategy (but they are not directly used in the reasoning process); and in IDM [Fink et al. 85], in which causal knowledge is used to solve difficult cases which are not solved by the heuristic one.

An interesting formalization of deep causal reasoning (and of its application to diagnostic problem solving) has been recently proposed by Pearl [Pearl 86][Geffner & Pearl 87][Pearl 87]. Pearl's new approach, based on probability theory, to evidential reasoning works through belief updating and propagation in a network of propositions [Pearl 86]. In such a network a conditional probability is associated with each link connecting two propositions. The belief updating and propagation scheme is able to modify the "degree of belief" associated with each proposition, when the evidence of some other proposition is modified or introduced. The approach can be successfully used to model causal diagnostic problem solving. In such an interpretation nodes represent diagnostic hypotheses, states of the modelled system and their observable manifestations: when evidence is gathered about some manifestations, the belief propagation scheme is able to determine the corresponding evidence (belief) for diagnostic hypotheses. Such a technique has been used in some systems - see, for example, the MUNIN system [Andreassen et al. 87].

Because of its clear semantic and mathematical soundness Pearl's approach also gained popularity in the section of the Artificial Intelligence community which has always been sceptical about the adoption of numerical methods to simulate human approximate reasoning. Nevertheless, the real applicability of this approach to model complex domains is still in question, mainly because of the large number of conditional probabilities which have to be supplied by the designer of the system.

A very different approach to the design of deep diagnostic systems is that based on the use of a "*ontological representation*" of the system to be diagnosed. From a very abstract point of view such an approach corresponds to giving a precise description of the structure and function of the system to be diagnosed. In order to deal with this form of knowledge complex forms of qualitative reasoning have been designed and applied to the diagnostic task (a brief overview of the qualitative reasoning techniques that have been recently proposed will be given in the next section). The approach has proven very useful in the design of many systems, in particular as regards the specific task of electronic circuits (and appliances) troubleshooting. Among the more interesting proposals Davis' "reasoning from first principles" [Davis 83] methods for deriving the behavior of a physical system from its structure and function [Davis 84] and Milne's "theory of responsibilities" [Milne 85] should be mentioned (for an overview, see [Bobrow 1984][Chandrasekaran & Milne 85]).

More abstract and formal schemes for deep reasoning have been recently proposed. The recent logical formalizations of deep diagnostic reasoning given by Reiter [Reiter 87] and de Kleer and Williams [de Kleer & Williams 87], which extend, in various directions, the original logical approach to deep reasoning proposed by Genesereth [Genesereth 84], are very interesting in this area. They have both, and independently, developed a formal theory of diagnosis from first principles, given a description of the structure of a physical system and the behavior of its constituent components. They propose an approach philosophically similar to Reggia's "covering set" [Reggia et al. 83], to discover the minimal set of faulty components which can explain an incorrect behavior of the system.

Particularly interesting in Reiter's approach is the complete logical formalization of the diagnostic problem: the correlation between the components of a system (that is, its structure) and the behavior of each single component is represented by a set of logical formulae SD (in particular, for describing the normal behavior of a component the special predicate "abnormal(<component>)" is used in its negated form). Given a set of observations OBS, a diagnosis consists of a set Δ of components which are not correctly functioning, so that the set of formulae

$$SD \cup OBS \cup \{abnormal(c) \mid c \in \Delta \}$$
$$\cup \{\neg \ abnormal(c) \mid c \in COMPONENTS - \Delta\}$$

is consistent (where COMPONENTS is the set of components of the system). An efficient method for the computation of the minimal set Δ satisfying the above relationship is proposed. Moreover, the observation of the correlation between diagnostic and non monotonic reasoning (an interesting discussion about the non monotonicity of diagnostic problem solving and an alternative approach to the formalization of the diagnostic task can be found in [Ginsberg 86]) is very interesting. It is worth noting, moreover, that Reiter's formalization approaches and solves the problem of diagnosing multiple faults (remember that one of the basic assumptions in other approaches, e.g. Genesereth's one, is the single-fault assumption).

From the conceptual point of view de Kleer's and Williams' approach is not very different, even if less completely logically formalized than Reiter's. Very interesting in this case is the analysis of "measurement theory" - i.e. of the problem of selecting an optimal set of tests to confirm/reject a diagnostic hypothesis.

1.3.2 THE IMPORTANCE OF QUALITATIVE REASONING

A very interesting characteristic of many of the approaches to deep reasoning (and specifically of the approaches based on "ontological models") is that they are based on *qualitative forms of reasoning* [Bobrow 84]. To understand better what this means let us present a simple example. Consider a set of differential equations and suppose we want to analyze the behavior of the particular system they model. A quantitative analysis corresponds to finding the mathematical solution of the set of equations so that the precise numerical variation of each state variable (and globally of the system), in response to a precise external perturbation, is determined; a qualitative analysis corresponds to deducing the sign and, in some cases, the order of magnitude of such variations, without solving any equation mathematically (usually propagation of constraints techniques [Sussman & Steele 80] are used in these cases).

It should be clear that whilst a quantitative analysis can be very complex, or even impossible (both from the theoretical and practical point of view), a qualitative one is simpler, less expensive and more interesting from an Artificial Intelligence point of view. In fact, the human approach to the analysis of physical systems is qualitative: precise quantitative analyses are performed only in doubtful or ambiguous cases, i.e. when the qualitative one fails. Consider, for example, an engineer who is performing the analysis of an electric circuit: he/she certainly would reason abstractly in terms of the sign of the "potential difference" in the different points of the circuit and would analyze it more precisely only if this were not be sufficient.

Complete and interesting examples of qualitative reasoning are naive physics, in which an approach to the analysis of physical systems is proposed and developed [Hayes 79][Forbus 84], common-sense arithmetic [Simmons 86], theory of confluences [de Kleer & Brown 84], mythical causality [de Kleer & Brown 86] and comparative statics [Iwasaki & Simon 86].

Moreover, particular attention deserves to be paid to Kuipers' method of qualitative simulation (QSIM algorithm) [Kuipers 84]. This method permits the analysis of the behavior of a physical system represented through mathematical models and has been suggested by the author for application to deal with causal knowledge (e.g. in medicine [Kuipers & Kassirer 84]).

Among the various approaches to qualitative reasoning (and more specifically to qualitative causal reasoning), certainly the most interesting for the purpose of deep knowledge-based expert systems design are de Kleer and Brown's and Iwasaki and Simon's ones. de Kleer's and Brown's theories of "confluences" [de Kleer & Brown 84] and of "causal ordering" [de Kleer & Brown 86] provide powerful mechanisms for the analysis of the behavior of a system. In particular, the first approach allows the analysis of the evolution of the state of a system through the analysis of the sign of the derivatives ("confluences" in de Kleer's terminology) of a set of state variables. The theory of causal ordering instead permits the determination of the causal correlations within the same set of variables through a "propagation of constraints" technique [Sussman & Steele 80]. A slightly different approach is Iwasaki's and Simon's method of "comparative statics" which allows the analysis of the effects of an external perturbation in a system modelled through a set of "qualitative" differential equations. Great interest is aroused in these approaches to the analysis of systems with "feedback", i.e. systems in which there are circularities in the set of cause-effect relationships. An interesting proposal for the analysis of such systems can be found in PEPTIDE [Weld 86].

The use of mathematical techniques plays an important role in many of the approaches designed for deep reasoning (such as, for example, the ones discussed above). Some other systems are more strictly based on mathematical modelling, among them, those presented in [Kuipers 84] [Kuipers & Kassirer 84][Kunz 84][Cramp et al. 85]. The idea is that the correlations and relationships between the constituting components of a physical (mechanical or even physiological) system can be described by a set of mathematical relations (equations or identities). The analysis of these models can be used to foresee the behavior of the system itself or to diagnose the causes of an unexpected functioning. Obviously, the use of the complete power of mathematical models would be too heavy from a computational point of view and far from the actual way of reasoning of domain experts, so techniques for qualitative analysis have been developed (see, for example, "common-sense arithmetic" [Simmons 86]).

All these methods are very powerful, but they have not yet found practical application in expert systems, the sort of application that has been found by the approaches discussed in the previous section.

1.4 THE ADVANTAGES OF COMBINING HEURISTIC AND DEEP REASONING

In the previous sections we have described various different approaches to deep knowledge representation and reasoning. In particular, we have noted that many formalisms have been developed, but few of them have found practical application to real world problems. The point that appears quite clearly from an analysis of such approaches is that they are very powerful (from the point of view of both knowledge representation and reasoning capabilities), but they are very complex and difficult to use in large domains [Kahn 84]. More specifically, if we wanted to build a diagnostic system based only on causal knowledge (e.g. in a medical domain) we would have to build a very large deep model and directly reason in it, at a very low level of detail. This means that we would not have any form of focalization and would directly reason in terms of causal/temporal relationships between the system's states. This would be very difficult and does not correspond to the effective behavior of a domain expert who certainly uses some forms of experience (heuristics), at least to focus deep reasoning.

A possible solution to these problems is to build systems based on different levels of representation, so that reasoning can be performed at different levels of abstraction as, for example, in ABEL [Patil 81]. More specifically, it has been recently argued by many researchers that an ideal scheme for diagnostic systems should be based on the combination of heuristic and deep reasoning.

Starting from the seminal work of Patil in the ABEL system, some approaches to the combination of such different forms of reasoning have been recently presented. A simple example of such an architecture has been recently proposed by Fink et al. [1985] in IDM, a system for diagnosis in mechanical domains. In Fink's approach, deep knowledge based on cause-effect relationships is used only when heuristic rules fail to find a solution, with the aim of deriving from a deep analysis new heuristic rules for such new cases. Similarly in [Steels & van de Velde 85][Van de Velde 86] a causal model is used to solve a problem when a rule-based heuristic level fails to solve the problem itself. In ACES [Pazzani 87] a functional model is used to confirm the hypotheses generated by a heuristic rule-based system: when a hypothesis is disconfirmed by the deep level, a learning mechanism is started to correct the heuristic level (failure-driven learning). In MDX2 [Sticklen & Chandrasekaran 88], the hierarchical classification approach of MDX [Chandrasekaran & Mittal 83a] is augmented by the adoption of a functional model which is used as a confirmatory module. In CASEY [Koton 88] the causal reasoning scheme proposed by Long is supplemented with a module performing a form of "case-based reasoning" [Kolodner & Kolodner 87].

In this book we present a complex diagnostic architecture in which heuristic and causal reasoning are strictly connected and actively cooperate during the diagnostic process. Our scheme derives from an analysis of the behavior of domain experts who use both experience and deep knowledge to produce diagnoses and explain them precisely, and who are able to acquire and modify their heuristics from deep reasoning. More particularly, we believe that heuristic knowledge can be used to produce (where possible) initial diagnostic hypotheses, to be confirmed, discriminated and explained using deep reasoning (in a certain sense, heuristics are used to focus reasoning on deep knowledge). Moreover, deep causal models can be used for tutorial purposes, i.e. to provide a user with precise descriptions of the modelled domain. Such an architecture presents several advantages over deep based ones, as will be described in the next chapters. In particular, some of the efficiency problems arising with the use of deep models are solved through the adoption of the heuristic component to focus deep reasoning; precise and deep explanations can be generated, based on causal/temporal relationships.

2

THE CHECK PROJECT

2.1 THE EXPERIENCES OF THE LITO PROJECT

At the Dipartimento di Informatica of the Universita' di Torino, the research activity in the field of expert systems in medicine [Torasso 85][Milanese et al. 85] dates back to 1978, when some of us were requested to develop a (sort of) consultant system in the domain of the evaluation of the function of the liver. By analyzing the characteristics of the domain with the help of expert physicians and by taking into account our previous experience in clinical decision making [Saitta & Torasso 81], we realized that it would be worthwhile to develop a consultation system by adopting Artificial Intelligence techniques and, in particular, the (at that time) emerging methodologies of expert systems. The result of these initial efforts was LITO1 [Lesmo et al. 80] [Lesmo et al. 84c], a rule-based expert system able to evaluate the degree of impairment of the liver function by reasoning on clinical data and by requesting laboratory tests only in the case of real suspicion of liver impairment. Even if the main tool for representing knowledge is production rules (in particular, fuzzy production rules since LITO1 makes use of fuzzy logic for dealing with uncertainty), LITO1 can be regarded as a hybrid system since it makes use of semantic nets formalisms for representing and organizing data (findings and laboratory tests).

In 1983 we decided to investigate the problem of complex control strategies in diagnostic expert systems and, with the advice of some expert physicians (the same who cooperated with us in the development of LITO1), we started work on the design of LITO2 [Cravetto et al. 85a][Cravetto et al. 85b]. The main goal of this research project was the development of an expert system able to diagnose hepatic diseases by modelling (at least to a certain extent) the diagnostic reasoning followed by an expert physician.

In many medical domains (and hepatology is one of them) the control strategy has to be quite complex since the physician is able to make diagnostic hypotheses, on the basis of few findings, to verify the hypotheses, to ask for additional data, to disregard a hypothesis if it does not gather sufficient evidence, etc. [Kassirer & Gorry 78]. In the domain of liver diseases, the interaction of the different diagnostic hypotheses must be taken into account because more than one disease can co-exist within the same patient, and in many cases causal and/or associational relationships hold between different hypotheses. It was almost immediately apparent that the implementation of a control strategy able to deal with the problems mentioned above would result in a rule-based system which was too cumbersome.

For this reason we decided to adopt, for developing LITO2, a formalism based on the notion of "frame" [Minsky 75]. However, the decision to model the diagnostic reasoning of the physician did also force us to investigate what kind of data the physician bases his/her decisions on. We realized that different kinds of data are used at different stages of the diagnostic process and that laboratory test results are generally used to confirm a diagnostic hypothesis rather than to achieve it.

When in mid 1985 the LITO2 system could be considered finished, we realized that it was more complex than anticipated [1], but such complexity was the result of an in-depth analysis of the domain at knowledge level [Newell 82]. However, this increased complexity did not require, during the development of the system, any major modifications to be made to the architecture since the frame formalism is powerful enough to accommodate different kinds of knowledge.

In particular, three different kinds of knowledge appear in each frame related to a different diagnostic hypothesis:

-    *Prototypical knowledge,* i.e the manifestations typically associated with a disease. This can be seen as a form of prediction of the status of the patient suffering from a given disease, a prediction expressed in terms of symptoms, signs, outcome of laboratory tests.

---

[1] Notice that this result is common to many other expert systems in which various kinds of knowledge and behavior have been added during the evolution in order to meet some requirements (see MDX for example [Chandrasekaran & Mittal 83b] [Sticklen at al. 85]).

-    *Control knowledge*, i.e. the kind of knowledge that enables the system to decide when a particular diagnostic hypothesis must be activated, what must be done if it is not confirmed by data gathered afterwards, and what kind of processing must be carried on if the hypothesis reaches a sufficient level of confidence.

-    *Structural knowledge*, which specifies the connection existing between different hypotheses, e.g. specialization, generalization, alternatives, etc.

Moreover, we were able to distribute the control among frames themselves, so that changes in the control strategy required only minor changes in the slots devoted to representing the control without affecting the "inference engine". The analysis at knowledge level has provided a rich set of concepts and relations (examples of the former are diagnostic hypotheses, triggers, major and minor findings, etc., whilst those of the latter are causal, mutually exclusive, supporting, concomitant relationships). This rich vocabulary has proven very useful in analyzing other domains (related to industrial problems, especially troubleshooting and computer components integration), so we have devoted further efforts to providing a more accurate semantic of the formalism. In particular, our main goal was to provide general guidelines for organizing different kinds of knowledge.

Despite the many fine features (at least from our point of view) of LITO2, we realized that many of the remarks made to "heuristic" systems (see section 1.3) hold also for LITO2. In particular, we realized that in some special cases LITO2 concludes with multiple different diagnoses and the evidence degrees of these diagnostic hypotheses are quite similar. However, the problem does not lie in the particular method adopted for combining evidence or in some flows in the knowledge base (so that a revision of the knowledge source could avoid the problem), but depends on the lack of a deep causal level in which causal reasoning at the pathophysiological level can contribute to discriminating between different diagnostic hypotheses.

These considerations, together with the desire to develop a valid and general framework for diagnostic expert systems, stimulated the design of CHECK (Combining HEuristic and Causal Knowledge), a diagnostic expert system able to combine heuristic and causal reasoning in solving diagnostic problems [Molino et al. 86][Torasso & Console 87] [Console & Torasso 88c] [Console & Torasso 88e].

2.2 THE MAIN GOALS OF CHECK

Let us discuss briefly the motivations which have led us to the design of

CHECK's architecture. Many of the considerations we shall make derive from analysis of the limitation of traditional diagnostic architectures and from an analysis we have made of how expert physicians solve the cases that are presented to them. This analysis provides very instructive suggestions on both the types of knowledge and the control strategies needed in diagnostic expert systems (moreover, it provides guidelines for the design of the man-machine interaction component and for its relationships with the control strategy, as will be discussed in chapter 9).

Let us briefly summarize the main results of such an analysis to introduce the main design issues of CHECK.

Expert diagnosticians tend to solve problems using experience knowledge first - that is, by directly associating observations (findings) with diagnostic hypotheses. Consider medical diagnosis: initial data volunteered by the patient evoke some initial diagnostic hypotheses in the physician's mind (on the basis of his/her experience of previous similar cases); new and more specific data are then required by the physician to confirm/reject such initial hypotheses and to refine them. The important point is that, generally, more then one diagnostic hypothesis is activated in parallel, so that differential processes are used in the first confirmation phase. These observations have some basic and important consequences on the design of a diagnostic system:

-    Some form of experience knowledge has to be represented - in particular, stereotypical descriptions of the possible malfunctions considered by the system are needed, connecting the malfunctions themselves to their typical (prototypical) manifestations. Moreover, some form of control specific knowledge to evoke hypotheses and to differentiate among them is needed.

-    A multi-step hierarchical control strategy is needed, but some form of parallelism in activating and considering diagnostic hypotheses to perform differential diagnosis is mandatory (the lack of such forms of parallelism is one of the limitations of many heuristic architectures operating diagnosis through an establish-refine cycle).

Experience knowledge is necessary for the solving of diagnostic problems, but it is not sufficient for several reasons. More specifically, we have noticed in section 1.3 that heuristic knowledge does not permit us to solve complex (new or unusual) cases or to discriminate precisely between competing diagnostic hypotheses. Moreover, it does not permit the generation of useful explanations.

Such observations have some interesting consequences for the design of an expert system, which can be summarized as follows:

- The forms of knowledge that can be useful for diagnosis do not necessarily coincide with those to be used for providing explanations (a similar consideration has been derived from a different analysis by Clancey [Clancey 85]).

- A deep level of knowledge representation and reasoning has to be combined with the heuristic one in order to solve unusual cases, confirm diagnostic hypotheses, differentiate and discriminate among them and generate precise explanations.

When designing a deep model of the behavior of a system, a fundamental point concerns the choice between the two possibilities of representing either the correct or the faulty behavior of the system to be diagnosed. Though the former approach has several advantages (and has been chosen by many researchers, e.g. [Fink et al. 85][Van de Velde 85]), we believe that the latter is more suited to the purpose of diagnosis, especially when complex systems have to be modelled. In many cases (e.g. medical domains), in fact, giving the model of the correct behavior is far more complex than giving that of the faulty behavior (and the resulting model itself is more complicated).

As far as the choice of the formalism to represent deep knowledge is concerned, some considerations are worth taking into account. Although the approaches based on "ontological representation" (e.g. "reasoning from first principles" approaches) are very interesting and powerful, they suffer from some limitation when they have to be applied to complex domains. In particular, when medical domains are considered, representing the structure and function of a physiological system seems to be very difficult (or even impossible). For this reason we have chosen to design a causal modelling formalism along the lines adopted in other complex diagnostic systems (e.g. ABEL). We believe that such an approach offers several advantages in terms of both modelling capabilities and suitability for application to different problems and domains, although it does not allow one to give as "deep" descriptions as can be given using other approaches ("ontological" ones). This will be discussed in more detail following the presentation of the formalism we have designed (chapter 12).

Another important point to be considered when building a two-level system concerns the relationship between the two levels. As noticed before the heuristic level should be able to solve typical cases, the point is to decide how it should behave on the other ones. In many systems the solution adopted is to provide the heuristic level with very strong and categorical classification schemes able to solve only "very typical" cases and rejecting as unsolvable all the other ones (e.g. [Fink et al 85] and [Van de Velde 85]). We believe that such a scheme is too restrictive in many cases, so it is better to provide the heuristic level with coarser prototypical descriptions: in this way the number of rejected cases is lowered even if the fuzziness in the distinction between diagnoses is augmented so that, in some cases, the system is unable to discriminate among them. This approach is more interesting for several reasons:

- In many cases one cannot assume to have a deep model covering all the malfunctions considered by the system (the causal evolution of some diseases in medical domains is doubtful or unknown). In such cases it is better to have some suggestions from the surface level than no response at all.

- The solutions proposed by the heuristic level can be used to focus reasoning at the deep one.

Some final considerations about the adoption of deep models in complex domains are worthwhile. What is probably realistic in the modelling of simple systems (for example, simple artifacts such as electronic circuits) - that is, the assumption that a complete model of the structure and behavior of the system can be given - is certainly not true when physical or physiological systems are considered. In such cases, in fact, for each level of modelling there are some important processes (or conditions) that cannot be represented since they require a deeper understanding of the system (which is sometimes not even known), so that deep level knowledge is often incomplete and some sophisticated form of common-sense reasoning is needed. Moreover, even if the chosen level of representation is not so deep, the causal process are not always known or certain and the resulting models are very complex. A confirmation of this difficulty is provided by the fact that many researchers advocate the adoption of probabilistic causal models for diagnosis in complex domains [Pearl 87][Andreassen et al. 87]. The important point is that one must be aware of such problems and limitations when approaching the problem and must deal with them when designing a particular deep-based architecture (and especially when one has to formalize deep reasoning).

The goal of CHECK is twofold:

- To show how it is possible to integrate two different forms of reasoning in an effective way. We believe that integration of the two levels is not restricted to some form of cooperation during the diagnostic process (see chapter 8), but that the knowledge about diagnostic hypotheses and diagnostic reasoning should be kept consistent at both levels.

- To introduce some form of approximate reasoning not only at the heuristic level (this is quite common in many diagnostic expert systems), but also at the deep one. However, we wanted to stress that at the deep level approximate reasoning cannot be based on numeric weights (whatever the framework is: probability theory, fuzzy logic, etc), but on a more qualitative logical approach. We feel that some form of non-monotonic common sense reasoning (non-monotonic "hypothetical reasoning" in particular) meets the requirements and therefore we developed such an approach by providing it with a sound logical basis (see chapter 8).

Obviously, CHECK was designed to maintain all the capabilities of heuristic reasoning (similar to those possible in LITO2), so that most diagnostic problems can be solved correctly in an efficient way, whereas analysis at the deeper level is required for solving complex cases in which the solution proposed by the heuristic level is not satisfactory. Moreover, the deep level can be used to provide the user with appropriate and precise explanations of the proposed diagnostic hypotheses or, more generally, about the specific domain of competence of the system.

To close this paragraph we aim at providing the reader with a basic outline of the overall architecture of CHECK, in order to make the following chapters easier to understand.

First of all, it is important to realize how the heuristic and the deep levels are integrated. Figure 2.1 shows that in CHECK we have three different kinds of entities - data, causal networks and heuristic descriptions of diagnostic hypotheses - and how each kind of entity lies on a different plane. Obviously at each level different kinds of relationships are defined: for example, at the level of diagnostic hypotheses relationships like "specialization", "generalization", "alternative", etc. are very useful.

Let us start our brief sketch from the "data" level. The experience gained during the development of LITO2 showed that not only must the knowledge about the diagnostic hypotheses be hierarchically organized, but also that the data must receive an appropriate structure [Mittal et al, 1984]. Data are structured in CHECK, i.e. classes of findings and hierarchies of classes are defined; each datum can belong to more than one class and multiple views of data are provided (e.g. the data organization used in the consultation process can be different from the one used during the reasoning process). The definition of classes of findings can be useful for many reasons - for example, for organizing the request for data in a reasonable way or for defining some form of "equivalence" between data with respect to a given diagnostic hypothesis (see chapter 3 for more details).

When used on a specific case, CHECK should act as a "consultant", able to suggest the diagnostic hypothesis (hypotheses) which accounts (account) best for the set of observations and findings gathered for the case under

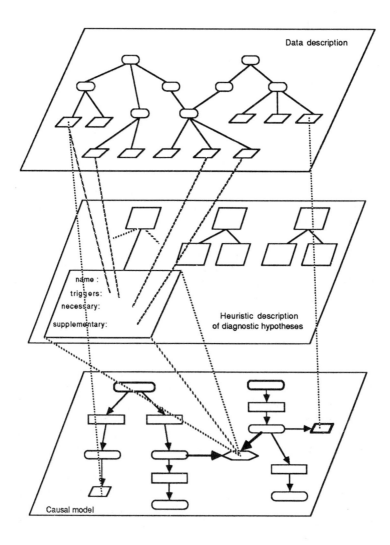

Figure 2.1 - The three levels of CHECK.

examination. CHECK provides mechanisms for a taxonomic classification of diagnostic hypotheses: "gross diagnostic classes", each of which can be specialized into a number of more specific ones which can be defined, i.e. a graph of diagnostic hypotheses at different levels of detail can be defined.

The resulting structural organization of diagnostic hypotheses is a useful tool for focusing the reasoning: in fact, CHECK, like most human experts, in the first place tries to establish a preliminary classification, and then refines it by identifying individual diagnoses. Not only is this mechanism useful for preventing the system from considering a large number of hypotheses, most of which should be rejected because they are completely (or almost completely) incompatible with actual data, but also for reducing the demands of additional data. In fact, the most specific findings will be requested by CHECK only when the diagnostic hypotheses which need them are to be activated.

In the heuristic representation (surface level), relationships between findings and hypotheses are represented by means of a hybrid formalism based on frames and production rules, with the aim of achieving a diagnosis easily (see chapter 4).

At the deep level the relationships connecting diagnostic hypotheses to findings are expressed via causal paths involving states and actions which represent states of the physical (or physiological) system to be modelled and activities which transform one state into another respectively (see chapter 7). The notion of state is fundamental in the causal network together with the one of "initial cause" which represents the starting point of a process which causes the physical (or physiological) system to exhibit a behavior different from the correct (or predicted) one.

In causal networks causal relationships play a major role, but other relations have to be defined in order to connect states with other kinds of entities (for example, HAS-AS-MANIFESTATION relationships, each one of which connects a state with a finding, i.e. with an external manifestation of the state itself). It is worth noting the strong correspondence between entities at the different levels (see figure 2.1). All the diagnostic hypotheses occurring at the heuristic level are in one-to-one correspondence with entities at the causal level which represent them. All findings occurring in the heuristic and in the causal models are defined in the data level, even if not all of them are necessarily used in the heuristic phase of diagnostic reasoning.

In the following chapters we will discuss in detail the knowledge organization and control strategy, looking separately at the two levels of knowledge representation (surface and deep) for ease of explanation. In the general description that follows emphasis is put on the problem of the interaction of the two levels (we shall return on this problem in the following chapters).

Surface level knowledge is invoked first to generate diagnostic hypotheses. This means that reasoning in the frame-system is performed (as will be discussed in chapter 5) and a solution generated. At this time the deep causal level is invoked to confirm and explain the conclusion. A portion of the global network which can explain the diagnosis from the ultimate causes to the final manifestations is searched and instantiated on the data describing the particular case under examination (see Chapter 8). During this activity, the diagnostic process makes heavy use of "hypothetical reasoning" (see chapter 8).

If the hypothesis can be confirmed, a complete and precise explanation is generated first, then unaccounted for and/or unexpected data are taken into account and correlated hypotheses are suggested (to the surface level or to the user, depending on their nature). In this way multiple-diagnosis solutions can be generated. If the hypothesis is rejected, alternative hypotheses to be considered are suggested to the surface level and control is passed to it.

Since knowledge acquisition is known to be a difficult (and boring) task, in chapter 9 we describe the tool we have developed for making it (a little) less difficult and error prone. Major emphasis is put on a graphical interface which allows the knowledge engineer to describe the causal network in a graphical form, and which is able automatically to translate the network into an executable code after having performed semantic checks on the consistency of the network itself.

Chapters 10 and 11 describe the implementation issues of CHECK. The diagnostic system is completely implemented in "Prolog+" (a graphical extension of C-Prolog for SUN workstations). Particular translation (preprocessing) techniques have been adopted to embed knowledge based systems within Prolog [Console et al. 86] [Console & Rossi 87] [Console & Rossi 88]. More specifically, the surface level has been designed using FROG (FRames in ProlOG), an environment for the development of knowledge based systems in Prolog we have designed [Console & Rossi 88], whilst object-oriented techniques have been adopted in the implementation of the deep level. Other modules of the CHECK environment (e.g. graphical interfaces and graphical editor for the knowledge acquisition phase) have been implemented in 'C' language and are linked together and to the expert system reasoning module (see chapter 11 for discussion).

Finally in chapter 12 we present a complete example of the application of CHECK and we discuss some extensions to CHECK's formalism that we are currently studying or developing.

3

DATA ORGANIZATION

Most expert systems assume a very simple organization of data since Working Memory is just a list of facts in which the usual structure for a single entity is provided by a list of "attribute-value" pairs. Although this organization is sufficient in some cases, it fails to realize that findings are not independent of each other and that findings are requested, analyzed and used in groups rather than in isolation. Recently, some approaches to data-base structuring in expert systems have been proposed. Of particular interest is the PATREC system [Mittal et al. 84], a knowledge directed database for the MDX diagnostic expert system [Chandrasekaran & Mittal 83b]. Not only is PATREC a repository of data, but it is also able to perform inferences (e.g. when there is access to data) and to maintain simple temporal information on data.

An interesting characteristic of CHECK is its ability to model data (this is not an innovative characteristic of CHECK, since we had already realized during the design of LITO1 that there was such a need, so in LITO1 a simple form of semantic network was introduced to represent the relations among findings and the characteristics of the findings themselves; see [Lesmo et al. 84c] for more details). This has been obtained mainly by introducing the concept of *class of data* and the possibility of defining taxonomic descriptions for representing the meaningful and useful groupings of findings. Notice that the leaves of these taxonomies correspond to single findings whereas the intermediate nodes correspond to some classes of findings. It is worth pointing out that, in general, more than one taxonomic description can be put into the data and the current version of CHECK is able to deal with multiple taxonomies which may share some of the leaves (that is findings) or even some of the intermediate nodes. This capability is very important since it allows one to accommodate different "views", that is the same reality can be analyzed from different points of view. For example, if we consider the field of medicine, a very usual way of organizing data involves the definition of classes as "past history", "symptoms", "signs", etc. However, alternative (but not mutually exclusive) groupings may refer to cost, ease of elicitation, invasiveness, etc. Therefore, multiple perspectives allow CHECK to use the most suitable taxonomic organization according to the phase in the diagnostic process.

Each class of data is represented by a simple frame-like structure. Two types of information are represented in such structures:

-   *Structural knowledge* which describes the position of the class in the data hierarchy. In particular, this description is formed by two slots: the *"specialization_of"* slot (containing the list of the superclasses of a class) and the *"generalization_of"* one (containing the list of the subclasses or of the specific findings of a class).

-   *Control knowledge* which is formed by different groups of slots which specify when and how data of a specific class should be asked for. Of particular interest here is the *"ask_after"* slot which specifies a list of classes (or of specific findings) that should be asked for before those in the class itself (the importance of this slot will be clear in a moment, when specific data frames will be discussed).

Knowledge about each single finding is represented by means of a frame-like structure. In particular each frame contains four types of knowledge:

-   *Structural knowledge,* which specifies the ancestors of the datum in the taxonomic organization (that is, the classes to which the datum itself belongs).

-   *Control knowledge,* which specifies how and when information about the finding should be asked for. Similarly important to the case of classes of data is the slot "ask_after", which allows the imposing of constraints on the order of the questions asked by the system.

-   *Prototypical knowledge,* which is the type of description permissible for the finding. In particular, a finding is characterized by a set of attributes, each one of which describes a particular feature of the finding itself. Some pieces of information are associated with each one of such attributes, e.g. a linguistic, numeric, fuzzy description, the set of admissible values (the numeric range in the case of a "numeric" finding), the measure unit and the set of expected values (in some cases we have a default value that can be used if nothing is known about the actual value).

-   *Interpretation knowledge,* which consists essentially of a set of rules which specify how to map (interpret or translate) the raw information about a datum obtained from the external world (usually provided by the user) into one which could be meaningful for the diagnostic system, i.e. the linguistic values which qualitatively characterize each attribute (feature) of the finding have to be computed, when possible.

At any given time some attributes may remain empty or may be filled in with a default value if no specific one is provided by the user. This computation of a linguistic description of the finding ("data abstraction") is performed by a set of *"translation" rules* which specify under which conditions a given interpretation of each attribute of a finding is possible by putting constraints on the set of values that the attribute itself can assume depending on each specific context. By context, we mean the values of other findings which may influence the description of the finding under consideration. For example, blood pressure is influenced by sex, age, etc. An interpretation of a raw datum is not possible unless the other findings influencing it are known (in this sense, not only is *control information* linked with classes, but with specific findings as well).

The interpretation rules play a very important role since they permit some form of qualitative abstraction. Clancey [1985] stresses that a significant portion of the knowledge about a domain is devoted to providing a more abstract (and qualitative) description of the data since raw data are not very useful in a direct match against the prototypical description of a diagnostic hypothesis. We believe that the introduction of interpretation rules is a simple and perspicuous solution to the problem of making the context explicit in reasoning about the data.

Notice that in medical diagnostic applications the above remarks are valid not just for subjective data (such as complaints) but also for laboratory tests. The lab tests are usually considered as "hard" data as opposed to "soft" data related to clinical history, symptoms, etc. However, in many cases the result of a lab test is not meaningful *per se,* but only in a context where other pieces of information concur in characterizing the status of a patient. It is apparent that the meaning of a lab test differs significantly on the basis of the sex, age, therapy, etc. of the patient under examination. We believe that it is not just the fact that physicians use linguistic terms like "abnormal", "increased", "very increased", etc. to qualify the lab tests The linguistic label (even if partially imprecise) associated with the lab test is useful both for abstracting from the particular numeric result of the lab test and for representing in a concise way the conclusion of an interpretation process. Such a linguistic term takes into account all (or at least the most important) aspects which concur in interpreting such a datum.

It is worth noting that the context is used also during data acquisition. If a datum about a particular case is provided by the user and its interpretation depends on other findings not yet furnished by the user, these are directly requested by CHECK.

The general form of a frame describing a datum is presented in figure 3.1. The description is based on the syntax of the high level knowledge representation language we have designed, which is in turn based on Prolog and which will be widely used in many parts of the book (for more comments about such a language see chapters 10 and 11).

---

finding <name> *is_a*
         specialization_of <list of classes>
         ask_after <list of findings>.

finding <name> *has_as_attributes* <list of attributes>.

attribute <name of an attribute> *of* <name of a finding>
         is_characterized_by
                  numeric_range [<real number>,<real number>]
                  measured_in <measure of unit>
                  linguistic_range <list of linguistic terms>
                  numeric_linguistic_mapping <name of an attribute>
                  default <a single linguistic term>.

numeric_linguistic_mapping <name of an attribute> *of*
         <name of a finding> :-
                  <linguistic term> *if* <conditions>,
                  ...
                  <linguistic term> *if* <conditions>.

Figure 3.1 - General form of the frame representing data.

In the first clause, information about the position of the datum in the hierarchy is represented together with *control* information ("ask_after" slot). Then there is a clause in which the attributes of the finding are listed and two clauses for each such attribute; these specify, first, the prototypical description of the attribute itself and, second, the *interpretation rules* for the values of such an attribute (mapping between numeric and linguistic values in particular). It is worth noting that when both a numeric and a linguistic value are associated with an attribute <name of an attribute>, they can be distinguished by using the "dot notation" and accessed through the names "<name of an attribute>.numeric" and "<name of an attribute>.linguistic".

Some remarks on data organization are worth making. A first point concerns the problem of inheritance in data hierarchies. When we first started to design the data structures of CHECK we introduced inheritance rules for the attributes of data (allowing us to associate attributes with classes of data). From the theoretical point of view this can be obtained without great problems and might allow more concise representations. However, in the design of specific (example) systems we noticed that inheritance in data hierarchies is, practically speaking, not very useful. That is because very often each datum of a diagnostic system has very specific attributes and such attributes have very different types of constraints on their possible values.

A second comment concerns the possibility of associating other kinds of slots with each frame describing data (classes) containing various kinds of specific information. In particular, when developing a (simple) natural language interface for data acquisition and explanation in CHECK, we noticed that specific linguistic information about the datum can be easily attached to the frame structure - for example, the syntactic structure of the expressions describing the datum. The resulting structure is very similar to the notion of entity used by Hayes in his "entity oriented parsing" [Hayes 84]. Other types of specific information can be attached to a frame in order to match other specific needs.

---

data_class risk_factors *is_a*
       specialization_of [clinical_data],
      generalization_of
          [chronic_alcohol_intake,
           administration_of_blood,
           exposure_to_hepatotoxic_agents].

Figure 3.2 - An example of data class.

In the following, we shall present some examples of frames describing classes of data and specific findings. Such examples are taken from the medical domain of liver diseases (which will be often used in the following). In particular in figure 3.2 the class of data "risk_factors" is reported.

In figure 3.3 the frame structure relative to the specific datum "tallness" is reported. Notice the use of the "interpretation" rules to map the numeric value of "tallness" in a more tractable linguistic one. This mapping depends on the sex of the patient (actually, this is a simplification since the linguistic value associated with tallness depends also on age, race, etc. [Lesmo & Torasso 87]), so that context information about sex is needed before asking questions about the tallness of a person.

---

finding tallness *is_a*
   specialization_of [general_data]
   ask_after [sex].

finding tallness *has_as_attributes* [value].

attribute value *of* tallness
   is_characterized_by
      numeric_range [100,250]
      measured_in 'cm'
      linguistic_range {short,medium,tall}
      numeric_linguistic_mapping value
      default medium.

numeric_linguistic_mapping value *of* tallness :-
   short *if* (sex=m, value.numeric < 160),
   medium *if* (sex=m, value.numeric $\geq$ 160, value.numeric < 180),
   tall *if* (sex=m, value.numeric $\geq$ 180),
   short *if* (sex=f, value.numeric < 150),
   medium *if* (sex=f, value.numeric $\geq$ 150, value.numeric < 170),
   tall *if* (sex=f, value.numeric $\geq$ 170).

Figure 3.3 - A simple example of datum.

Finally, in figure 3.4 an example of more complex data structures is reported: the frame for "fever" is presented to show a case in which more than one attribute is necessary to characterize a datum.

---

finding fever *is_a*
    specialization_of [symptoms].

finding fever *has_as_attributes* [intensity, duration].

attribute intensity *of* fever
    is_characterized_by
        numeric_range [35,43]
        measured_in 'celsius_grades'
        linguistic_range {absent,low,medium,high}
        numeric_linguistic_mapping intensity
        default absent.

numeric_linguistic_mapping intensity *of* fever :-
    absent *if* (intensity.numeric $\leq$ 37),
    low *if* (intensity.numeric $>$ 37, intensity.numeric $\leq$ 38),
    medium *if* (intensity.numeric $>$ 38, intensity.numeric $\leq$ 39),
    high *if* (intensity.numeric $>$ 39).

attribute duration *of* fever
    is_characterized_by
        numeric_range [0,60],
        measured_in 'days'
        linguistic_range {short,medium,long}
        numeric_linguistic_mapping duration
        default short.

numeric_linguistic_mapping duration *of* fever :-
    short *if* (duration.numeric $\leq$ 3),
    medium *if* (duration.numeric $>$ 3, duration.numeric $\leq$ 10),
    long *if* (duration.numeric $>$ 10).

Figure 3.4 - A more complex example of datum.

4

HEURISTIC LEVEL:
KNOWLEDGE REPRESENTATION

The relevance of prototypical descriptions (implemented via frame structures) in diagnostic expert systems (and, more generally, in problems of heuristic classification) has been recently recognized. Although already in the seventies some experimental systems like PIP [Pauker et al. 76] and CENTAUR [Aikins 83] showed that the capability of representing different kinds of knowledge (prototypical, structural, control) in a frame system offers several advantages, unfortunately, just in a few cases, mechanisms for evaluating the degree of match between the prototypical description contained in the frame and actual data have been proposed and most of them adopt quite *ad hoc* methods.

As stated above, different kinds of knowledge should be accommodated in a diagnostic expert system, especially in cases where the control structure is complex. Although the most usual type of knowledge stored in a frame system is relative to a prototypical description, the original idea of frame proposed by Minsky [Minsky 1975] and adopted in some systems, advocates the use of knowledge for deciding what to do both in the case of failure or success in the instantiation of the frame itself. For this reason the control knowledge is a relevant part of the domain knowledge.

In the following, after a brief discussion on CHECK's frame-system organization, we shall turn to describing in full detail the structure of CHECK's frames and considering the different types of knowledge that can be represented in them.

4.1 FRAME SYSTEM

In CHECK's heuristic level the frame system is organized in a hierarchical way. In such an organization, frames which represent diagnostic hypotheses at different levels of detail can be defined, which can be connected by different types of links. The hierarchy can assume the form of an acyclic graph in which at the top level there are coarse diagnostic hypotheses, whereas at the bottom level there are specific diagnostic hypotheses. The basic relation connecting the frames representing diagnostic hypotheses is the SPECIALIZATION one which connects frames representing general diagnostic hypotheses (classes of diagnoses) to frames representing more specific hypotheses (more restricted classes or specific diagnoses).

The resulting structural organization of diagnostic hypotheses is a useful tool in order to focus the reasoning process: in fact CHECK, like most human experts, in the first place tries to establish a preliminary classification, and then to refine it by identifying individual diagnoses. Not only is this mechanism useful in preventing the system from considering a large number of hypotheses, most of which should be rejected because they are completely (or almost completely) incompatible with actual data, but also in reducing the demands for additional data. In fact, the most specific pieces of information (e.g. data and/or clinical findings in a medical domain) will be requested by CHECK only when the diagnostic hypotheses which need them are to be activated.

As an example, consider the domain of liver diseases: we have defined ten gross diagnostic classes (e.g. cirrhosis, hepatitis, tumours,..) each of which has a number of specializations which represent specific diseases (for more details, see [Molino et al. 86]).

Besides mere SPECIALIZATION/GENERALIZATION relationships, other kinds of links can be defined to hold among frames in CHECK, in particular the ASSOCIATED and ALTERNATIVE relationships that connect a frame (diagnostic hypothesis) to associated and alternative ones (see the paragraph devoted to control knowledge in a frame for an in-depth discussion).

Notice that an organization similar to ours has been used in other systems (for example, MDX and CSRL [Bylander & Mittal 86]). The major difference regards the use of the hierarchy: in CHECK it is used just to organize knowledge about diagnostic hypotheses but no commitment is made to using it for searching for a solution in a diagnostic problem (on the other hand, the hierarchy is the main, if not the only, structure for controlling diagnostic reasoning in CSRL and MDX). Another point concerns the meaning of SPECIALIZATION. Nothing indicates that two diagnostic hypotheses, both specializations of the same diagnostic classes (that is, with the same father), are mutually exclusive.

4.2 FRAME ORGANIZATION

CHECK's frame-like structures have a complex form in which different types of knowledge are represented. The distinction between knowledge types is mirrored in the actual organization so that three major groups of slots can be identified when looking at a frame description:

- *structural* knowledge slots
- *prototypical* knowledge slots
- *control* knowledge slots

In the following, we shall first discuss the organization of the structural knowledge, then the prototypical description and finally the control knowledge.

4.2.1 STRUCTURAL KNOWLEDGE

The SPECIALIZATION and GENERALIZATION slots form the structural description part of a frame as they describe its position in the frame system. In particular, the SPECIALIZATION slot contains the names of the diagnostic hypotheses that are more specific than the one under consideration. The dual relationship is contained in the GENERALIZATION slot indicating which are the diagnostic hypotheses (immediately) generalizing the one under consideration.

4.2.2 PROTOTYPICAL KNOWLEDGE

In most systems the organization is very simple: the description of a diagnostic hypothesis consists of a group of features, each one of which is described in a slot of a frame. This means that implicitly all the descriptions contained in the slots are ANDed and that they are all at the same level, i.e. all of them have to be "necessarily" matched against data in order to instantiate the frame (evaluation functions, in order to allow partial match, are used in some systems). Such a rigid interpretation of the meaning of prototypical description is inadequate in many applicative domains.

The first way to make a prototypical description more flexible is to allow slots to describe not only the necessary features of the hypothesis. The experience of developing diagnostic expert systems [Cravetto et al. 85a] suggested the subdivision of a prototypical description into two parts: NECESSARY description slots and SUFFICIENT ones (a similar distinction can be found in PIP [Pauker et al. 76]). The meaning of this distinction is obvious: necessary conditions should be satisfied in order to confirm a diagnostic hypothesis, whereas a hypothesis can be established if one of the sufficient conditions is matched. It follows that in such a scheme NECESSARY conditions are ANDed, SUFFICIENT ones are ORed and the two groups, each one taken as a whole, are ORed in the global description of a hypothesis. Therefore, this organization is very powerful from a theoretical point of view, but it is not very useful in many practical domains since SUFFICIENT conditions are very difficult to define.

In many practical cases a slightly different organization can be very useful: instead of defining SUFFICIENT conditions, one can define SUPPLEMENTARY conditions (slots). SUPPLEMENTARY conditions allow the completion of NECESSARY ones by describing more specific features, that are not strictly necessary. The semantics of prototypical descriptions is now more complicated. SUPPLEMENTARY slots are implicitly ORed, since we can consider that the instantiation of even one of them can contribute to the confirmation of a hypothesis (we shall return later on the relationship between NECESSARY and SUPPLEMENTARY conditions).

Let us describe now how each single slot (NECESSARY, SUFFICIENT or SUPPLEMENTARY) is organized. In the following, for the sake of simplicity, we shall suppose that each finding is characterized by only one attribute, so that the name of the attribute can be omitted without problems of ambiguity.

Each slot of a CHECK frame contains, at a first approximation (we shall refine the discussion in the following sections when we shall define how uncertainty in prototypical descriptions is represented), a finding or, more precisely, a finding name and a list of its linguistic values that are compatible with the diagnostic hypothesis itself. In other words, each slot has the following form:

> finding_name : <list of linguistic values
>   compatible with the hypothesis>

A simple example of prototypical description, taken from a very simple mechanical domain (diagnosis of problems with a car) in which

NECESSARY and SUPPLEMENTARY conditions have been identified, is presented in figure 4.1.

FRAME: electrical problems

NECESSARY FINDINGS
  ignition: <impossible, faulty,>
  lights: <low_intensity, not_burning>

SUPPLEMENTARY FINDINGS
  battery_water_level: <low, medium>
  sparking_plugs_change:
              <between_20000_and_30000_km,
               more_than_30000_km>

Figure 4.1 - A simple prototypical description of the diagnostic hypothesis "electrical_problems".

In such a frame the diagnostic hypothesis "electrical problems" of a mechanical system has been represented. The meaning of this prototypical description can be paraphrased as "to have an electrical problem a car *must* have both an 'impossible' or faulty ignition and lights that do not work; moreover further evidence in favor of the disorder can be gathered if the water level in the battery is low and the sparking plugs are old".

A more structured and interesting example is the prototypical description of the class of diseases "cirrhosis" reported in figure 4.2.

FRAME cirrhosis

NECESSARY FINDINGS
  general_well_being:
              <normal, mild_alteration, average_alteration>

digestive_troubles:
        <absent, mild, average>
abdominal_pain:
        <absent, mild>
fever:
        <absent, mild, medium>
symptoms_duration:
        <less_than_1_week, less_than_1_month,
           less_than_6_months, more_than_6_months>
jaundice:
        <absent, mild, average, severe>
liver_volume:
        <normal, mild_increase, average_increase, severe_increase>
liver_firmness:
        <mild_increase, average_increase, severe_increase>
liver_surface_regularity:
        <normal, mild_altered, average_altered, severe_altered>
liver_pain:
        <absent, mild, average>
spleen_volume:
        <normal, mild_increase, average_increase>
ascites:
        <absent, mild, average, conspicuous>

SUPPLEMENTARY FINDINGS
less_than_1_year_protracted_daily_alcohol_intake:
        <medium, high>
more_than_1_year_protracted_daily_alcohol_intake:
        <medium, high>
prolonged_exposure_to_blood_or_blood_derivatives:
        <lasting_more_than_6_months>
inflammatory_bowel_disease:
        <present>
collagen_disorder:
        <present>
previous_acute_viral_hepatitis_or_jaundice:
        <present>

Figure 4.2 - A simple prototypical description of the diagnostic hypothesis "cirrhosis".

The idea is that one can diagnose "cirrhosis" in a patient if "all" NECES-SARY FINDINGS are present in the patient (the reason for which we have used "all" will be clear in the next section about partial match). Moreover, a further confirmation of the diagnosis can be obtained if at least one of the SUPPLEMENTARY FINDINGS is observed.

4.2.3 CONTROL KNOWLEDGE

The third kind of knowledge that is present in a CHECK's frame is *control knowledge*. Such information is constituted of five slots: TRIGGERS, VALIDATION RULES, ASSOCIATED HYPOTHESES, ALTERNATIVE HYPOTHESES and DEFAULT SPECIALIZATION.

TRIGGERS are activation rules; a frame is considered, that is to say it is moved into working memory and its instantiation is attempted, only if these rules are satisfied by actual data. In CHECK, the Knowledge Engineer can define different triggering rules, each of which is sufficient to evoke the frame (this means that they are implicitly ORed). A major problem in defining TRIGGERS concerns their level of specificity. Using very specific and precise conditions has the advantage of limiting the search space of the system, but, if the initial data provided by the user are not complete and precise enough, one risks excluding frames that should be considered. Conversely, if one defines large triggering conditions, the risk of losing frames that are worth considering decreases but the search space for the system is larger. The choice we have adopted in CHECK is that different types of triggering rules can be defined at different levels of specificity, which are then considered differently when triggers are evaluated. This is obtained through the use of "*relevance measures*": the idea is that one can define triggering rules with different relevance in characterizing the frame. A simple example (to be refined later in this section) of TRIGGER for the diagnostic hypothesis "cirrhosis" is the following:

> **TRIGGER:** ascites present <u>and</u>
> liver_volume increased <u>and</u>
> liver_firmness increased

This means that it is worth considering (activating) the diagnostic hypothesis "cirrhosis" in every context in which the patient has ascites and both his/her liver volume and firmness are increased.

The slot VALIDATION RULES plays a very important role in a frame description. It contains a set of production rules that should involve specific data to confirm or reject the instantiation of a frame. In particular, two completely different types of rules can be defined, namely CONFIRMATION and EXCLUSION rules. In the former group there are rules that can confirm the diagnostic hypothesis represented by the frame, in the latter are rules that can be used to exclude the hypothesis itself. The point now is to define the form that these rules have and which kind of knowledge they have to be based upon in order to be able to confirm or reject hypotheses. A first important point concerns the fact that CONFIRMATION and EXCLUSION rules must not be simultaneously applicable - that is, given a set of data either CONFIRMATION or EXCLUSION rules should be applicable (it may be the case, however, that no VALIDATION rule at all could be applied). Consider now one of the two groups of rules (e.g. CONFIRMATION rules, but the same considerations hold for EXCLUSION ones too): the rules in this group are implicitly ORed, i.e. the activation of each rule can validate the frame instantiation. Again, rules can have different specificity in validating a hypothesis, i.e. they can confirm (reject) it in different ways. This is also obtained by introducing the concept of relevance of rules (see next sections).

Let us turn now to the form of the premise of each VALIDATION rule (the consequent is obviously formed by one of the actions that "confirm" or "reject" the hypothesis). This premise is formed by two distinct parts:

-    *condition* part

-    *context of application*

The condition part is formed by a logical condition on data. In particular in the VALIDATION rules it is useful to take into account specific data. For example, in medical domains results of laboratory tests and examinations are typically used.

The context of application of a rule specifies when the rule is to be taken into account (i.e. when it can be applied). It is very useful to specify conditions on diagnostic hypotheses other than the one in which the rule itself appears (to take into account e.g. compatibilities or incompatibilities between different disorders). For example, the simultaneous presence of two disorders may be impossible if certain specific data are present, so one has to be excluded. However, in other cases the presence of a disorder can be confirmed if other disorders that could account for similar specific data have been proven to be absent (i.e. their NECESSARY FINDINGS have not been matched against data).

Consider, for example, the following EXCLUSION rule for the diagnostic hypothesis "cirrhosis" (remember that for the moment we are not considering uncertainty and relevance of rules):

> **exclude** <u>if</u> cholestatic_damage severe <u>and</u>
>   biosynthetic_damage mild
> <u>in context</u> cholestatic_jaundice present

A few comments on this rule. First, notice that specific data (results of the liver functional assessment) are used in the condition part of the rule. The meaning of the rule is intuitively the following: "the presence of cirrhosis has to be excluded if the disease cholestatic jaundice is present (has proven to be present or has been confirmed) in a patient, who has severe cholestatic damage and mild biosynthetic_damage" (actually the meaning is not so categorical, as will be discussed later in this chapter). VALIDATION rules are a simple mechanism to support multiple-diagnosing. They permit it to be taken into account, in fact, that the simultaneous presence of more than one disease can hide the presence of the typical manifestations of each one of them.

The slot ASSOCIATED HYPOTHESES contains a list of the hypotheses that are associated with the current one, i.e. the list of disorders that, in many cases, are present when the current one is present. This slot plays a very important role in CHECK's surface level inference strategy, as will be discussed in the next chapter. As an example, the ASSOCIATED HYPOTHESES slot of the frame "cirrhosis" has the following form:

> **ASSOCIATED HYPOTHESES:** chronic_cholestasis,
>   tumours.

The meaning of the slot ALTERNATIVE HYPOTHESES, which contains the list of disorders that are alternative to the current one, is completely different. This slot can be useful to suggest other hypotheses to be considered when the activation of the current one fails to match actual data. The hypotheses to be inserted in the slot are those which can be easily confused with the current one, i.e. which have a prototypical description similar to the current one. For example, in the case of the disease "cirrhosis", the list of ALTERNATIVE HYPOTHESES is the following:

> **ALTERNATIVE HYPOTHESES:** chronic congestion of the liver
>   chronic cholestatic syndromes
>   steatosis storage disorders

Let us finally consider the DEFAULT SPECIALIZATION slot, which obviously is present only in frames representing classes of diseases (i.e. which are not leaves in the frame system hierarchy). In this slot is contained the list of the specializations that are more commonly present when the generic disorder can be established. This slot is very useful in cases when, for example, the frame corresponding to a generic disorder can be instantiated on actual data (i.e. the general disorder can be confirmed) but no specialization frame can be activated (triggered). Nevertheless, it may be reasonable to try to activate the most common specializations (using a sort of default reasoning) which are contained in the DEFAULT SPECIALIZATION slot. For example, the DEFAULT SPECIALIZATION slot of "cirrhosis" has the following form:

> **DEFAULT SPECIALIZATIONS:** alcoholic cirrhosis,
> post-hepatic cirrhosis

4.3 REPRESENTING UNCERTAIN KNOWLEDGE

So far we have discussed the organization of CHECK's frames in a simplified way. In particular we have left out all the considerations concerning the representation of uncertain knowledge. It should be clear that assuming that prototypical descriptions must be categoric is in itself a severe limitation. Moreover, such an assumption has the consequence that, in order to instantiate a frame (that is, to classify a given situation), the match between the frame and actual data must be complete. The problem then is to give more flexible prototypical descriptions, so that a formal technique for their partial match with data could be defined [Torasso & Console 89]. We shall discuss in this section the problem of defining fuzzy prototypical representations, with which precise semantics are associated; moreover, we will introduce the concept of *"relevance measures"*. The mechanisms for combining evidence values will be presented in chapter 6.

4.3.1 DEFINING FUZZY PROTOTYPICAL
DESCRIPTIONS

Let us consider the prototypical component of a CHECK frame. When we defined the form of slots we noticed that each one of them is formed by the name of a finding and the list of its possible linguistic values that are fully compatible with the hypothesis represented by the frame. The concept of compatibility used above is a categorical one, i.e. we have defined a way of giving categorical prototypical descriptions. An obvious way of making such descriptions fuzzy is to modify the interpretation of the term "compatible": instead of interpreting it on the binary set {yes,no} (that is, a linguistic value for a finding is compatible or not with the hypothesis), we could interpret it on possibility measures. This means that we can associate with each possible linguistic value of a finding, a "compatibility degree" with the hypothesis. For sake of simplicity we will assume that the values of a finding are linguistic terms, that they can be defined in a crisp way and that they are mutually exclusive. In some cases this assumption may result in a limitation since sometimes the values could be more correctly represented by means of fuzzy linguistic terms [Zadeh 83]. In any case, the extension of our system to the fuzzy case does not require any major modification to the model, since it would be sufficient to define an operator for combining the possibility value of the linguistic term with respect to the fuzzy linguistic variable representing the finding with the compatibility degree of the pair <finding, linguistic value>. With this interpretation a list of pairs with the following form:

$$<\text{linguistic\_value } V_{ij}, \text{ possibility\_value } \mu_{ij}>$$

is associated in each slot with the finding F_i. The interpretation of each slot is the following: the fact that the finding F_i takes the (linguistic) value V_{ij} is compatible with the hypothesis H with possibility value μ_{ij} (following Zadeh's Possibility Theory [Zadeh 78]).

In order to make the subject clear, we will consider again the simple example of the prototypical description relative to the diagnostic hypothesis "electrical problems" in a car troubleshooting domain discussed above reporting a possible fuzzy representation in figure 4.3.

FRAME: electrical problems

NECESSARY FINDINGS
   ignition: <impossible,1> <faulty,0.8> <normal,0.1>
   lights: <normal,0.1> <low_intensity,0.7> <not_burning,0.9>

SUPPLEMENTARY FINDINGS
   battery_water_level: <low,1> <medium,0.6> <high,0.1>
   sparking_plugs_change: <less_than_10000_km,0.2>
                          <between_10000_and_20000_km,0.5>
                          <between_20000_and_30000_km,0.8>
                          <more_than_30000_km,1>

Figure 4.3 - The fuzzy prototypical description of the diagnostic hypothesis "electrical_problems".

For the sake of simplicity, just two NECESSARY and two SUPPLEMEN-TARY conditions are reported; the interpretation of the slots is the following: the condition that "ignition" is "faulty" is compatible with the diagnostic hypothesis "electrical problems" with a possibility value 0.8, whereas the condition that "lights" are "normal" is compatible with the hypothesis with a possibility value 0.1.

It should be clear from the comparison of figures 4.1 and 4.3 that the possibility of associating compatibility degrees in [0,1] with each linguistic value of a finding makes the prototypical model much more flexible. The major problem is how such compatibility degrees are to be combined in a global evidence of the match between a frame and actual data (this subject will be discussed in chapter 6).

In particular two problems must be solved: (1) determining the evidence of each group of findings (i.e. NECESSARY and SUPPLEMENTARY ones) and (2) combining the evidence values obtained from each group of findings (chunk of knowledge). As far as the second problem is concerned it is obvious that SUPPLEMENTARY conditions cannot be used as SUFFICIENT ones: they cannot confirm a hypothesis by themselves. This means that they can only augment the degree of match of NECESSARY slots and actual data, giving a more precise specification of the hypothesis. Moreover, the way in which they contribute to the confirmation must be dependent on the degree of satisfaction of NECESSARY conditions: in a certain sense SUPPLEMEN-TARY conditions cannot influence the global evaluation too much if the match of NECESSARY conditions and actual data is poor (see section 6.2).

4.3.2 INTRODUCING RELEVANCE MEASURES

In many parts of the preceding discussion we have noticed that the introduction of the concept of "relevance" could be very interesting in a prototypical description. For example, we pointed out that different triggering rules have different relevances in the activation of a frame (i.e. that there are triggering rules that should contribute more than others to the activation of a frame). Similarly, we noticed that each CONFIRMATION (EXCLUSION) rule should influence the validation of a frame in a specific way. To respond to a need such as making prototypical descriptions more flexible, we introduced the concept of "relevance measure" (of data, rules, slots, etc.) into our model [Torasso & Console 89]. In the following we will first present the concept in a very general way, then we shall discuss how it has been used in CHECK's knowledge representation formalism.

The concept of "importance" of data was introduced in the expert system

CENTAUR [Aikins 83] in order to weigh differently the contributions of the subframes (components) in the evaluation of a frame.

We have introduced "*relevance measures*" to weigh the importance of data (or conditions on data) and we use them in a different and more systematic way compared with CENTAUR. Consider a generic condition (e.g. a condition to be evaluated during the instantiation of a slot), and suppose that a conjunction of data (values of findings) must be tested. Information about these data may be uncertain or incomplete, so that fuzzy evaluation has to be used. Often data to be tested have a different relevance in the evaluation of the condition; certain data may be necessary, other less important. It would be nice if a general evaluation function could account for this information.

We propose to associate with each atomic condition in a complex condition a "relevance measure" (RM) in the interval [0,1]: a value close to 1 indicates that the atomic condition has a great relevance, conversely a value close to 0 indicates a low relevance. Obviously, this relevance measure is context dependent, i.e. the same atomic condition can have different relevance values in different contexts. It is worth pointing out that for the sake of simplicity we assign a relevance measure just to each atomic condition and the global evidence degree is evaluated by taking into account the relevance and the evidence degree of each atom. In principle, it should be possible to assign a relevance measure to each combination of atomic conditions, but in most cases this would cause an unbearable increase in the complexity of the system (especially for the domain expert or the knowledge engineer who are in charge of providing reasonable estimates of the relevance measure). In particular in the prototypical description we decided to assign a relevance measure to each finding and not to each pair <finding, linguistic value> (see next paragraph for more comments).

We can distinguish between two evidence values for each datum: "observed evidence" and "corrected evidence". We will denote with "observed evidence" the evidence of a datum (finding) provided by the user (or derived by the system from the evidence of other findings). Corrected evidence values are context dependent values; they are obtained by combining the observed evidence and the relevance of a datum in each particular context. These corrected values are those which are used in the evaluation of complex conditions; they are computed in such a way that evaluations will rely more on relevant data.

The idea in the evaluation of a complex condition, e.g. a conjunction of literals is that its evaluation should mainly depend on important literals, so that, for example, the fact that the evidence of important literals is close to 0 should lead to an evaluation of the conjunction which is close to 0. On the other hand, the fact that the evidence of unimportant literals is close to 0 should have a minor influence on the evaluation of the conjunction. A complete discussion of the functions to combine "observed evidence" and "relevance measure" to get the "corrected evidence" of a literal will be given in chapter 6.

Let us now turn to the problem of using relevance measures in a prototypical description. We shall reconsider here each one of the groups of slots of CHECK's frames, discussing how in each one of them the introduction of such a new parameter contributes to making the formalism much more flexible and powerful (see also [Torasso & Console 89] for a discussion).

PROTOTYPICAL DESCRIPTION

In the prototypical description (NECESSARY and SUFFICIENT or SUPPLEMENTARY descriptions) a relevance measure is associated with each single slot.

Consider, for example, NECESSARY findings slots; the fact that a relevance measure (RM) is associated with each one of them means that they do not all have the same "strength of necessity". Some findings are strictly necessary (RM close to 1), others have a lower strength of necessity (RM close to 0). Similarly, in the case of SUFFICIENT descriptions the relevance of a slot represents its "strength of sufficiency" in characterizing the frame. In the case of SUPPLEMENTARY findings, the meaning of relevance measures is different and more complicated. The interpretation given for SUFFICIENT descriptions can be adapted to the case of SUPPLEMENTARY ones. In fact, consider the group of SUPPLEMENTARY findings slots: the conditions contained in these slots are ORed, so the instantiation of even one of them can be sufficient to contribute to the better specification of a hypothesis. It follows that relevance measures can again be considered as sufficiency measures. What has changed from the case of SUFFICIENT descriptions is the scope of sufficiency: in the case of SUFFICIENT slots the scope is the frame, in the case of SUPPLEMENTARY slots, the scope is limited to the group of slots itself. More complicated functions (that will be discussed in the next section) are to be used to combine evidence values obtained from NECESSARY and SUPPLEMENTARY slots.

As an example of simple complete prototypical description consider again the one used in figures 4.1 and 4.3. In figure 4.4 that description has been augmented, associating a relevance measure with each one of the slots. Notice that whereas the slot "faulty ignition" has great relevance in giving a necessary characterization of the disorder, the slot "lights" has a lower one.

It is worth pointing out, to avoid misunderstandings, that from the semantical point of view there is a complete difference between a NECES-SARY FINDING with a low strength of necessity and a SUPPLEMENTARY one.

Notice that we have associated a "relevance measure" with each slot, i.e. with each finding. An alternative approach would have been that of associating a "relevance measure" with each pair <finding,linguistic-value>. This possibility is certainly very interesting and would make the representation even more flexible and powerful, but it is very complex since it requires a great number of estimates of relevance measures to be provided by the knowledge engineer. It should be pointed out, however, that the functions for evidence combination we have designed (described in chapter 6) can also be adopted in this case without any modification.

FRAME: electrical problems

NECESSARY FINDINGS
ignition: <impossible,1> <faulty,0.8> <normal,0.1>
relevance: 1
lights: <normal,0.1> <low_intensity,0.7> <not_burning,0.9>
relevance: 0.5

SUPPLEMENTARY FINDINGS
battery_water_level: <low,1> <medium,0.6> <high,0.1>
relevance: 0.7
sparking_plugs_change: <less_than_10000_km,0.2>
                       <between_10000_and_20000_km,0.5>
                       <between_10000_and_30000_km,0.8>
                       <more_than_30000_km,1>
relevance: 1

Figure 4.4 - The fuzzy prototypical description of the diagnostic hypothesis "electrical_problems" with "relevance measures".

TRIGGERS

A "relevance" measure can be associated in this case with each triggering rule. As we have noted before, triggering rules are implicitly ORed, so the satisfaction of many triggers (even if each of them has relatively low relevance) causes the activation of the frame corresponding to the hypothesis. It is worth noting that in this revised model the satisfaction of just one trigger with a low relevance is not sufficient for activating the hypothesis (this is a powerful method for preventing the activation of too many hypotheses).

VALIDATION RULES

A "relevance measure" is associated with each VALIDATION rule too, i.e. to each CONFIRMATION and EXCLUSION rule. In the former case, the measure can be interpreted as the "strength of confirmation" of the rule and in the latter as its "strength of exclusion". This means, in the case of CONFIRMATION rules, that the more relevant a rule is, the greater is its influence on increasing the evidence of the hypothesis in the validation process.

4.4 A COMPLETE EXAMPLE

In the preceding sections we have defined CHECK's surface level knowledge representation schemes in full detail. We have argued that prototypical descriptions are very useful in representing hypotheses in a diagnostic system and we have proposed a very flexible and powerful approach for representing prototypical knowledge. To close this chapter we will present a complete example of a complex frame: in particular, the frame corresponding to the coarse diagnostic hypothesis (i.e. class of diseases or "syndrome") "cirrhosis" in our liver diseases expert system is reported in figure 4.5.

FRAME: cirrhosis

TRIGGERS:
   ascites present <u>and</u> liver_volume increased <u>and</u> liver_firmness increased
      relevance 1
   jaundice present <u>and</u> ascites present
      relevance 0.8
   ascites present
      relevance 0.6

liver_volume increased <u>and</u> liver_firmness increased
   relevance 0.6
jaundice present
   relevance 0.4

NECESSARY FINDINGS
general_well_being: <normal,0.8>
                    <mild_alteration,1>
                    <average_alteration,1>
                    <severe_alteration,0.4>
   relevance 0.7
digestive_troubles: <absent,1>
                    <mild,1>
                    <average,1>
                    <severe,0.2>
   relevance 0.7
abdominal_pain: <absent,1>
                <mild,0.8>
                <average,0.4>
                <severe,0.2>
   relevance 0.6
fever: <absent,1>
       <mild,1>
       <medium,0.8>
       <severe,0.4>
   relevance 0.6
symptoms_duration: <less_than_1_week,0.8>
                   <less_than_1_month,1>
                   <less_than_6_months,1>
                   <more_than_6_months,1>
   relevance 0.7
jaundice: <absent,1>
          <mild,1>
          <average,1>
          <severe,1>
   relevance 1
liver_volume: <normal,0.8>
              <mild_increase,1>
              <average_increase,1>
              <severe_increase,1>
   relevance 1
liver_firmness: <normal,0.1>
                <mild_increase,0.8>
                <average_increase,1>

                              <severe_increase,1>
    relevance 1
liver_surface_regularity: <normal,1>
                               <mild_altered,1>
                               <average_altered,1>
                               <severe_altered,0.7>
    relevance 0.8
liver_pain: <absent,1>
               <mild,1>
               <average,0.6>
               <severe,0.2>
    relevance 0.7
spleen_volume: <normal,1>
                      <mild_increase,1>
                      <average_increase,1>
    relevance 0.8
ascites: <absent,1>
         <mild 1>
         <average,1>
         <conspicuous,1>
    relevance 1

SUPPLEMENTARY FINDINGS
less_than_10_year_protracted_daily_alcohol_intake:
               <medium, 0.6>
               <high, 1>
    relevance 0.7
more_than_10_year_protracted_daily_alcohol_intake:
               <medium, 0.8>
               <high, 1>
    relevance 1
prolonged_exposure_to_blood_or_blood_derivatives:
               <lasting_more_than_6_months,1>
    relevance 0.5
inflammatory_bowel_disease:
               <present,1>
    relevance 0.5
collagen_disorder:
               <present,1>
    relevance 0.5
previous_acute_viral_hepatitis_or_jaundice:
               <present,1>
    relevance 0.5

VALIDATION RULES
    exclude if cytolitic_damage absent and
            cholestatic_damage absent and
            biosynthetic_damage absent and
            increased_reactivity absent
            in_context -
            relevance 1

    exclude if cytolitic_damage severe
            in_context acute_hepatitis present or
                            acute_congestion_of_the_liver present
            relevance 0.8

    exclude if cholestatic_damage severe and
            biosynthetic_damage absent and
            increased_reactivity absent
            in_context -
            relevance 0.8

    exclude if cholestatic_damage severe and
            biosynthetic_damage mild
            in_context cholestatic_jaundice present
            relevance 0.4

    exclude if cytolitic_damage average and
            biosynthetic_damage absent and
            (increased_reactivity average or
             increased_reactivity severe)
            in_context chronic_hepatitis present
            relevance 0.4

    confirm if (cytolitic_damage absent or
            cytolitic_damage mild) and
            (cholestatic_damage absent or
            cholestatic_damage mild) and
            (biosynthetic_damage average or
            biosynthetic_damage severe) and
            increased_reactivity average
            in-context -
            relevance 1

ASSOCIATED HYPOTHESES: Chronic_hepatitis
                                    Tumours

ALTERNATIVE HYPOTHESES: Chronic_congestion_of_the_liver
Chronic_cholestatic_syndromes
Steatosis_storage_disorders

SPECIALIZATIONS: Alcoholic_cirrhosis
Autoimmune_cirrhosis
Haemocromatosis
Wilson's_disease
Post-hepatic_cirrhosis
Toxic_cirrhosis
Porphyrias
Cryptogenic_cirrhosis

DEFAULT SPECIALIZATIONS: Alcoholic_cirrhosis
Post-hepatic_cirrhosis

Figure 4.5 - The complete frame describing the diagnostic hypothesis "cirrhosis".

5

HEURISTIC LEVEL:
INFERENCE STRATEGY

In this chapter we will discuss how reasoning is performed at the heuristic level in CHECK; i.e. we will present the control and the inference strategy we have designed in the frame system. It is worth noting that the reasoning scheme we are going to present has been strongly influenced by the experience of LITO2.

As noted before (see chapter 2), the heuristic (surface) level of CHECK is invoked first with the aim of producing one (a set of) diagnostic hypothesis, so that all the initial phases of user consultation and data acquisition are charged to the surface level control structure. In the following pages we shall first briefly discuss the initial consultation (data acquisition) phase (more details about the actual organization of this phase and the techniques we have adopted for building a friendly interface will be given in chapter 9, describing man-machine interaction in CHECK), then we shall present the global search strategy in CHECK's frame system and the inference strategy adopted in each frame.

It is worth making some points before starting the discussion: the entire presentation that follows abstracts from the techniques used for the management of uncertain knowledge and evidence combination (that is, uncertain reasoning). This means that we shall refer to generic evidence evaluation and combination functions in the following pages (e.g. when we make assertions like "the evidence of NECESSARY FINDINGS" is computed, we mean only that some function should be used to evaluate such an evidence degree without specifying which). This corresponds to how CHECK's control and inference strategy is practically realized: it is completely parametric with respect to the evidence combination schemes adopted, so different combination criteria can be designed and experimented with. Moreover, we believe that, for the sake of clarity, it is better to separate the description of the control and inference strategies (given in this chapter) from that of the particular evidence combination scheme we have designed (given in the next chapter).

5.1 GENERAL OVERVIEW

The first important phase when the system is activated concerns data acquisition. This means that data relative to a particular consultation (case) have to be obtained from the external world. In CHECK, it is important to distinguish between two different phases of data acquisition: a *passive* phase and an *active* one. In the first one, the system "passively" receives data from the user and in the second the system is active and requests data, asking questions of the user. More details about these two phases, their organization and motivations for such a choice will be given in chapter 9.

For the purpose of this section it is only important to point out that the initial consultation phase is the passive one: the user is presented with a set of menus through which he/she can select which findings are present in a given case. For each selected finding new menus are popped up to fill in the attributes of the finding itself: if the user provides a numeric value for an attribute of a finding then the interpretation rules (remember that "interpretation rules" are associated with each finding in the data hierarchy - see chapter 3 on data organization) are activated to compute the corresponding linguistic value. It is worth noting that, in order to make the interpretation rules operate correctly, in some cases the user is requested by the system to fill in the description of other findings (in fact, it may be the case that information about other findings is necessary in the interpretation rules for a finding). The findings of the initial menu, which are not selected by the user, are assigned a default value. In this initial phase, only very general data are requested by the system - that is the minimum set of data which are sufficient to evaluate the triggering conditions of the higher level diagnostic hypotheses, other data are successively asked for by the system when actually needed (e.g. during the activation process of a frame or during the evaluation of validation rules).

The important point to consider here is that data acquisition in CHECK is not merely an input-output operation, but that an initial, simple form of reasoning on data is performed. More particularly, the data provided by the user are abstracted (for example, using the interpretation rules associated with a datum in its frame in the data hierarchy) and the corresponding prototypical descriptions (in the data hierarchy) are instantiated. Moreover, when initial data have been acquired from the user, very simple checks of their consistency can be performed, using the interpretation rules as test rules.

Let us now briefly analyze the general lines of the reasoning process in CHECK's heuristic level. In this section we will give an abstract description of the overall process, associating with each abstract problem solving phase its correspondent at the implementation level (e.g. the conceptual phase of "considering a diagnostic hypothesis" corresponds to the actual operation of "activating a frame"); in the more accurate description that follows, the two levels of description will be often interleaved.

After initial data are provided by the user the system starts the search phase in the hypotheses hierarchy for a solution (diagnostic hypothesis). The search strategy we have adopted in CHECK is a very special one based on a high parallelism in the consideration of the hypotheses at every diagnostic abstraction level. More particularly, a parallel form of heuristic guided breadth-first search in the hierarchy has been adopted which allows us to realize (simple) forms of differential reasoning at every diagnostic level (e.g. when specializing a given diagnostic hypothesis). This means that highest level hypotheses, corresponding to coarse diagnoses, are taken into account and matched against data of a specific case first; then all of those which have been instantiated are specialized (that is, their descendants in the hierarchy are considered) and so on, until a solution (a set of solutions) is found (that is some specific diagnoses - some leaves in the hierarchy of hypotheses - are confirmed on the data of the specific case under examination).

In the following we shall analyze in detail these different phases of reasoning, starting with the phase of "awakening and activation of hypotheses (corresponding at the implementation level to the "triggering and activation of frames" phase). It is worth noting that, during the reasoning process, diagnostic hypotheses may be activated more than once: different forms of reasoning on the hypothesis are performed in each such activation (that is, different control slots of the frame corresponding to the hypothesis are considered in each activation). For example, highest level coarse diagnostic hypotheses (and similarly all the other ones which are not leaves in the hierarchy) are first awakened (that is, the corresponding frames are triggered), then considered for matching against data (frames are activated for instantiating their prototypical description slots), then activated for validation (that is, validation slots of a frame are activated) and finally for diagnostic refinement (during each one of these phases all the frames at a given diagnostic level are activated in parallel).

For the sake of simplicity, in the following presentation we shall limit the discussion of the control strategy to the case in which only two levels of diagnostic hypotheses are present in the system (that is: coarse diagnostic hypotheses and specific diagnoses). The extension to the general case of systems with more levels of hypotheses is straightforward: it is sufficient, in fact, to iterate at every intermediate level the reasoning scheme we shall define for coarse diagnostic hypotheses in our two-level example system). Limiting the discussion to such a form of system has the advantage that a complete description of the control strategy can be given.

5.2 TRIGGERING AND ACTIVATION OF DIAGNOSTIC HYPOTHESES

The first phase after data acquisition consists of the triggering and activation of higher level frames (diagnostic hypotheses). Initial data, in fact, activate the *triggering rule slots* of such frames: those frames whose triggers are satisfied and for which the global relevance of the triggers exceeds a given threshold, are inserted in an "*agenda*" of hypotheses to be considered.

The frames in the agenda are then selected and activated. In this first phase the activation of a frame corresponds to an attempt to instantiate its prototypical description (NECESSARY and SUPPLEMENTARY FINDINGS slots) against data. In particular, the instantiation of NECESSARY FINDINGS is attempted first; then, if it succeeds, SUPPLEMENTARY FINDINGS are taken into account as well. In this phase two different evidence values are computed (one for NECESSARY FINDINGS and one for SUPPLEMEN-TARY ones), they are then combined to obtain an (initial) global degree of evidence for the hypothesis. It is worth noting that this evidence value will be successively refined in the VALIDATION process, as will be discussed in the next section.

The instantiation of each single slot consists simply of testing whether the actual values of the attributes of the finding contained in the slot are compatible with the diagnostic hypothesis (this test returns a compatibility degree value, to be combined with the relevance of the slot, to compute its corrected evidence - see chapter 6). During this instantiation process it may be the case that no information about a finding is present in the system, since in the initial consultation only very general data are provided by the user (that is, data to test triggering rules are inserted in the initial form to be filled by the user). If information about a finding is not yet present, the system asks the user about the finding itself in a special pop-up window (see chapter 9).

At the end of the triggering and activation phase an agenda, containing the frames which have been instantiated, is built by the system (again, this agenda is a ranked one - in fact, with each frame is associated its instantiation evidence).

5.3 VALIDATION PROCESS

One of the most interesting reasoning processes in CHECK's heuristic level is the *validation process,* whose aim is at confirming/rejecting the diagnostic hypotheses generated in the activation process using specific data and differentiating among them. This process immediately follows the activation one - that is it operates on the agenda of instantiated frames built by the activation process. The validation process is a highly parallel one since its main task is to discriminate between all the hypotheses at a given diagnostic level, using specific data (results from the evaluation of liver function assessment in our medical system operating in the domain of liver diseases) and information about the associations (correlation and compatibilities) or incompatibilities between hypotheses.

Before the main part of the process begins there is another operation which is performed by the control strategy of CHECK: the activation of frames which are *associated* with instantiated ones (i.e. which are contained in the ASSOCIATED HYPOTHESES slots of instantiated frames). The idea is the following: if a hypothesis H_i has got high evidence, then all hypotheses H_j associated with it (listed in the ASSOCIATED-HYPOTHESES slot) are considered and the system tries to match them against data, independently from triggering rules.

Since an associational link exists between H_i and H_j (in some cases a causal relationship connects the two hypotheses), H_j can never be disregarded if the hypothesis H_i has been established with a high degree of evidence. This means that H_j is directly activated (without considering the triggering phase) and, if the activation is successful, it is inserted in the agenda of instantiated frames to be validated. This mechanism is an important aspect of the parallel search between classes of CHECK since it takes into account interactions and connections between diagnostic classes in the search process.

After the activation of associated frames, the main part of the validation process begins: each instantiated frame in the agenda is activated again and control is passed to the VALIDATION RULES slot. This means that either a CONFIRMATION·or an EXCLUSION rule is activated and the evidence of instantiation of the frame is respectively increased or decreased. The entity of the increase (decrease) depends on the evidence of the rule and on its relevance. If no rule can be activated, the instantiation of the frame remains unchanged.

To verify whether each single CONFIRMATION (EXCLUSION) rule in a frame can be activated, its context of application is tested first, then the specific conditions in the premise of the rule are evaluated. Notice again that this may lead to asking the user further questions (very specific data are, in fact, used in the VALIDATION rules which were not needed in the preceding phases).

The important point to consider in the validation process is that the system is able to differentiate between diagnoses and to reason on the diagnostic problem more globally. This is due to the parallel searching and instantiation at every diagnostic level and to the possibility of specifying different types of interrelations between frames in the "context of application" of the VALIDATION rules. The possibility of operating at such a global level and of discriminating between possible diagnostic hypotheses is very important in producing more reliable solutions. It is worth noting that this differentiation is not possible in systems which use a pure "refinement process" to produce diagnoses (as, for example, in the early version of MDX or in CSRL).

The final result of the validation process is that a set of frames (diagnostic hypotheses) is inserted in the agenda and with each of them a final instantiation plus validation evidence is associated (the mechanism for combining two such values is described in chapter 6).

5.4 SPECIALIZATION PROCESS

The last phase of frame activation in CHECK's heuristic level is the specialization one. In particular, specialization is applied to all frames inserted in the agenda by the validation process - that is, to all frames whose instantiation has been confirmed in the validation process. The specialization process of a frame is a simple one and consists mainly in the activation of its subframes. In particular, the subframes of the frame to be specialized are triggered and a new agenda of frames to be activated is built. Otherwise, if no subframe can be triggered, DEFAULT SPECIALIZATION frames are taken into account. On this new agenda the inference process starts from the beginning - that is, the frames are activated (instantiated), validated and, in turn, specialized (if they are not leaves in the hierarchy).[1]

---

[1] Notice the resemblance of our specialization process with the MDX (or CSRL) refinement process.

If a frame is a leaf in the hierarchy, its activation is concluded after the validation process and, if confirmed, the frame is considered as a possible solution to be further confirmed and, eventually, explained by the deep level.

5.5 DISCUSSION

To close this chapter we show in figure 5.1 a scheme of the strategy adopted at each diagnostic level to determine the set of hypotheses compatible with the data observed in a specific case. It should be noted that the control strategy briefly outlined in this section fits Clancey's definition of "Heuristic Classification": data provided by the user are abstracted (e.g. linguistic values are obtained from numeric ones), solutions are heuristically searched (using a heuristic match in a frame system) and refined.

One of the peculiarities of CHECK is its way of performing differential (and possibly multiple) diagnosis by means of "parallel" searching at the corresponding diagnostic level. We believe that only such a form of (limited) parallelism can solve the problem, furthermore the techniques adopted are simpler and clearer than others, e.g. those proposed recently in the new version of the MDX system [Sticklen et al. 85]. In this system mechanisms for simple differential and multiple diagnosis are added on top of a pure depth-first search in a hierarchy of hypotheses.

It is important to point out that, although a breadth first (parallel) search in the frame system hierarchy has been adopted, the effective search space of the system in any specific case (consultation) is not very large - that is, search is focused so that we do not have serious problems of inefficiency (as might be imagined). The focusing of the search derives mainly from the pruning of the search space which is done in different phases of the reasoning process: first, triggering rules are able to exclude hypotheses (that is, to prune the search graph) at a very early stage, then the instantiation process and the evaluation of the degree of match of frames and actual data allows for the exclusion of other hypotheses. Finally, in the validation process the activation of EXCLUSION rules allows for other forms of pruning. This means that we use different forms of heuristics which allow us to work in a reasonable search space.

Consider, for example, the case of LITO2 (the heuristic system from which the surface level of CHECK has been borrowed): the specific application we have built ·in the domain of liver diseases has ten diagnostic classes and about eighty specific diseases. The evaluation of the performances of the system has shown that, on average, only less than half the high level frames (coarse diagnostic hypotheses) pass the triggering phase and are considered

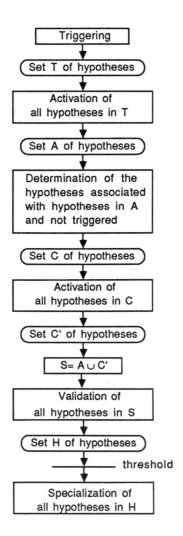

Figure 5.1 - Scheme of the inference strategy at each diagnostic level.

for activation, and that usually only two or three of them pass the activation and validation process (usually most of the others are already excluded when NECESSARY FINDINGS slots are evaluated). As regards specific diseases the system, on average, considers between five and ten of them, but only two to five (at worst) pass the validation process (and consequently should be passed on to the deep level for further confirmation). These figures show that we have a high focusing in the search - that is, we have designed a breadth-first differential process which gives reliable solutions without losing too much in efficiency.

Another important feature of the search strategy we have chosen is that it takes into account the associational relations between diseases in every case and not only when a particular value for a finding is not accounted for by a single chosen disease (there is no need for "can't account for", "re-establish" or "expected but not found" messages between diseases typical of the new version of MDX [Sticklen et al. 85]).

6

APPROXIMATE REASONING

In this chapter we shall discuss the mechanisms of evidence evaluation we have designed in order to provide a way of ranking diagnostic hypotheses on the basis of their "fitness" with the data describing the particular case under examination [Torasso & Console 89]. The goal of ranking hypotheses does not imply that we believe that a final decision on the choice of the correct diagnosis can be taken on the sole basis of the resulting evidence degrees of the competing hypotheses (some authors point out that the selection of the correct diagnosis has to be approached with methods of decision theory, in which the notion of utility plays a very important role [Lau & Pauker 85] [Langlotz et al. 86]).

We believe that the evidence evaluation mechanisms we have introduced in CHECK provide the system with a powerful heuristic focusing mechanism since they allow the system to disregard most of the diagnostic hypotheses that have been activated. In particular, the mechanisms we are presenting have been partly borrowed from the evidence combination schemata that have been investigated in past years for rule systems [Lesmo, Saitta, Torasso 84a,b] [Lesmo, Saitta, Torasso 85].

Unfortunately, results for rule-based systems are only partially useful in frame-based systems, mainly because in a frame each chunk of knowledge is stored in a separate group of slots according to its meaning, whilst in most rule-based systems production rules are not grouped according to the role they play. If we consider the structure of a diagnostic hypotheses it is apparent that the different parts of the description (NECESSARY FINDINGS,

SUPPLEMENTARY FINDINGS, etc.) play very different roles and consequently the evidence combination mechanism must take into account such a difference. In particular, two problems should be faced:

-    the evaluation of an evidence degree inside each chunk of knowledge since the different descriptions are implicitly or explicitly related via logical connectives (as occurs in NECESSARY FINDINGS or SUPPLEMENTARY ones);

-    the evaluation of a global evidence degree for the diagnostic hypothesis on the basis of the different evidence degrees gathered by the hypothesis by considering the different chunks of knowledge.

In our approach the first problem is made more difficult because of the introduction of relevance measures, which on the other hand allow the system to weigh the importance of the single components inside the global description.

In the following paragraphs we shall first deal with this problem and then we shall provide the semantics of the logical connectives used for evaluating the evidence inside each chunk of knowledge. In section 6.2 the problem of combining evidence degrees coming from different knowledge sources will be addressed.

6.1 INFLUENCE OF RELEVANCE MEASURES ON EVIDENCE EVALUATION

The way in which observed evidence values and relevance measures are combined depends on the logical connective used to form a complex condition starting from the atomic ones (for the sake of simplicity, we will assume here that we have conditions formed using only one type of connective, AND or OR, without any loss of generality). The combination can be expressed introducing a function $f_{CONNECTIVE}$ with the following type:

$$f_{CONNECTIVE} : D_{EV} \; x \; D_{RM} \rightarrow D_{EV}$$

where D_{EV} represents the domain of evidence and D_{RM} the domain of relevance measures.

The (corrected) evidence obtained by applying $f_{CONNECTIVE}$ to the pair <observed_evidence, RM> of a fact is the same as that used in the fuzzy evaluation of the complex condition. The general requirements for the function $f_{CONNECTIVE}$ are reported in (1) and (2) for the two cases of AND and OR connectives respectively.

(1)
$$f_{AND}(e,0)=1$$
$$f_{AND}(e,1)=e$$
$$f_{AND}(0,m)=1-m$$
$$f_{AND}(1,m)=1$$
$$f_{AND}(e,m)\geq e \quad \text{if} \quad 0 <e <1 \quad \text{and} \quad 0 <m <1$$

(2)
$$f_{OR}(e,0)=0$$
$$f_{OR}(e,1)=e$$
$$f_{OR}(0,m)=0$$
$$f_{OR}(1,m)=m$$
$$f_{OR}(e,m)\leq e \quad \text{if} \quad 0 <e <1 \quad \text{and} \quad 0 <m <1$$

The first operand of both f_{AND} and f_{OR} represents the observed evidence of an atomic condition and the second one the relevance measure of the finding occurring in the atomic condition.

These formulae deserve a brief comment. Consider the case of the AND connective (dual considerations hold for the OR connective) and imagine a formula in which many atomic conditions are conjuncted (suppose different relevance measures are associated with each one of them). Corrected evidences have to be computed in such a way that these two rules hold:

- if a datum is important, the evidence of the complex condition has to depend directly on its evidence;

- if a datum is not important, its observation has to contribute to the evaluation, whilst the lack of its observation must not be determinant in the evaluation.

This means that the lack of observation of data with low relevance has to be 'neutralized': the global evaluation must depend on the other conditions. This 'neutralization' must be inversely proportional to the relevance value: if the relevance is 0, the neutralization must be total. For this reason observed evidences have to be increased by f_{AND}, whose limit has to be the constant function $e = 1$ for $m \rightarrow 0$. Note that if all relevance measures are '1', the usual evaluation of AND conditions (without relevance measures) can be obtained.

Dual considerations hold in the case of f_{OR}: in this case evidence values have to be decreased and the limit for $m \rightarrow 0$ is the constant function $e = 0$.

Notice that an importance measure m=1 for a condition which should be ANDed with other ones, means that the condition is strictly necessary. On the contrary m=1 for a condition to be ORed with other ones indicates that the satisfaction of the condition itself is sufficient for the satisfaction of the OR condition.

Obviously the criteria expressed in (1) and (2) are not sufficient to constrain the form of the formulae which define f_{AND} and f_{OR} : there are several families of functions satisfying (1) and (2). In (3) and (4) we report two possible definitions:

(3)
$$f_{AND}(e,m)=m^*e+(1-m)$$

$$f_{OR}(e,m)=m^*e$$

(4)
$$f_{AND}(e,m)=e^2(m^2-m)+e(2m-m^2)+(1-m)$$

$$f_{OR}(e,m)=e^2(m-m^2)+m^2e$$

The formulae (3) are very simple and linear, whilst the formulae in (4) allow one to obtain more interesting corrections of the observed evidence values, with a greater computational effort. In any case, the choice between (3) and (4) (or other possible definitions compatible with (1) and (2)) does not significantly alter the global evaluation mechanism. As regards these formulae it is worth noting that Sanchez [Sanchez 87] arrived at similar conclusions about the influence of relevance measures, starting from a very different problem (intelligent information retrieval).

Once the revised evidence degree has been evaluated for the elementary conditions, we have to use formulae for deriving the evidence degree of complex descriptions. Since in each chunk of knowledge elementary conditions are related together by means of logical connectives (in some cases this connection is implicit as in NECESSARY FINDINGS and in SUPPLEMENTARY ones), we use the evidence evaluation mechanism developed for evaluating the evidence degree of complex logical formulae occurring as antecedents in production rules [Lesmo, Saitta, Torasso 84a,b] [Lesmo, Saitta, Torasso 85]. In particular, the semantics of "AND" logical connective are given by the formula:

$$(5) \qquad e(\text{AND } (T_1 \ T_2 \ ... \ T_n \ )) = \alpha+\beta * (\beta-\alpha)$$

where $\alpha = \prod_{j=1}^{n} e(T_j)$ and $\beta = \min_{j=1}^{n} e(T_j)$

The resulting evidence degree consists of the product of the evidence degrees of the n elementary terms increased by a quantity which is a part of the difference between the minimum (β : upper bound) and the product (α : lower bound) proportional to the minimum.

The semantic of the NOT operator is given, as is usual in possibility theory [Zadeh 78], as:

$$(6) \quad e(\text{NOT } T) = 1 - e(T)$$

As regards the OR operator, the definition is given according to the De Morgan's laws:

$$(7) \quad e(\text{OR } (T_1 \ T_2 \ \dots \ T_n)) = e(\text{NOT } (\text{AND } ((\text{NOT } T_1) \ (\text{NOT } T_2) \ \dots \ (\text{NOT } T_n)))$$

It is worth noting that the interpretation of logical connectives has some resemblance to the one of possibility theory, even if the formulae defining the semantics of the logical connectives are not the usual ones (MAX for OR and MIN for AND). There are several reasons for not adopting the standard formulae: the major objection is the insensitivity of the result to the evidence degrees of all the different conditions, apart from the one that has the maximum value in an OR-ed expression (or the minimum in an AND-ed expression). In fact, if one wants to characterize the match between a given condition and some input data, it is unrealistic to assume that a sequence of n low values (let us say 0.2) fits equally as well as a sequence of (n-1) elementary conditions matched perfectly, followed by a condition which is poorly matched (with a value of 0.2); on the contrary, it seems reasonable to assume that if many conditions are poorly matched, the global degree of match goes below the individual minimum. For an accurate analysis of the properties of the formulae (5) and (7) and a comparison with the standard ones, see [Lesmo, Saitta, Torasso 85].

Furthermore, the mechanism described in [Lesmo, Saitta, Torasso 85] provides the system with the capability of evaluating the evidence degrees of complex expressions which involve not only logical connectives (AND, OR NOT), but also quantified expressions. In particular mechanisms for evaluating expressions like "AT LEAST n elements in class C satisfy property P" have been defined and used extensively in the LITO systems. The introduction of quantifiers like "AT LEAST n", AT MOST n", "EXACTLY n" proved to be very useful in augmenting the expressive power of the rules and in making them very perspicuous (see [Yager 83] for a similar approach).

Quantified expressions have also been used in some cases in the heuristic level of CHECK, particularly in TRIGGERS and VALIDATION RULES, since they provide a compact way of expressing the fact that the presence (or the absence) of a given number of findings belonging to a given class is relevant for establishing or rejecting a diagnostic hypothesis. Notice that in recent years we have also investigated the problem of evaluating expressions containing fuzzy quantifiers [Lesmo & Torasso 87]. Even if the introduction of such a kind of quantifiers could significantly extend the expressive power, we preferred to avoid their introduction in the surface level of CHECK because their evaluation is strongly influenced by the context and in some cases the heuristic level of CHECK has not enough knowledge to characterize the context in a correct way.

6.2 AN HEURISTIC APPROACH TO EVIDENCE COMBINATION

In this section we will describe how evidence degrees obtained from different chunks of knowledge can be combined to compute the global evidence degree of diagnostic hypotheses [Torasso & Console 89].

In most rule-based expert systems the problem of evidence combination is solved in a heuristic way, since many subtle questions arise when one has to define a precise semantic for this kind of operation [Bylander & Mittal 86] [Zadeh 86]. What is important to note here is the fact that evidence combination mechanisms are usually "additive" in nature - that is, the global evidence degree is never lower than the maximum of the evidence degrees of the single chunks of knowledge. In other words the evidence of a hypothesis is strengthened if more than one knowledge source provides evidence for it.

A formula widely used for combining evidence is the Bernoulli formula (initially proposed in the MYCIN system, it has been adopted in the EMYCIN shell [Van Melle 79] and has also been used in other systems, for example MORE [Kahn et al. 85]):

$$(8) \qquad e_1 +_f e_2 = e_1 + (1-e_1)*e_2$$

In this case the two evidence degrees are to be considered in the same way: no single value is in a privileged position. This seems to correspond to the case in which a diagnostic hypothesis is described by means of NECESSARY FINDINGS and SUFFICIENT FINDINGS; in such a case a frame can be instantiated (a diagnostic hypothesis can be established) if either all the NECESSARY FINDINGS have been properly matched or one of the SUFFICIENT FINDINGS is satisfied.

It should be clear that the formula (8) cannot be used to combine the evidence degrees obtained from the match of NECESSARY and SUPPLEMENTARY FINDINGS with actual data. In fact, let us suppose that the match between NECESSARY FINDINGS and actual data has completely failed (that is e(N) = 0), then it would be sufficient to have the match of one of the SUPPLEMENTARY FINDINGS (provided that its relevance measure is equal to 1) with one datum of the case under examination in order to obtain the complete confirmation of the hypothesis (that is, the resulting evidence degree is equal to one).

What we need is a different operation ("unfair addition") in which one of the operands (e.g. the first) is in a privileged position. Acceptable results for such cases can be obtained by using the following additive operator (the first operand is the privileged one):

$$(9) \qquad e_1 +_u e_2 = e_1 + (1 - e_1)^* e_1^* e_2$$

This operation is obviously not commutative, but it is associative. If we assume that e_1 is the evidence degree coming from NECESSARY FINDINGS and e_2 the one from SUPPLEMENTARY findings, we find that the contribution of SUPPLEMENTARY findings depends on the degree of match of NECESSARY ones and actual data. In other words the increment of the overall evidence due to SUPPLEMENTARY FINDINGS is modest if the evidence degree obtained by NECESSARY ones is low.

The formulae (8) and (9) represent two extreme examples of the degree of fairness used in evidence combination. In particular, (8) represents the perfect "fair" case since both contributions are treated equally, whilst (9) represents the "unfair" case since the first contribution is the privileged one. We can make a generalization from these two extreme cases by introducing an evidence combination mechanism which makes use of a parameter λ representing the degree of fairness. Therefore, the resulting formula for evidence combination is

$$(10) \qquad e_1 +_\lambda e_2 = e_1 + (1 - e_1)^* e_2^* g(e_1, \lambda)$$

in which the correcting factor $g(e_1, \lambda)$ is characterized by the following behavior:

$g(e_1, 1) = 1$ (perfect fairness)
$g(e_1, 0) = e_1$ (unfair case)
$g(e_1, \lambda) = X$ with $e_1 < X < 1$ when $0 < \lambda < 1$

Among the many possible formulae which exhibit such behavior we have chosen the following definition:

$$(11) \qquad g(e_1, \lambda) = e_1 + (1 - e_1) * \lambda$$

By varying λ we can obtain an evidence combination scheme which assigns less or more predominance to the first contribution.

The evidence combination mechanism is more complex than we have discussed so far since in the characterization of a diagnostic hypothesis we do not have only NECESSARY and SUPPLEMENTARY FINDINGS but also VALIDATION RULES. Since the role of these rules is to provide a significant contribution to the establishment or rejection of the diagnostic hypothesis, the evidence mechanism previously introduced should be extended to cover the contribution of VALIDATION RULES. In particular, we have to devise a method which takes into account CONFIRMATION and EXCLU- SION RULES. It is apparent that the role of EXCLUSION RULES is different from that of other knowledge sources, and therefore the assumption of an "additive" scheme is not appropriate since the satisfaction of the EXCLUSION RULES by the actual data of the case under examination can- not leave unchanged the evidence degree of the diagnostic hypothesis. On the contrary, the satisfaction of at least one of the EXCLUSION RULES should cause the rejection of the diagnostic hypothesis - that is, its evidence degree should be reduced[1]. In order to take into account the intuitive semantics of EXCLUSION RULES, a new operator for evidence combination should be defined. This operator is essentially "multiplicative" since the global evidence degree of the hypothesis should not be decreased in case the evidence gath- ered by EXCLUSION RULES is null.

If we assume that the additive operator is defined by (8), the "fair" multi- plicative operator ("unfair" one can be defined in a similar way) has to be defined as:

$$e_1 \; O_f \; e_2 = e_1 * e_2$$

Therefore, the evidence degree of the hypothesis H is obtained as

$$e(H) = ((e(N) +_u e(S)) \; O_f \; [1 - e(ER)]$$

where $e(N)$ represents the evidence degree gathered by NECESSARY

---

[1] It is worth noting that we preferred to use just one number to represent the evidence de- gree of a hypothesis. In some systems two different measures have been introduced: one for representing the evidence in support of the hypothesis, the other for the evidence against the hy- pothesis. There are several advantages in taking these two measures separately (see, for example, [Rollinger 83]), but most of the advantages are lost when the two measures are combined in a single value in order to provide the system with a ranking of the hypotheses. Since the ranking of the hypotheses is of paramount importance in diagnostic problem solving and a lot of difficulties arise when one wants to define a total ordering and each hypothesis is represented by a pair of values (positive and negative evidence) we thus decided to limit ourselves to just one evidence value.

FINDINGS, e(S) the one of SUPPLEMENTARY FINDINGS and [1-e(ER)] represents the evidence degree of the negation of the EXCLUSION RULES. In fact, the evidence degree of the hypothesis H is not decreased in the case of e(ER)=0, that is when none of these rules is satisfied. In fact, as stated in chapter 4, the EXCLUSION RULES are implicitly OR-ed and their evidence degree e(ER) is computed according to formulae (3) and (7).

Finally, CONFIRMATION RULES have to be taken into account. They can increase the evidence in favor of a hypothesis (their contribution depends on the evidence of their match and on their relevance measure), but they cannot reverse the confidence about a hypothesis; this means that the satisfaction of a CONFIRMATION RULE is not sufficient to establish a hypothesis if the evidence degree of the hypothesis itself obtained by considering NECESSARY FINDINGS, SUPPLEMENTARY FINDINGS and EXCLUSION RULES, is low . Therefore this behavior can be expressed by adopting the unfair additive operator defined in (9). It is worth remembering that the condition part of EXCLUSION RULES and CONFIRMATION RULES is designed in such a way that they are mutually exclusive, i.e. no CONFIRMATION RULE can be applied when one of the EXCLUSION RULES has been satisfied. Nevertheless, the following formula for the evaluation of a hypothesis takes into account all the separate chunks of knowledge:

$$(14) \qquad e(H) = (((e(N) +_u e(S)) \; O_f \; [1 - e(ER)]) +_u e(CR))$$

where e(CR) represents the global evidence gathered by the CONFIRMATION RULES.

A graphical scheme of the evidence combination mechanism is shown in figure 6.1.

6.3 EVIDENCE COMBINATION: AN EXAMPLE

To conclude this chapter we will discuss a simple example of an application of the evidence combination scheme we have designed. Let us consider more particularly the simple car troubleshooting example ("electrical_problems") frame discussed in chapter 4 and which is reported in a slightly extended version in the following (figure 6.2).

Suppose now we are trying to instantiate the frame reported above on the following case:

ignition faulty
lights normal

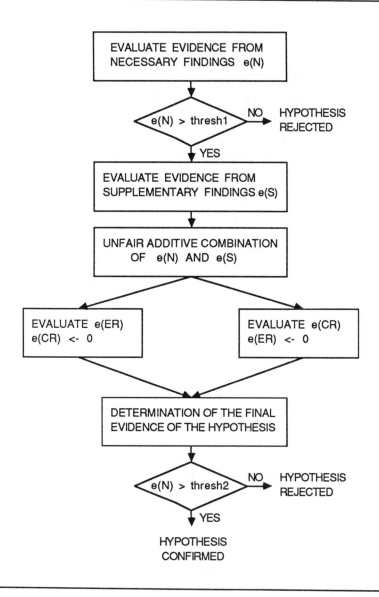

Figure 6.1 - Evidence Combination (scheme).

battery_water_level medium
sparking_plugs_change between_20000_and_30000_km
starting_engine dumb

To instantiate the frame, NECESSARY FINDINGS slots have to be instantiated first. Let us consider, for example, the "ignition" slot. From the

---

FRAME: electrical problems

TRIGGERS
ignition(status,impossible)
relevance 1
ignition(status,faulty) <u>and</u> lights(intensity,abnormal)
relevance 1

NECESSARY FINDINGS
ignition: <impossible,1> <faulty,0.8> <normal,0.1>
relevance: 1
lights: <normal,0.1> <low_intensity,0.7> <not_burning,0.9>
relevance: 0.5

SUPPLEMENTARY FINDINGS
battery_water_level: <low,1> <medium,0.6> <high,0.1>
relevance: 0.7
sparking_plugs_change: <less_than_10000_km,0.2>
<between_10000_and_20000_km,0.5>
<between_20000_and_30000_km,0.8>
<more_than_30000_km,1>
relevance: 1

VALIDATION RULES
exclude <u>if</u> starting_engine(firing)
<u>in context</u> carburettor_problems(present)
relevance 0.8

confirm <u>if</u> starting_engine(dumb)
<u>in-context</u> not(transmission(present))
relevance 0.7

Figure 6.2 - A simple diagnostic hypothesis.

prototypical description we know that the compatibility degree of the value "faulty" for the finding "ignition" (remember that when findings have a unique attribute, the name of the attribute can be omitted) is 0.8. A corrected evidence value for the slot has to be computed to be used in the global evaluation of NECESSARY FINDINGS. Since NECESSARY FINDINGS are ANDed the function "f_{AND}" (formula (3)) is used to compute such corrected evidence. Since the relevance of the slot "ignition" is 1, the resulting corrected evidence for the slot itself is 0.8. Similar considerations apply to the slot "lights", whose corrected evidence is 0.55. By combining these two values with the formula (5) (as noted, NECESSARY FINDINGS are ANDed), we obtain the final evidence value e(N)=0.5005 for such a group of slots. It is worth noting that, although the compatibility of the linguistic value "normal" for the finding "lights" is very low, the influence of this value on the degree of match of necessary findings is limited by the low importance of the finding itself.

Consider now the SUPPLEMENTARY FINDINGS slots and, in particular, the "battery_water_level" one. In this case the compatibility degree of the value "medium" for the finding "battery_water_level" is 0.6 and a corrected evidence value for the slot has to be computed taking into account its relevance. Using the function "f_{OR}" (formula (3)) (remember that SUPPLEMENTARY FINDINGS slots are ORed), we obtain the final value 0.42 for the evidence of the slot. Applying similar considerations to the slot "sparking_plugs_change" we obtain the evidence value 0.8. These two values are then combined using the formula (7) (they are ORed) to get the final evidence value 0.8672 for the SUPPLEMENTARY DESCRIPTION of the frame.

The two evidence values obtained from the match of NECESSARY and SUPPLEMENTARY FINDINGS with actual data have then to be combined in the final value representing the degree of match of the prototypical description part of the frame and actual data. As noticed above, an "unfair" additive operator (formula (9)) is used to combine these values. In the specific case we are discussing, the total evidence of the match of the prototypical description of the frame and actual data is 0.7177. Note that the influence of SUPPLEMENTARY FINDINGS on the global degree of match is limited.

Let us briefly analyze now how the evidence value of the frame is modified during the VALIDATION process. Suppose that in the specific example we are considering the frame "transmission" has not been activated (instantiated), so the context of application of the CONFIRMATION rule of the frame "electrical_problems" is satisfied. Since the premise of the rule is also satisfied by actual data, the rule can be activated (notice that in this case, as expected, the EXCLUSION rule associated with the frame is not applicable, since at least its premise is certainly false). The final evidence of the frame can be computed using the formula (14) in which:

$$e(ER) = 0$$
$$e(CR) = 0.7$$

so that the final expression for the evidence is:

$$e(H_{electrical\_problems}) = (0.7177 \; O_f \; 1) +_u 0.7 = 0.8595$$

Such an evidence value is the final one for the diagnostic hypothesis "electrical_problems".

The mechanisms introduced for evidence combination are essentially heuristic since they have not been derived by a unifying mathematical theory, but have been suggested by a careful examination of the way human experts try to explain on what basis they increase or decrease their confidence in a given hypothesis, by taking into consideration different pieces of knowledge.

In any case, the actual scope of the evidence combination mechanism is limited, since it is used essentially as a focusing mechanism to find out the most promising hypotheses and to rule out the others. The real decision about the validity of a given diagnostic hypothesis is taken at the deep level in which a causal explanation is searched for, by using sound logical inferences.

7

CAUSAL LEVEL:
KNOWLEDGE REPRESENTATION

The causal knowledge is mainly used in CHECK to perform a deep and precise validation of a diagnostic hypothesis with respect to the overall causal model and to provide explanation facilities about cause-effect relationships. Moreover, as previously outlined, this deep knowledge base might be used also directly to question the system about its knowledge content.

The knowledge representation formalism we have designed for the deep level of CHECK is based upon the use of causal networks. From a very abstract point of view, a causal network is formed by a set of nodes (representing different entities, such as states, hypotheses or findings), connected by different kinds of relationships.

The aim of this chapter is at providing a precise description of the knowledge representation formalism we have adopted. In particular, we first give a description of the basic constituents of the formalism, following the abstract distinction between nodes and relationships. This means that we shall discuss which are the possible types of nodes that can be used in CHECK's networks, what they represent in the modelling of a physical (physiological) system and which kinds of relationships can be defined to hold among them (examples in this part will be taken from both mechanical and medical domains). We shall then analyze how networks formed using such specific components can be used to model complex domains, providing again detailed examples.

In the following, we shall use both linguistic and graphical descriptions to present examples of components and parts of the network. The graphical descriptions have been produced using a causal network editor (NEED) we have developed for CHECK - this will be fully described in chapter 9. The language in which the linguistic descriptions are given is based on Prolog and allows us to describe very simply the nodes and relationships in the network. It is worth noting that the language is defined in such a way that by interpreting the net's descriptions as Prolog procedures (associating the obvious natural meaning with the defined operators, as "causes", "caused_by", etc.) one can have an idea of how reasoning will be performed in the modelled system. For these reasons we believe that such linguistic descriptions are very self-explanatory, so they will be widely used in the following.

7.1 CAUSAL NETWORK: NODES

Different types of nodes are defined in CHECK's causal networks to represent different objects in the deep model of a physical (physiological) system. More particularly, five types of nodes can be used to model a particular system, namely *HYPOTHESES, STATES, ACTIONS, INITIAL CAUSES* and *FINDINGS*.

7.1.1 HYPOTHESES

The nodes of type "HYPOTHESES" correspond to the diagnostic hypotheses considered by the system. As noted before, each hypothesis node is strictly connected to the frame that represents the same hypothesis in the surface (heuristic) level. That has various consequences: first, all the information contained in the (instantiated) frame can be used while reasoning at the deeper level; second, we will see in the following that the connection between frames and hypothesis nodes has a great impact on the organization of the reasoning strategy in the network (particularly when a heuristic hypothesis has to be confirmed and explained at a deep level). There is also the possibility of introducing in a causal network "HYPOTHESES" nodes which do not correspond to frames in the surface level. Such nodes can be useful to represent diagnostic hypotheses that are outside of the specific domain modelled in a causal network, and they are useful to suggest correlated or alternative diagnostic hypotheses to be considered or for taking into account unexpected findings (as will be discussed in chapter 8).

The presence of nodes corresponding to diagnostic hypotheses in a deep causal model could be surprising. The concept of "diagnostic hypothesis" is, in fact, at a very different knowledge level with respect to the other concepts used in our model such as, for example, the concept of "state". Diagnostic hypotheses are "artificial" concepts created to give a name to a specific situation (state or combination of states) in which a system can be at a given time. In other words, each diagnostic hypothesis is an abstraction built to characterize a typical (or frequent) faulty behavior of a system. This meaning is maintained in our model, as will be clear when "DEFINED_AS" relationships are discussed.

7.1.2 STATES AND ACTIONS

Most of the nodes in a network represent states of the modelled system. From an intuitive point of view the concept of "state of a physical (physiological) system" is obvious: a state represents a possible situation in which the system can be at a given time. It is important to distinguish between the concept of "*global state*" of a system and that of "*partial state*" (or "local state"). Whilst a "global state" aims at representing a situation in which the modelled system as a whole can be at a given time, "partial states" are used to represent the situations in which the different components of a system can be. In the latter case, the "global state" is defined as a combination of "partial states". The main difference between global states and partial ones is that in the first case a system can be, at any one time, in one and only one state, whilst in the second case more that one state can be simultaneously present. It should be clear that the descriptions given in terms of partial states are simpler (since they are partial descriptions of the modelled system) and more flexible than the descriptions given in terms of "global states" (many of the approaches to causal modelling proposed so far are based on the representation of "partial states", see, for example, [Patil 81][1] [Fink et al. 85][Steels 85]).

Usually states are characterized by a set of "*state variables*" which represent different attributes (features) of the state itself. Each variable can assume values in a predefined set of legal ones. Moreover, state variables are often connected, i.e. the values they assume at a given moment are strictly correlated (consider [de Kleer & Brown 84] for discussion of the "intra-state" behavior in a physical system).

The analysis of "intra-state" behavior of a particular system is certainly interesting, but usually more interest is generated by the study of the "inter-state" one. In the latter case, the state transitions of a system are studied so that its global evolution can be followed or predicted. State transitions are

---

[1] In particular in ABEL a specific structure, the PSM (Patient Specific Module), is used to represent the global state of the patient as a combination of partial pathophysiological states.

usually caused by some action (event or perturbation) internal or external to the system.

"STATES" nodes in our causal networks are intended to represent the states of the modelled system, whilst "ACTION" nodes represent the events causing state transitions. More specifically, each "STATE" is intended to represent a "partial state", i.e. to give a partial description of the modelled system which is globally described by a combination of "STATES". Each state is characterized by a set of *state variables* (or attributes), which can assume *qualitative* values within predefined ranges. This means that in CHECK we are interested in modelling the behavior of a system in a qualitative way. More particularly, qualitative reasoning techniques are used to set the values of state variables during a particular consultation.

An example of linguistic description of a state in a mechanical system is shown in figure 7.1. It is worth noting that only part of the linguistic description of a STATE has been shown in figure 7.1 - that is, only the clauses defining its internal structure (attributes and their possible values).

---

state engine_temp *has_attributes* [intensity].

attribute intensity *of* engine_temp
    has_admissible_values [medium, high, very_high].

attribute intensity *of* engine_temp :-
    <instantiation_scheme>.

Figure 7.1 - An example of a STATE in a mechanical domain .

The definition is formed by a group of clauses: the first clause defines the name of the STATE and lists its attributes, then a pair of clauses is used to define each attribute (the first one lists the admissible values the attribute can assume, in the second the instantiation scheme for the attribute is defined).

Notice that the STATE "engine_temp" ("engine temperature") is characterized by one attribute: its intensity. Such an attribute is intended to represent the value of the temperature. The attribute is in turn characterized by the set of values it can assume ("admissible values") and by an instantiation scheme.

Such a scheme can be used to instantiate the attribute when a specific case is being analyzed.

"ACTION" nodes have been introduced to represent "*state transformation functions*", i.e. the mechanisms (or the events) which induce state transitions. In a certain sense, the introduction of "ACTION" nodes is a way of giving better characterizations to cause-effect relationships between states. The meaning of "ACTION" nodes will become clearer in the next section, when relationships between nodes will be discussed (in particular, when CAUSAL relationships will be presented, see section 7.2.1).

7.1.3 FINDINGS

Another important type of nodes in CHECK is that of "FINDING" nodes. To comprehend what they represent, consider a generic physical system: we observed before that such a system is, at any given time, in a specific state, i.e. states completely characterize a system internally. In general the internal states of a system are not directly observable. It may happen, however, that being in a certain state has some effect on the system itself which is observable from outside, i.e. it may have "manifestations". For example, in a mechanical system (engine) the state "engine_temperature high" may have as a manifestation "vapour", or in the pathophysiological model of liver diseases the state "presence of fluids in the peritoneum" may have as a manifestation "ascites". "FINDING" nodes in CHECK represent observable conditions (data) in the modelled system, i.e. manifestations of its internal states (which we assume are not directly observable).

It is important to consider now which is the correlation between findings used in the deep level and in the heuristic one. We have noted in chapter 3 that data (findings) are structured in CHECK (i.e. classes of data and hierarchies of classes are defined) and that each datum (class) is represented by a frame-like structure. This data hierarchy is shared by the two levels of the system; some data are used in both levels, which consequently refer to the same data structures (it is worth noting that the two levels can operate or access the same data at different levels of detail, i.e. some attributes of a datum may be used only by the deep module such as, for example, time specific information). Furthermore, there are data specific to the deep level: they usually refer to very specific information which is not used in the heuristic reasoning.

An important distinction has been made in CHECK (in the deep component of CHECK in particular) between two different major groups of findings: those which are easy to observe or verify in the modelled system and those which require an in-depth (physical) analysis of the system to be observed. To be clearer, consider the example of a medical domain: to the first group belong all clinical findings, data from history, etc.; to the second one, histological findings which require costly and invasive examinations of the patient. Similarly, in a mechanical domain "histological" manifestations are those which require the accessing of the internal structure of the modelled artifact to be observed.

The distinction is very coarse but it has a precise meaning in the way diagnosticians operate. Let us return again to the medical example: a physician considers the possibility of performing histological examinations on a patient only as an ultimate possibility, e.g. to have some final confirmation or to solve some very doubtful case. Similarly, a diagnostic system should be able to use histological data when it is present, i.e. when voluntarily provided by the user, but should ask for them only if it is strictly necessary and after consulting the user. We shall see in the following that this distinction has many important consequences on the reasoning component of CHECK, so "histological" data are treated in a very special way (see next chapter).

The frame-like structure defining findings has been fully described in chapter 3 and corresponds to the linguistic descriptions created by the network editor NEED in correspondence to FINDING nodes.

7.1.4 INITIAL CAUSES

The last group of nodes in CHECK is formed by the so called "INITIAL CAUSES". These nodes represent the possible original causes of a disorder, or, better, of the disorders considered in a given model. In a certain sense they can be considered as the initial perturbations which can cause the presence of a disorder, i.e. starting the causal process which can lead the modelled system to a faulty behavior. To be more precise, consider some simple examples: in a pathophysiological model of liver diseases, one of the initial causes of "alcoholic cirrhosis" could be "alcohol_intake protracted and intense"; in a mechanical model possible alternative or concomitant initial causes for an "engine burnout" could be "piston_rings_used_up" or "pistons" ("worn pistons", see figure 7.18).

"INITIAL CAUSES" nodes play a very important role in the diagnostic reasoning in a causal network - in fact, one of the most interesting points for confirming (explaining) the presence of a disorder in a specific system is to establish one (or a combination) of its possible initial causes and to recognize the process which has led from such causes to the disorder itself.

---

initial_cause pistons *has_attributes* [wear_state].

attribute wear_state *of* old_pistons
    has_admissible_values [low, medium, high].

Figure   7.2   -   Linguistic   description   of   the
INITIAL_CAUSE "old_pistons".

---

initial_cause alcohol_intake *has_attributes* [intensity, duration].

attribute intensity *of* alcohol_intake
    has_admissible_values [normal, medium, high, very_high].

attribute duration *of* alcohol_intake
    has_admissible_values [months, few_years, many_years].

Figure 7.3 - The INITIAL_CAUSE "alcohol_intake".

It is worth noting that with each INITIAL CAUSE node is associated a set of variables which give a better specification of the initial perturbation represented by the node. Notice that information about "INITIAL_CAUSES" (about their attributes in particular) can be obtained, at least in some cases, from the user since they correspond to findings that can be verified on the specific case under examination. In other cases their presence can be only hypothetically assumed. This is very important in designing (and formally justifying) a reasoning scheme on the network (see next chapter). Let us consider, for example, the INITIAL_CAUSE node "pistons" taken from a mechanical model (figure 7.2). A complete characterization of such INITIAL_CAUSE can be given only if the "wear_state" of the pistons is known.

As a further example, the description of the INITIAL_CAUSE "alcohol_intake" in a medical domain (pathophysiological model of liver diseases) has been reported in figure 7.3. In this case a complete characterization of the "alcohol_intake" can be given only if its duration and intensity are known.

7.2 CAUSAL NETWORK: RELATIONSHIPS

In the previous section we have presented the possible basic components (nodes) of CHECK's causal networks. The next point is to describe which relationships can be defined to hold among such kinds of nodes, that is to say, which *arcs* can be defined in the network formalism. It will be clear from the following that relationships between nodes in CHECK are represented by means of complex structures, i.e. they cannot be considered simply as predicates holding among nodes.

7.2.1 TYPES OF RELATIONSHIPS

Basically six types of arcs can be used in CHECK to define relationships between nodes, namely *CAUSAL, HAM* (Has As a Manifestation), *SUGGEST, DEFINED_AS, FORM_OF* and *LOOP*. Each type of arc can connect only particular nodes, as is discussed in the following.

CAUSAL ARCS. Causal arcs are used in CHECK to model cause-effect relationships between states. From an abstract point of view they connect two states, say "A" and "B", to represent "A causes B". The peculiarity of CHECK's causal arcs is that each one of them has a complex structure involving a node of type ACTION and two sub-arcs: a STATE-ACTION sub-arc and an ACTION-STATE one. In such a model causal relationships between states are augmented with information about the events (actions) which cause the state transitions (see figure 7.4).

The major advantage of the definition of a causal arc as a complex structure is that it allows a first (very simple) form of abstraction in the analysis of a network. In fact, at an abstract level, only cause-effect relationships between states which are not further specified could be presented to be elaborated into more complex structures involving the ACTION node. On the other hand, there are pieces of information which are difficult to represent and manipulate at such a level of detail. In particular, we refer to relationships in the causal model: whilst it is possible to represent temporal constraints on cause-effect relationships between states, in many cases it is difficult to represent such information at a lower level of detail, i.e. on STATE-ACTION and ACTION-STATE subarcs.

Before considering the examples, it is worth making a few remarks on the language used to describe the network. The description of a CAUSAL arc between two STATES S_1 and S_2 involving an ACTION "A" is divided into three clauses (suppose that S_1 is the only cause of S_2 and that S_2 is the

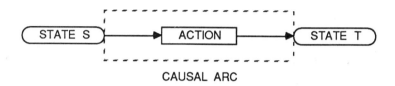

Figure 7.4 - Structure of a CAUSAL arc.

only consequence of S_1):

-       a clause listing the "consequences" of the STATE "S_1":
        causes S_1 :-
        S_2 through_action A *if* <condition>
        where <condition> is the condition on the CAUSAL relationship (rela-
        tionships in CHECK causal models can be conditioned, a complete dis-
        cussion on such conditions is reported in the next section).

-       A clause defining the STATES in which the ACTION "A" initiates and
        to which it leads (this clause is not useless, as could appear from the
        example below - see in particular the discussion about LOOP arcs):
        action A *initiated_in_state* S_1 *lead_to_state* S_2.

-       A clause listing the "causes" of the STATE "S_2". This clause is similar
        to that describing the "consequences" of "S_1".
        caused_by S_2 :-
        S_1 through_action A *if* <condition>
        where <condition> is again the condition on the CAUSAL relationship
        (which is duplicated to improve the declarative reading of the group of
        clauses).

        Consider as an example the model of a mechanical engine; a cause-effect
relationship can be defined between the two states "lack of lubricating oil"
and "engine_temperature" through the action "friction", as reported in figure
7.5.

The corresponding linguistic description is the following:

causes oil_lack :-
    (engine_temp *through_action* friction *if* true).

action friction *initiated_in_state* oil_lack
               lead_to_state engine_temp.

caused_by engine_temp :-
    (oil_lack *through_action* friction *if* true).

Figure 7.5 - A simple example of CAUSAL arc in a mechanical domain.

If the STATE S_1 has more than one consequence and, similarly, the STATE S_2 has more than one cause, the clauses described above become more complex. In particular:

- in the right part of the clause listing the "consequences" of the STATE "S_1", for each consequent STATE "S" there is a predicate with the form
          S *through_action* <action> *if* <condition>
  where <action> is the name of the action connecting "S_1" to "S" and <condition> is the condition on the CAUSAL arc.
- Similarly, in the right part of the clause listing the "causes" of the STATE "S_2", for each causing STATE "S" there is a predicate with the form
          S *through_action* <action> *if* <condition>
  where <action> is the name of the action connecting "S" to "S_2" and <condition> is the condition on the CAUSAL arc.

As a further (more complex) example consider, in our pathophysiological model of liver diseases, the causal path from the state "alter_liver_struct" (alteration of the liver structure) to the state "extrahepatic_shunts" reported in figure 7.6.

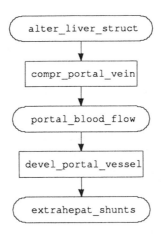

Figure 7.6 - A causal path in the pathophysiological model of liver diseases.

It is worth making a brief comment on the role of ACTION nodes. The ACTION node "A" associated with the CAUSAL arc connecting the states "S_1" and "S_2" represents the functional transformation describing how the values of the attributes of the state "S_2" depend on the value of the attributes of the state "S_1". As an example the ACTION "friction" reported in figure 7.5 represents the following functional transformation between the attribute "severity" of the state "oil_lack" and the attribute "intensity" of the state "engine_temp" (we shall refine the example in the following):

    oil_lack(severity,low) $\Rightarrow$ engine_temp(intensity,medium)
    oil_lack(severity,medium) $\Rightarrow$ engine_temp(intensity,high)
    oil_lack(severity,high) $\Rightarrow$ engine_temp(intensity,very_high)

Further examples of ACTION nodes and CAUSAL arcs will be given in chapter 9 (see figure 9.7).

HAM ARCS. Arcs labelled HAM (Has As a Manifestation) connect "STATES" nodes to "FINDING" ones. The meaning of the relationship they represent is that the finding is an (observable) external manifestation of the state which it is connected to by means of a HAM arc. Using again our mechanical and medical examples: "oil_gauge" is a manifestation of the state "oil_lack" (figure 7.7), whilst "ascites" is a manifestation of "transudation of fluids in the peritoneum" (if some conditions are satisfied, see figure 7.8).

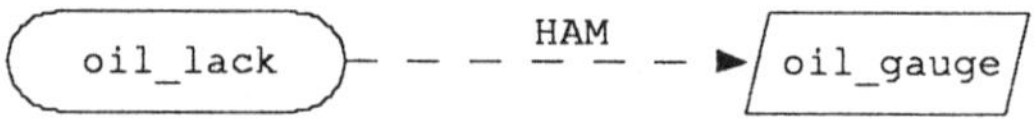

The corresponding linguistic description is the following:

ham oil_lack :- *manifestation* oil_gauge *of* oil_lack.

Figure 7.7 - "HAM" relationship between the STATE "oil_lack" and the FINDING "oil_gauge".

It is worth noting that with each HAM relationship connecting a STATE "S" and a FINDING "F" is associated an "attribute-compatibility" scheme. The role of such a scheme is to describe the relationships between the values of the attributes of "S" and the values of the attributes of "F" specifying which specific instances of "F" are compatible with each instance of "S". Taking as an example the HAM relationship between the STATE ""oil_lack" and the FINDING "oil_gauge" reported in figure 7.7, the following "attribute-compatibility" scheme describes the relationship between the attributes of the two nodes:

    oil_lack(severity,low) - oil_gauge(colour,normal)
    oil_lack(severity,medium) - oil_gauge(colour,yellow)
    oil_lack(severity,high) - oil_gauge(colour,red)

HAM relationships are of primary importance during the reasoning process in CHECK, in particular in the hypothetical reasoning component (see chapter 8).

LOOP ARCS. One of the most interesting features of CHECK is the possibility of defining loops in the deep causal model of a specific physical or physiological system. This is accomplished through a particular kind of arc: the

LOOP arc. Structurally a LOOP arc is similar to a CAUSAL one, i.e. it is characterized by the presence of an ACTION node and two subarcs, so it connects two states. Also the meaning of the two kinds of arcs is similar to a certain extent: they both represent cause-effect relationships but LOOP arcs have the special feature of closing loops in the network.

---

ham transudation :-
      manifestation ascites *of* transudation.

manifestation ascites *of* transudation :-
      transudation(intensity, high).

Figure 7.8 - Linguistic description of the "HAM" relationship between the STATE "transudation of fluids in the peritoneum" and the FINDING "ascites". Notice that a condition is associated with the arc (for discussion of the meaning of conditions see section 7.2.2). The idea is that the manifestation is present only if the condition is satisfied.

We believe that it is very important to be able to represent circularities in a causal model. In many practical cases, in fact, physical (or physiological) processes manifest circularities, i.e. a particular state is periodically reached (established) as a result of a series of events (consider the discussion of "systems with feedback" given in [de Kleer & Brown 86] [Iwasaki & Simon 86] and the PEPTIDE system [Weld 86] as an example of the interest in how to treat circularities in the behavior of an artifact).

In our experience of the design of complex pathophysiological models the capability of representing circular processes has proven very useful or even mandatory. In particular, two major classes of circular processes have been encountered in the design of such models. In the first one, the reaching of a state starts a causal process returning to the state itself which has the effect of modifying (usually increasing or decreasing in a monotonic way) some attributes of the state itself. In many cases such states have manifestations which are observable only after the circular process has been repeated a number of times - that is, after some attribute (state variable) has reached a given threshold (remember that we have only linguistic values for state variables). As an example, consider the following (simplified) scheme of the

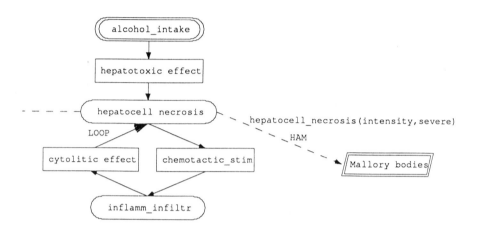

Figure 7.9 - An example of loop in the pathophysiological model of liver diseases.

"necrosis" loop, typically present in many patients. Only when the "necrosis" is intense, the histological finding "Mallory bodies" is observable in a patient; traversing the loop has the effect of increasing the "necrosis" (figure 7.9). A slightly different possibility concerns the case in which a circular process has the effect of maintaining the presence of a particular state: when the process interrupts itself (e.g. for an external perturbation, typically a therapeutic intervention in medicine) it has the effect that the state itself ceases to be present.

Not only are circular processes necessary in medical pathophysiological models, but also in the representation of the behavior of physical systems or specific artifacts. As an example, in figure 7.10 a simple loop describing the behavior of a mechanical engine is reported: engine temperature continues to increase as long as the engine continues to work in abnormal conditions (e.g. such as a lack of lubricating oil).

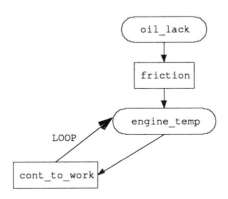

the corresponding linguistic description is the following:

causes engine_temp :-

    ...

    engine_temp *through_action* cont_to_work.

action cont_to_work

    initiated_in_state engine_temp *loop_to_state* engine_temp.

Figure 7.10 - Simple example of LOOP in a mechanical
domain. Notice that the description is similar to that of
CAUSAL arcs and that the clause specifying the
STATES connected through the ACTION "cont_to_work"
contains the information which characterizes the arc as a
LOOP one (so that the clause is not useless).

To simplify the reasoning process in the presence of circular causal
models, we have imposed a limitation on the form loops can have in CHECK.
More precisely, we allow only "structured loops", i.e. loops in which there is
a "head state" which is the only entry and exit point in the loop. Structured
loops can be nested, exactly as loops can be nested in structured programming
languages (i.e. we perform the same tests performed in verifying the struc-
turedness of a program). This limitation, combined with the fact that each

attribute of a state can assume only a finite set of linguistic, qualitative values, is important for several reasons - in particular, for simplifying the complexity of CHECK's reasoning component. With these assumptions, in fact, a loop can be traversed only a finite number of times: either the instantiation value of a state variable remains unchanged after the traversing of a loop (a new traversal of a given loop is useless when, after a traversal of the loop, the values of the variables characterizing the state which is both the origin and the termination of the loop itself, remain unchanged), or its value is increased (decreased) until a (linguistic) threshold is reached. It should be clear that with this limitation we are not able to model the behavior of oscillating systems. Moreover, the assumption is important in the construction of the logical model of a causal network used to design a complex form of common sense reasoning (e.g. hypothetical reasoning, see chapter 8). The examples of loops reported in figures 7.9-7.10 are correct structured loops that are definable in CHECK (it is worth noting that the tests of the presence of loops and of their correctness are completely performed by the network editor NEED in the knowledge acquisition phase - see chapter 9).

SUGGEST ARCS. "SUGGEST" arcs connect STATES (or FINDINGS) to HYPOTHESES nodes. The meaning of the relationship they represent is the following: the presence of the state suggests the analysis of the hypothesis as a collateral (concomitant) or an alternative one. In particular, a hypothesis can be suggested as concomitant with the one currently analyzed if they are compatible and the current one can be confirmed. Otherwise, if the current hypothesis cannot be confirmed, established states can suggest alternative ones to be considered. It is worth noting that such suggested hypotheses must be outside the domain of competence of the system (e.g. in the pathophysiological model for liver diseases suggested hypotheses must be external to the liver domain). "SUGGEST" arcs are very useful to suggest further diagnostic hypotheses to be investigated.

DEFINED_AS ARCS. "DEFINED_AS" arcs are structurally similar to "SUGGEST" ones in the sense that they connect "STATES" (or better, sets of STATES) to "HYPOTHESES" nodes, but they have a completely different meaning. They are used to represent the fact that a certain diagnostic hypothesis is defined as the presence of a particular state (or combination of states) in the modelled system. More precisely, since conditions can be attached to "DEFINED_AS" arcs imposing constraints on the values of the attributes of the defining states, a diagnostic hypothesis is defined as the presence of a particular state having some specific attribute values (that is, as the presence of an instantiated state). The arc does not mean that the presence of a hypothesis can be concluded from the presence of a state, but more correctly it represents a "*definitional*" relationship. We observed in the previous section that the concept of "diagnostic hypothesis" is an "artificial" one and that it is at a very different knowledge level with respect to the other concepts used in our modelling formalism. This difference is reflected in the semantic of the "DEFINED_AS" relationship: "HYPOTHESES" are *defined concepts*, i.e. a diagnostic hypothesis is confirmed *if and only if* the states defining its presence can be established. To be more precise, consider the medical example of "alcoholic cirrhosis". Such a disease can be defined as an "intense and diffuse structural alteration of the liver". This definition can be represented by connecting the state "alteration_of_the_liver_structure" to the "HYPOTHESES" node "cirrhosis" (see figure 7.11) by means of a "DEFINED_AS" relationship, imposing, on the relationship, the condition that the structural alteration must be intense, diffuse and due to alcohol_intake (conditions on INITIAL_CAUSE nodes can be associated with DEFINED_AS arcs).

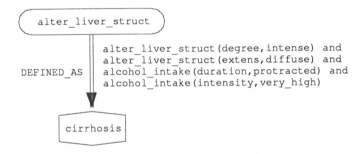

the corresponding linguistic description is the following:

hypothesis alcoholic_cirrhosis *defined_as* alter_liver_struct :-
      alter_liver_struct(extension,diffuse),
      alter_liver_struct(degree,intense),
      alcohol_intake(duration,protracted),
      alcohol_intake(intensity,very_high).

Figure 7.11 - An example of DEFINED_AS relationship in a medical domain.

Notice that the relationship is defined as a clause in which the premise represents the condition on the relationship itself. As a further example, consider the diagnostic hypothesis "burnout" in the mechanical domain of car troubleshooting: it can be defined as the presence of a "very high engine temperature" (see figure 7.12).

---

hypothesis burnout *defined_as* engine_temp :-
  engine_temp(intensity, very_high).

Figure 7.12 - An example of DEFINED_AS relationship in a mechanical domain.

FORM_OF ARCS. "FORM_OF" arcs connect HYPOTHESES nodes in the causal network. They represent a generalization (specialization) relationship between the connected nodes. FORM_OF relationships, as DEFINED_AS ones, are at a very different level with respect to the other ones introduced in our formalism (nevertheless they can be useful in the reasoning process and in the generation of explanations).

To conclude this section, here is a table in which the different types of arcs definable in CHECK are listed together with a summary of the types of nodes they can connect and the kind of relationship they represent.

RELATIONSHIPS BETWEEN NODES			
Arc type	From node	to node	meaning
causal	state	state (through action)	cause-effect
ham	state	finding	manifestation
defined_as	state	hypothesis	definition
suggest	state or finding	hypothesis	suggestion
loop	state	state (through action)	cause-effect
form_of	hypothesis	hypothesis	specialization

Table 7.1

7.2.2 CONDITIONAL RELATIONSHIPS

So far we have presented the relationships which can be defined in CHECK as unconditioned ones. CHECK's deep level knowledge representation formalism allows a condition to be attached to each arc. The condition must be verified when the arc itself is traversed. These conditions can impose various kinds of restrictions on the traversal of the arc when the network is used in the analysis of a particular case. From the syntactic point of view, the condition must be expressed as a formula of first order logic with equality (moreover, order relationships between numbers are also defined). From the semantic point of view the principal types of restrictions that can be imposed through the use of these conditions are the following:

-    Given an arc "A" exiting from a node "N", conditions on the values of the attributes of "N" can be attached to the arc "A".

-    conditions on which initial causes have been established in a particular case.

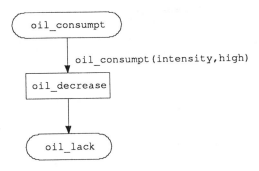

Figure 7.13 - An example of condition on a CAUSAL arc.
The transition between the states "oil_consumption"
and "oil_lack" depends on the intensity of the
"oil_consumption".

The possibility of associating conditions with each relationship has proven very useful in the modelling of complex domains. As an example in figure 7.13 we have reported a simple conditional CAUSAL arc in the mechanical model of car troubleshooting.

It is worth noting that we must reduce the expressive power of the condition definition in order to be able to provide precise semantics of the formalism (and to formalize completely the reasoning scheme in the networks) and to reduce computational complexity. In particular, we must restrict the types of conditions that can be used, not allowing the expression of conditions on data or on other entities, for example other states different from the one from which the arc exits.

Other conditions that can be used to augment the expressive power of the formalism are those that can be associated with a node and that concern the arcs entering the node. In particular all the entering arcs sharing the same type can be connected by means of a logical condition. For example, in this way the causes of a STATE can be defined as concomitant (ANDed) or disjuncted (ORed)[2].

To be more precise, if the arcs entering a node are ANDed we consider them as a single arc. Consider, for example, the simple relationship in figure 7.14. The relationship between "A", "B" and "C" is considered in CHECK as a single "CAUSAL" relationship, with exactly one associated "ACTION". Moreover, all the other pieces of information that can be associated with an arc (e.g. conditions) are associated with the complex CAUSAL relationship as a whole.

Conversely, when the "CAUSAL" arcs entering a state are ORed an "ACTION" is associated with each one of them independently. It is important to point out, however, that if the ORed causing states are not exclusive, the possibility of their simultaneous presence must be taken into account. Suppose, for example, that a state "S" is caused by the state "S_1" or the state "S_2". If "S_1" and "S_2" are not mutually exclusive, in the instantiation scheme for "S" the possibility of the simultaneous presence of "S_1" and "S_2" must be considered (that is, different instantiations of "S" can be obtained in the three cases "S_1 present", "S_2 present", "both S_1 and S_2 present"). More specifically three different functional transformation schemes are associated with the complex causal transition (see figure 7.15). This facility is very useful to diagnose multiple-faults, as will be discussed in the next chapter.

---

[2] In the following we use the convention that arcs entering in a node are implicitly ORed, if nothing different is explicitly indicated.

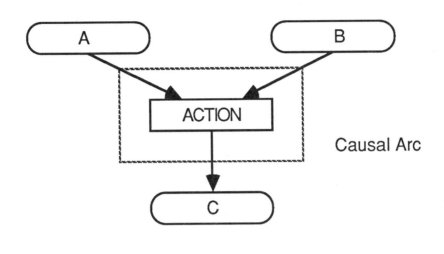

Figure 7.14 - A causal relationship in which the two causing
states "A" and "B" of state "C" are ANDed. The relationship
is considered in CHECK as a single CAUSAL arc with just one
associated ACTION.

7.2.3 NECESSARY AND POSSIBLE RELATIONSHIPS

Causal models have often been used in such a way that some basic
assumptions about the characteristics of the domain to be modelled should be
satisfied. Unfortunately, in most cases these assumptions have not been made
explicit. Let us consider, for example, the choice of the level of detail of the
model: this choice is, in many cases, quite arbitrary (or at least domain and
task dependent), since, in most cases, it is possible to provide different levels
of description for a given domain. However, in many practical problems (e.g
models of physical or physiological systems), only processes and conditions at
some level of abstraction can be represented because of the inherent complexity of the system or because of the ignorance of the underlying mechanisms
(as often occurs in biological systems). Even a system like ABEL [Patil 81],
which uses multiple levels of description has to limit in some way the grain
size of representation (in ABEL the lowest level is the pathophysiological

one). Putting such a bound is the only way to constrain the complexity of the causal model; moreover, this corresponds quite often to limitations of the capability of human experts who may be in trouble when they have to reason at too deep a level (e.g. biochemistry may not be in the field of expertise of a physician).

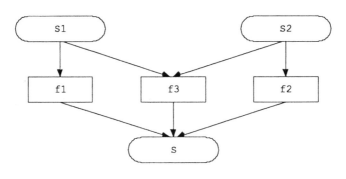

Figure 7.15 - The causal dependency of the state "S" from the states S_1 and S_2.

Moreover, there are several other reasons for which it can be interesting (or necessary) to omit the representation of some conditions in a model: they can be difficult or even impossible to formalize or to quantify properly, or they may depend on data specific to a particular case under examination which are very difficult or even impossible to gather, or which depend on external processes not considered by the system. As an example, consider the case of a pathophysiological model and imagine a transition which critically depends on the individual susceptibility of a patient to a particular agent, which is impossible to model and investigate.

A typical example taken from our pathophysiological model of liver diseases is the following: an elevated and protracted intake of alcohol may cause "necrosis" through the action "cytotossic action", but this strongly depends on the individual susceptibility of each particular patient to alcohol. Such a condition cannot reasonably be represented in a model, but it is important to mark in some way that the transition does not necessarily occur - that it is possible that in a heavy drinker (or even a cirrhotic patient) "necrosis" might not have become established.

The problems arise when we concentrate on a given level and assume that we have perfect and complete knowledge at this level by disregarding the influence of the underlying mechanisms in conditioning the actual transition from one state to another. Since, in most cases, the reasoning on causal models is carried out in a categoric way, this may lead to a given state or situation being unconditionally established even if, in the real world, this state only occurs in some cases. This can happen because the establishment of some relationships in a particular case may critically depend on conditions or the activation of processes which are not explicitly represented.

Failure to recognize the *possibility* of such a transition (by assuming its *necessity*) may provoke serious errors when the causal model is used to verify a diagnostic hypothesis in a particular case, since the model predicts that a given situation necessarily *has* to occur in the case under examination, whereas in reality this situation just *may* occur. This may lead to the establishment of states (or even to the confirmation of diagnostic hypotheses) in cases in which they should not be established (confirmed).

These considerations might suggest the use of probabilistic reasoning (for example, the one adopted in CASNET [Weiss et al. 78] or in [Pearl 86][Pearl 87]), but we believe that a non-numerical approach based on non-monotonic logic is more adequate for deep reasoning systems.

In order to overcome the problem we propose the introduction of a distinction between *necessary* and *possible* relationships in a causal model, and a particular form of *hypothetical reasoning* to cope with them. In particular, we will introduce the distinction between necessary (**MUST**) and possible (**MAY**) arcs: the latter are used to model relations which are conditioned but whose conditions are not expressible at the level of abstraction of the model (or which are unknown). In particular, each kind of arc (except for DEFINED_AS ones) can be labelled as a MAY one in CHECK.

Figure 7.16 - MAY relationships.

Since the meaning of MUST arcs is straightforward, we shall describe more precisely the meaning of MAY arcs: let us consider a simple causal relation (figure 7.16) between two states, say "A" and "B". For the moment we will ignore the presence of ACTION nodes, looking more abstractly at cause-effect relationships.

The meaning of the relation can be expressed as "A may cause B". This means that in some cases it might happen that state "B" could result as a consequence of the presence of state "A". More precisely, we can say that there are some conditions on the transition between "A" and "B" which have not been represented in the system and on which the transition itself depends. In some sense labelling the transition between "A" and "B" as a MAY one is a way of expressing the ignorance in the actual conditions and processes underlying the relationship itself (more comments in chapter 8).

An example in which the possibility of labelling arcs as MAY ones can increase the expressiveness of the model is reported in figure 7.17 (taken again from a pathophysiological model).

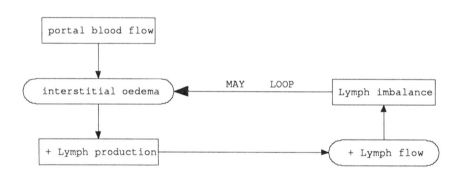

Figure 7.17 - A complex example involving MAY relationships in a medical domain.

In this case the loop which maintains the presence of the state "interstitial oedema" as an effect of increased lymph production and flow, and the imbalance between formation and absorption of lymph, is only a possibility in a patient. In fact, the transition between "lymph_flow increased" and "interstitial oedema" (through the imbalance between formation and absorption of lymph) strongly depends on the entity of the production of lymph and on the specific characteristics of the "lymphatic vessels" of a particular patient, which are not modelled at the level of abstraction of our representation.

To produce a slightly different example, we will return to the model of "burnout problems" in a mechanical engine. A possible cause of the lack of lubricating oil in an engine is the presence of a hole in the oil cup from which the oil might have spilled. The presence of such a hole in the cup might be the result, for example, of being struck by a stone while travelling on unsurfaced roads. It is important to be aware, however, that such events do not necessarily cause the presence of a hole in the oil cup (this could, in fact, depend on many other conditions, such as the type of stone, the speed of the car, etc., which are not easily expressible in the model - see figure 7.18).

We believe that recognizing that every model of a physical (or, in particular, physiological) system is not complete, in the sense that it is limited to a certain level of abstraction, is of primary importance. All the information that is below the level of abstraction of the model, though very important or even critical, is not represented. The limitation is obviously necessary due to the finiteness of models and for complexity or computational problems. The introduction of the distinction between strictly necessary and possible relationships, and the introduction of particular forms of common-sense reasoning (hypothetical reasoning, which is described in chapter 8) to deal with them, allow us to solve such "cut (and lack) of information" problems. In a certain sense, such solutions correspond to the definition of a deep, qualitative form of uncertainty in causal models, in the same way that hypothetical reasoning is a sophisticated and qualitative form of approximate reasoning.

7.3 EXAMPLES OF CAUSAL MODELS

In this section we wish to summarize the description of CHECK's deep level knowledge representation formalism, presenting some structured and complete examples of causal models. More specifically, we shall first present a simple brief example of modelling in a mechanical domain ("burnout problem" in an engine), then we shall present some parts of the very complex network we have designed for a pathophysiological model of liver diseases

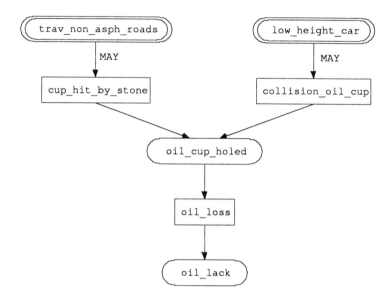

Figure 7.18 - An example of MAY relationship in a mechanical domain.

(in particular, we shall give a simplified description of that part of the network that concerns the disease "alcoholic cirrhosis" and, more generally, "cirrhosis"). These examples are intended to give a practical description of CHECK's knowledge representation formalism, showing how it can be successfully used in the deep and precise modelling of real-world domains and situations.

In figure 7.19 an example of a complete network for "burnout problem" and "melting problem" in a mechanical engine is reported. Some of the possible ultimate causes of such a problem have been considered, describing the process that leads to the state "engine_temperature_increase high" which is a definition of "burnout". Moreover, a few main consequences of the disorder (leading to the other disorder "melting" which can be considered as an evolution of "burnout" have been considered.

More interesting for understanding the real power of our scheme of causal knowledge representation, is the example reported in figure 7.20 It reports a simplified description of (part of) the pathophysiological model of the liver disease "alcoholic cirrhosis". The two arcs entering the STATE "alter liver struct" (alteration of the liver structure) whose origin is not displayed comes from the STATES "post_necrotic scarring" and "pseudolobular regeneration". The only ultimate cause of the disease is "alcohol intake protracted and intense". Several paths from such an INITIAL CAUSE node to "alteration of the liver structure diffuse and intense" have been considered, together with the conditions and constraints for their traversal. For the sake of simplicity the description of the internal structure of the states has been omitted and each state is characterized only by its name - note also that all the consequences of the state "alteration of the liver structure" have been omitted.

7.4 DISCUSSION

It is worth saying a few words to conclude this section. A first important point is to observe that our representation of causal knowledge is a qualitative one, that is, states and their relationships are characterized in a qualitative way. A second observation concerns the difference between general and instantiated networks. Consider the definition of "STATE" nodes in our formalism. Since each state is characterized by a set of state variables, a "STATE" node represents a family of states of the modelled system rather than a single state. The specific states in the family can be determined simply by instantiating the attributes of the STATE node, i.e. associating specific values with them. A causal network could be designed defining directly the cause-effect relationships between instantiated states, but this would result in a very large and cumbersome model. Abstracting groups of instantiated states in more general ones is mandatory in order to constrain the complexity of the resulting model. On the other hand, this has the consequence that the reasoning process is more complicated, since the problem of the instantiation of the network on the specific case under examination has to be taken into account.

A more interesting observation concerns the problem of representing "time". The concepts of "time" and "causation" are in fact strictly correlated [Shoham 87] and discussion about causality completely abstracted from the notion of time can be meaningless.

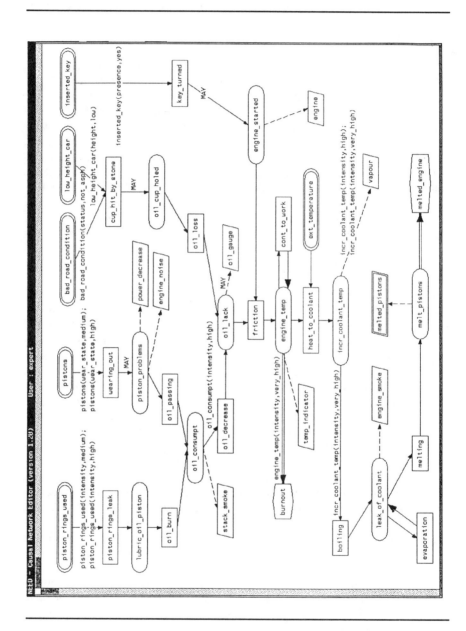

Figure 7.19 - The complete network for the diagnostic hypothesis "burnout".

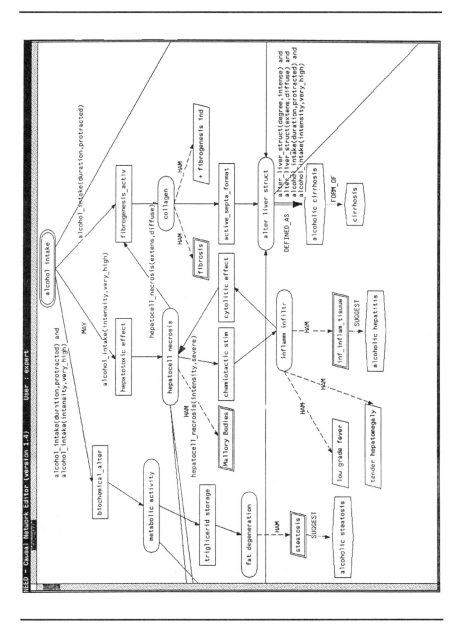

Figure 7.20 - Part of the pathophysiological model of the causes of "alcoholic_cirrhosis".

It should be clear that it is very important to add time information to causal models, because not considering time correlations, differences and delays may lead to incorrect reasoning on a causal model. Consider, for example, the very simple causal model in figure 7.21. It should be clear that unless "A" and "B" are present simultaneously, "C" cannot be established in any given case: temporal correlations between states and events should be taken into account while reasoning on a network to solve such problems.

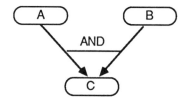

Figure 7.21 - A Simple causal relationship.

An important problem on which we are presently working is how to represent and deal with temporal information in causal models. In particular, we aim to give a qualitative representation of time relationships (or attributes), discriminating between very general classes of time intervals (e.g. "seconds", "minutes", "days", ...). The most complex problem with such a representation is how to define formal rules for combining time information concerning different events and relationships in order to obtain a complete causal-temporal description of the evolution of a physical (physiological) system. Another interesting point, strictly connected with the representation of time, is that of distinguishing between reversible and irreversible states. We are presently investigating such a subject for CHECK's networks. We shall return on this subject in the conclusion of the book (chapter 12).

8

CAUSAL LEVEL:
INFERENCE STRATEGY

8.1 USES OF CAUSAL KNOWLEDGE

In this chapter we will discuss how reasoning is performed at the causal level of CHECK. The discussion is logically divided into two distinct parts: in the first one we give an overview of the different uses of CHECK's causal knowledge, distinguishing between a *general use*, independent from the data of a particular consultation, and a *particular use*, in which a specific case is analyzed; in the second part of the chapter we shall turn to presenting, in a detailed way, how reasoning is performed on causal knowledge. In general use the deep level is used to provide general (tutorial) explanations regarding the domain which the system operates upon; in a specific case the deep level is used in strict conjunction with the surface (heuristic) one to confirm a diagnosis and to provide precise explanations.

8.1.1 GENERAL USE

The "general use" of CHECK's causal network allows the user to navigate the causal knowledge base; in this way he/she can get information about the possible deep causes and evolutions of diagnostic hypotheses. In particular, the user can access the general network in three different ways, corresponding to three different types of nodes: HYPOTHESES, FINDINGS and INITIAL CAUSES. In order to simplify the interaction, all the other nodes are not directly accessible to ask for explanations (this is reasonable considering that a user generally does not know which are the intermediate states constituting the evolution of the modelled system). On the other hand, when a portion of a causal network has been displayed by the system in response to some request of the user, each node (i.e. also intermediate states) can be accessed in the network to get further information and explanations (e.g. about the prototypical structure of the node). In each one of the cases the explanations are built by considering the general knowledge coded in the network, without taking into account any particular information.

Let us consider some examples of the possible explanations that a user can get from the system in each one of the cases listed above, in order to have a basic idea of what can be provided by the system. For the sake of clarity all the examples that we will look at in this section are taken from our medical application in the domain of liver diseases.

Access to HYPOTHESES

The user can access the system at hypothesis level to get information about the possible deep causes and evolution of the malfunctioning represented by the hypothesis itself. For example, by accessing the hypothesis node "alcoholic cirrhosis" in the liver diseases diagnostic system, the user can ask about the possible ultimate causes of the disease and for an explanation of the processes that lead from those causes to the disease itself. He/she can then ask about the possible manifestations of the disease or get information about diseases that are often correlated with "alcoholic cirrhosis".

Access to FINDINGS

A different kind of access to the general network is that at finding level. In this way the user can get information about the nature of the finding and about its possible causes. Moreover, the user can ask which are the hypotheses that can account for the presence of the finding and obtain, in this way, a description of the possible causal processes that can explain the presence of the finding, given a particular disease.

Access to INITIAL CAUSES

Initial causes can be accessed to generate two kinds of general explanations: first the user can get information about the node itself and its meaning, then he/she can ask which are the diagnostic hypotheses that are causally connected to the initial cause itself.

It is interesting to consider how the net is traversed and the explanations produced in these cases. First it should be noted that an extensive traversal of the network is needed when general explanations are requested, since, as no particular case is considered, the conditions on the arcs cannot be evaluated. This has the important consequence that the explanations that are generated have conditional and/or hypothetical parts (derived from the consideration of MAY arcs).

It is worth noting that no advanced form of reasoning is needed in the traversal of the causal network to realize the functionalities discussed in this section. Each response to a request by the user corresponds to a display of some portion of the global network. The specific explanation generated by such a traversal is displayed by the system using the graphical interface discussed in chapter 9.

Apart from the case of simple navigation of a knowledge base, other more complex and interesting forms of case-independent reasoning can be performed on a causal network. In particular a very attractive possibility is that of using a causal model to analyze simulated situations [Console et al. 88a]. Such a form of reasoning has not received much attention so far even though it can be used to generate very interesting explanations.

Let us discuss more precisely which are the possible interactions between CHECK and its users during the analysis of simulated cases. First of all it is important to define the precise meaning of a simulated situation in CHECK's formalism. A simulated situation can be characterized as a partial description of a case or, in other words, as a description of a generic case. By applying this definition to CHECK's causal modelling formalism we have that a simulated situation can be characterized as follows:

-    a set (possibly empty) of instantiated (partially instantiated) findings or initial causes;

-    a set (possibly empty) of multi-instantiated findings or initial_causes;

where an instantiated finding (initial cause) is a FINDING (INITIAL_CAUSE) node whose attributes are filled in with unique values; a partially instantiated finding is a FINDING node in which some attributes may be not instantiated; a multi-instantiated finding is a node in which some attributes may be filled in with a n-pla of (alternative) values. Since the cases of partially instantiated and multi instantiated nodes are generalizations of the fully instantiated nodes, we shall concentrate on the fully instantiated nodes case.

Given a simulated situation, different forms of explanation can be requested by a user. More specifically the user can access the network in the

three different ways discussed above (i.e. access to INITIAL_CASE, FIND-
ING and HYPOTHESIS nodes) to ask for more sophisticated types of explanation than those listed before. For example, by accessing an
INITIAL_CAUSE node the user can ask for explanations of the consequences
of partially instantiated initial perturbation; by accessing a FINDING node the
user can analyze which initial perturbation and/or diagnostic hypotheses
account for a (partially) instantiated finding.

The generation of these forms of explanation requires the adoption of
complex forms of reasoning. Basically, constraint propagation techniques
must be adopted in order to analyze a simulated situation. At present the
module devoted to the generation of such a kind of explanations has been
only partially implemented (in particular we have implemented the functionalities connected to the access to INITIAL_CAUSE nodes).

8.1.2 USE IN A PARTICULAR CASE

A different possibility is to use the causal network during the consultation on a particular case. This corresponds to the use of the causal model to
provide a deep and precise validation of diagnostic hypotheses generated at
the surface (heuristic) level and to construct precise explanations. In particular, if the hypothesized diagnosis has been confirmed on the network, a complete and precise explanation can be generated for the user of the malfunctioning in the modelled system, its possible deep causes and causal evolutions, and its possible consequences and manifestations. Moreover, associated
or alternative hypotheses can be suggested and the inquiry of the' causal
knowledge base on the particular case under examination can be allowed
(with modalities similar to those discussed in the preceding section; notice,
however, that in this case the instantiated network is used to provide explanations). If a diagnostic hypothesis cannot be confirmed, the reasoning on the
net is not useless; in fact, it may happen that part of the network that has
been instantiated could be used for the analysis of other hypotheses (or to
suggest other hypotheses).

Let us consider now how the two levels communicate and, in particular,
how the deep level is invoked by the surface one. As stated before, the
heuristic level is activated first to generate diagnostic hypotheses. We have
noted that a HYPOTHESIS node in the network is associated with each
frame, so that when a hypothesis has to be confirmed (and eventually
explained) the corresponding node is called and reasoning in the network
starts from that node. All its possible deep causes are collected and paths
from them (or from just one of them, if it is sufficient) are searched, analyzing the conditions on the arcs and the action mechanisms. After the causes of

a hypothesis have been confirmed, its consequences are analyzed. In other words, the system searches for a portion of the complete causal network that gives an explanation of the hypothesized disease in terms of deep causes (initial states).

To make the description clearer a complete example of how a causal network is used to confirm a diagnostic hypothesis will be presented in the final chapter of the book.

8.2 REASONING IN THE CAUSAL NETWORK

Let us now discuss how reasoning is performed in the causal model in order to to achieve the functionalities presented in the previous section. In particular we shall concentrate our attention on the use of the system on a particular case, i.e. on the case in which the network is used in a specific consultation to confirm and, eventually, explain a diagnostic hypothesis.
In this case the problem to be solved is to search for a portion of the global network which can account for the diagnostic hypothesis to be confirmed from its initial causes to its ultimate manifestations. The important point is that such a portion of the network has to be instantiated on the specific case under examination. This means that, fundamentally, the problem is to discover the initial causes of the malfunctioning corresponding to the diagnostic hypothesis and to reason on the states (which internally characterize the modelled system) on the causal evolution from the initial causes to the states defining the malfunctioning itself and on those on the causal evolution from the states defining the malfunctioning to their ultimate consequences and manifestations. The instantiation of such states is based on prototypical information and the observation of their external manifestations.

The whole process is further complicated by the presence of MAY relationships, for which a particular treatment is needed. In the next section we shall give a more precise description of the overall reasoning scheme, particularly concentrating on the special scheme of *hypothetical reasoning* we have designed to deal with possible relationships in a causal model.

Some consideration is worthwhile before starting the discussion. We believe that one of the major criticisms that can be correctly ascribed to many of the reasoning schemes that have been recently developed (in expert systems in particular) is that they are lacking in a precise, formal definition (this is particularly true when deep reasoning systems are considered). In recent years (and particularly in the last few months, since this interest is rapidly growing) some researchers have proposed interesting formalizations of different forms of reasoning using approaches based on mathematical logic (see, for example, [Genesereth 84][Ginsberg 86][de Kleer 86][de Kleer & Williams 87][Reiter 87] for a logical formalization of diagnostic reasoning). In particular, different forms of classical and non-classical logic have been used for such formalizations and many different approaches to non-monotonic reasoning (whose need is often advocated, especially for diagnosing) have been proposed (e.g. Mc Dermott and Doyle's "non-monotonic logic" [McDermott & Doyle 80][McDermott 82], Reiter's "default logic" [Reiter 80], McCarthy's "circumscription principle" [McCarthy 80] [McCarthy 86], Moore's "autoepistemic logic" [Moore 85]).

In the design of the deep level of CHECK we realized that the introduction of a formal logical basis to the reasoning component is necessary in order to be able to give a precise and non-ambiguous definition of both the operations performed by the system and the results that can be obtained. This is particularly critical for the form of hypothetical reasoning we have designed to deal with MAY relationships. For this reason we have decided to design a complete logical model of the deep level reasoning processes (and obviously of a causal model), based on a particular form of non-monotonic logic. We shall not give in this book the complete logical details of such a model; an outline will be given at the end of this chapter. The interested reader can find an accurate and precise description in [Console & Torasso 88d] and in [Console & Torasso 89].

8.2.1 OVERVIEW OF THE INFERENCE STRATEGY

Let us now describe informally the main steps of the deep level inference strategy that are performed when a diagnostic hypothesis "H" is passed from the surface level to the deep one for confirmation.

Before starting the discussion about CHECK's inference strategy, a few comments on the problem of multiple-fault diagnosis and on the possibility of performing such a complex form of diagnostic reasoning in CHECK are worthwhile. Let us analyze, more precisely, which are the characteristics of CHECK's causal modelling formalism that directly support the possibility of diagnosing multiple faults.

-      No limit has been imposed on the position of the states defining a diagnostic hypothesis. Thus a state defining a diagnostic hypothesis can be a consequence (i.e. correlated by means of a sequence of CAUSAL relationships) of another state defining a different diagnostic hypothesis. The causality relationships between hypotheses are captured in this way very naturally. Moreover, this allows multiple-fault diagnosis to be carried out in the case of associated (causally correlated) hypotheses.

- As we noticed in chapter 7, the arcs entering a node (e.g. a STATE or a FINDING) can be logically connected and, in case of disjunction (OR), no assumption has been made about their independence. However, the formalism encourages the possibility of specifying the effect of the presence of more than one of the causes. Thus the influence of independent evolutions (of different malfunctionings) can be taken into account.

- The presence of "state variables" and of "finding attributes" is very important, especially as far as FINDING nodes are concerned. If the presence of a state can account only partially for the observation of a finding, other states have to be searched for in order to account for it completely. Consider the case reported in figure 8.1. Suppose that the finding "F" has two attributes "x" and "y" for each one of which {a,b} is the set of admissible values and that in the specific case we are considering we have observed that both attributes assume the value "b". Suppose moreover that we have the following relationships between the values of the attributes of S_1 and S_2 and those of "F" (we are assuming, for the sake of simplicity, that S_1 has one attribute whose only admissible value is s_1 and that S_2 has only one attribute whose only admissible value is s_2):
a) the observation of the pair of values {a,b} is compatible only with

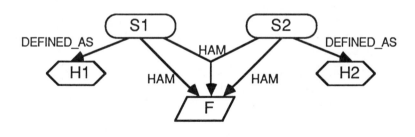

Figure 8.1 - Complex interaction on the finding F of the states S_1 and S_2 defining the hypotheses H_1 and H_2.

the value s_1 of the attribute of the state S_1

b) the observation of the pair of values {a,a} is compatible only with the value s_2 of the attribute of the state S_2

c) the observation of the pair of values {b,b} is compatible only with the presence of both states S_1 and S_2 and more specifically with the value s_1 of the attribute of the state S_1 and the value s_2 of the attribute of the state S_2.

In such a case in order to completely account for the observed finding "F" we have to combine the presence of the two states S_1 and S_2, so that {H_1, H_2} is a two-fault diagnostic hypothesis accounting for our observed datum.

In this way CHECK is able to perform multiple-fault diagnosis. However, for the sake of simplicity, the following discussion is limited to the case of a single malfunctioning diagnosis (it is important to note that this can be easily and naturally generalized to the case of multiple-fault diagnosis).

As we noticed above (see chapter 7), to each frame in the heuristic level corresponds a HYPOTHESIS node in the deep one: reasoning on the network starts from the node corresponding to the diagnostic hypotheses that must be confirmed. When a hypothesis node is activated for confirmation, the system searches for the set of states which define the presence of the malfunction corresponding to the hypothesis node, using DEFINED_AS arcs. In this way the problem of confirming a diagnostic hypothesis is reconducted to the problem of establishing the presence of a group of states. Two different analyzes of the network have to be made to confirm the presence of a state:

-   establishing the presence of a group of INITIAL CAUSES and of causal paths from such initial causes to the state itself, which explain the causal evolution from the initial perturbations to the presence of the given state;

-   establishing the presence of the strictly necessary consequences of the state (it is sufficient to establish the necessary consequences of a state; unnecessary ones can be used as a further confirmation).

The first step concerns searching for INITIAL CAUSES. Schematically the process is as follows: first the system searches backwards from the state defining the hypothesis to be confirmed (that is, cause-effect relationships are used in a reverse way - from the effect to the cause - in this search process) for the INITIAL CAUSES nodes which are connected to the state itself. After such nodes have been found (or assumed)[1], reasoning is performed in a forward way on the causal network starting from the INITIAL CAUSES nodes and trying to instantiate the network. It is important to note that backward traversing of the network is used only for searching for nodes; all the reasoning steps are performed forwards.

Ignoring for the time being the presence of MAY relationships, which will be discussed in the next section, the instantiation process proceeds as follows. A state "S" can be instantiated (and consequently confirmed) if:

-       its causing states have been confirmed (in particular, since the CAUSAL arcs entering a STATE S can be logically connected, it is not necessary that all states that can cause S should be confirmed).

-       the conditions on the arcs from the instantiated causing states are satisfied;

-       its strictly necessary manifestations are present.

In such a case the state "S" can be instantiated, that is its attributes (state variables) are set with a specific linguistic value, depending on the instantiation values of the causing states (the procedure to determine the instantiation value of an attribute is associated with the ACTION node entering the state "S"). Instantiating a STATE corresponds to predicting the presence of its manifestations (if any): if such findings are observed in the case under examination the causal path which has been considered to instantiate the state is confirmed, otherwise alternative paths have to be considered (or an inconsistency is detected).

It is worth pointing out that non-histological and histological findings are treated differently in this reasoning process. In particular information about histological findings must be volunteered by the user, so that when no information is known about a predicted finding the user is requested to provide such pieces of information (if they are known) unless the finding is a histological one. In the case of a histological finding a question is asked of the user only if the finding is needed to confirm some portion of the reasoning process (or, better, if the finding is the only one which can provide some form of confirmation during the hypothetical reasoning process). It should be clear that, on the contrary, a state cannot be confirmed if one of the conditions listed above is not satisfied [1] - that is, if some of its causing states have not been confirmed, or the conditions on an arc entering the state are not satisfied, or if one of its necessary manifestations cannot be observed.

The general idea is that states on a causal path (which cannot be directly

---

[1] Remember that information about "INITIAL CAUSES" nodes can, at least in some cases, be directly deduced from the data of the specific system under examination, see previous chapter. In the other cases the presence of INITIAL CAUSES can be only hypothetically assumed.

observed in the modelled system) can be established, given the presence of initial perturbations, by observing their external manifestations and reasoning on their causing states.

The analysis of the consequences of a state to be confirmed (for example a state defining the presence of a diagnostic hypothesis) is similar to the process discussed above (the only difference is that in this case the backward search for INITIAL CAUSES is obviously not needed), that is, paths from the state are followed forwards for instantiation on the particular case under examination.

In this way, if all the states defining the presence of a diagnostic hypothesis (i.e. connected to the HYPOTHESIS node by DEFINED_AS arcs) can be established in the reasoning process on the network, the diagnostic hypothesis can be confirmed at the deep level. An explanation for the user can be generated, considering the portion of the network that has been instantiated to confirm the hypothesis itself. More specifically, a graphical explanation is generated; for a complete description see chapter 9.

On the other hand, if one of the states which define the presence of the hypothesis is not confirmed the hypothesis is rejected. It is worth noting that during the whole confirmation process questions may be asked by the system in order to obtain information about unknown findings from the user.

Reasoning on the causal network is not completed when a diagnostic hypothesis passed by the heuristic level has been confirmed or rejected. There are in fact three other important tasks that are accomplished by the system:

- *Analysis of unexpected and unaccounted for data.*
  When a diagnosis has been confirmed it may be the case that some of the data of the particular case under examination are not accounted for (explained) by the hypothesis itself, that is none of the states which have such findings as manifestations is included in the instantiated portion of the network. It could be interesting in such cases to analyze which other malfunctions, which have not been included in the diagnostic hypothesis, can account for them and to consider such malfunctions as correlated diagnoses. More particularly, if one hypothesis can account for some unaccounted for findings, the system tries to establish it as a diagnosis concomitant with the confirmed one (if they are not incompatible). When concomitant hypotheses cannot be confirmed, or in general when not all the findings are accounted for at the end of the reasoning process, the system warns the user about the presence of such findings.

-   *Analysis of SUGGEST arcs.*
    As discussed in chapter 7, SUGGEST arcs relate STATES of the net-work to diagnostic hypotheses, external to the domain of competence of the system, which are worth investigating if the state is confirmed. Such suggested hypotheses are directly provided by the system to the user in the explanation generated by the system in response to a confirmed diagnosis.

-   *Generation of alternative hypotheses.*
    If a diagnostic hypothesis cannot be confirmed, the system searches for alternative hypotheses to investigate. Alternative hypotheses can be discovered by analyzing the data of a particular consultation and look-ing for the hypotheses that can account for them. The system can also use information in the heuristic level (remember that frames and HYPOTHESES nodes are connected). In particular, the ALTERNA-TIVE CLASSES slot associated with the frame corresponding to the unconfirmed diagnostic hypothesis can be accessed. Moreover, it may be the case that some (incomplete) portion of the network has been instantiated on the particular case under examination, but such an instantiated portion is not sufficient to confirm a diagnostic hypothesis. In this case the analysis of the instantiated portion of the network and of the SUGGEST arcs exiting from the instantiated STATES can be used to get other alternative hypotheses to be considered (or suggested to the user).

This discussion completes our brief and informal overview of CHECK's deep level inference strategy. In the following section we shall analyze the hypothetical reasoning scheme we have designed to deal with MAY relation-ships and we shall outline how the overall reasoning process has been logi-cally formalized.

8.2.2 HYPOTHETICAL REASONING

In this section we want to outline the hypothetical reasoning scheme we have designed (for more detail, see [Console & Torasso 89]).

At the beginning of section 8.2 we advocated the introduction of a pre-cise logical basis to the causal level reasoning component. An important feature of the logical system we have designed to formalize both CHECK's causal modelling scheme and reasoning process is that different sets of predi-cative symbols have been introduced in order to represent the different enti-ties of the causal modelling scheme (in other words, the alphabet of predica-tive symbols has been partitioned in different subsets). The distinction corresponds to a different role played by the different entities in the reasoning process. Let us briefly sketch now how the logical model of a causal network can be built.

-   Each "STATE", "FINDING" and "INITIAL_CAUSE" can be characterized as an atomic formula. More specifically, different sets of predicative symbols are used for each type of node. If a "STATE" ("INITIAL_CAUSE" or "FINDING") has 'n' attributes, a n-ary predicative symbol is used to model it in the logical system.

-   CAUSAL relationships are modelled by a complex implication formula. In particular, ACTIONS are modelled as *functions* which allow us to express the attributes of the caused state in terms of those of the causing one. As an example, consider the example of figure 8.2 in which a simple cause-effect relationship between the states "S_1" and "S_2" depends on the action "A" and the condition "C". The corresponding logical formula is the following (assuming that "S_1" has two attributes ("x" and "y") and "S_2" has only one):

$$S_1(x,y) \land C(x,y) \Rightarrow S_2(f(x,y))$$

Notice that a function "f" is used to model the action "A".

-   HAM relationships can be modelled similarly using implication formulae, except that they do not involve functions (no action, in fact, is involved in HAM relationships). As an example, consider the HAM relationship between the state "S" and the finding "m" reported in figure 8.3; the corresponding logical formula is the following (assuming that "S" has two attributes and "m" one):

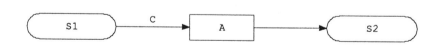

Figure 8.2 - A simple cause-effect relationship.

$$S(x,y) \Rightarrow m(z)$$

- MAY relationships are modelled through the introduction of an "assumption literal". We noticed above that labelling a relationship as a MAY one corresponds to abstracting some processes or conditions underlying the relationship itself (or expressing ignorance of such processes or conditions). This can be represented by introducing a "generic condition" (distinguishable from the other ones by the use of an "assumption" predicative symbol), which models the abstracted (ignored) ones. As an example, suppose that the cause-effect relationship of figure 8.2 is a MAY one (instead of a conditioned one). In such a case the relationship is modelled by the following formula (in which an "assumption" literal α has been introduced):

$$S_1(x,y) \wedge \alpha \Rightarrow S_2(f(x,y))$$

Notice that no logical correspondent is defined for DEFINED_AS relationships. This is in accordance with the observation that such relationships are at a different knowledge level with respect to the other ones, so it is not necessary to model them logically and to reason on them (they are just definitions).

The interesting point is now how to give a logical characterization of the causal reasoning process. In order to deal with MAY relationships and with the generic conditions associated with them in the logical model, we have designed a *hypothetical reasoning* scheme. The general idea is that the generic conditions associated with MAY relationships can be treated as *hypothetical assumptions* in the reasoning process.

Figure 8.3 - A simple HAM relationship.

Let us suppose for a while that we could give a deep causal model for the possible disorders of a particular system in a complete and fully detailed way, i.e. using only necessary (MUST) relationships (we believe that this is not a realistic case, even if it may be the case that in the modelling of very simple physical artifacts one could describe the behavior of the system in full detail). In this case the reasoning process to instantiate the network (or part of it) on actual data is relatively simple. In fact a sort of "categorical" reasoning can be performed which can lead to two different and opposite situations:

- The network can be successfully instantiated, that is complete necessary paths from initial causes to a hypothesis node and to its final manifestations can be found and instantiated. This means that *all* the manifestations of the states on these paths are present in the particular case under examination.

- The network cannot be instantiated on actual data, that is, a discrepancy is found between the causal model and the system under examination. More particularly, such discrepancies arise when a necessary manifestation of a state is discovered to be absent in that particular case.

It is worth noting that such a form of reasoning corresponds very strictly with the classical forms of categoric logical reasoning, and in fact can be easily formalized using classical logic.

The problems become more difficult when one allows for the use of possible (MAY) relationships in a causal model, when the considerations given above cannot hold. The main problem is that categorical reasoning is no longer sufficient, and more flexible and powerful approaches are needed. In the same way as the introduction of MAY relationships corresponds to defining a qualitative form of uncertainty in the model, then, in a certain sense, a qualitative form of approximate reasoning is needed to cope with such models.

To solve this problem we have designed a reasoning formalism based on the concepts of "*assumption*", "*possible world*' [Kripke 59] and "*hypothetical reasoning*" [Rescher 64][Gabbay & Reyle 85]. Intuitively a world is formed by a set of formulae which hold (or which are supposed to hold) in it, whilst an assumption is a fact that is supposed to hold, but for which there is no direct evidence (proof). Moreover worlds are closed under deduction. A world can be, at any given time, in one of the following three states:

- *confirmed*, that is, all the formulae in the world have been proven to hold;

- *inconsistent*, that is the world contains some contradiction;

- *hypothetical*, that is the world contains some hypothetical assumption.

Hypothetical reasoning is a scheme of reasoning designed to deal with *assumptions*, *"possible worlds"* and *"state transitions of worlds"*.

The interesting point is how to use hypothetical reasoning to deal with possible (MAY) relationships in a causal model. The discussion that follows is a rather informal and simplified one (all the logical details have been omitted for the sake of simplicity; the interested reader is referred to [Console & Torasso 89] for more details). Let us start the informal discussion by considering the simple example of figure 8.4. Suppose we have established the presence of "A" in a world W and we want to analyze the consequences of "A". In the model it is represented that "A may cause B", i.e. that some condition underlying the transition has not been represented; let us call "α" this condition. The literal "α" represents a generic condition or, in other words, the ignorance about the actual condition underlying the transition (remember the discussion of section 7.2.3).

The basic step of our reasoning process in such a situation is to create a "possible world" W_1, accessible from W, in which "α" is introduced as an assumption, i.e. W and W_1 differ in that "α", which is unknown in W, is assumed to hold in W_1 (note that W is augmented monotonically, so all assertions which hold in W hold in W_1). Reasoning is then performed in the hypothetical world W_1, in which, obviously, "B" can be derived as a consequence of "A", so the consequences of "B" can be analyzed. All the reasoning in W_1 is dependent on the assumption "α", so one of the major problems is that of defining how an assumption can be confirmed or rejected, while

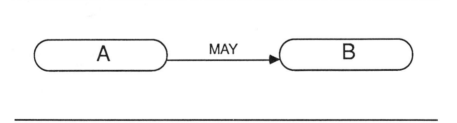

Figure 8.4 - A cause-effect MAY relationship.

reasoning in the possible world W^* created by introducing the assumption itself (or in some world created from W^*). This corresponds to the problem of discovering whether the possible world W_1 is consistent (i.e. to be confirmed), or inconsistent.

In our formalism, the process of confirmation or rejection of hypothetical assumptions is based on the analysis of the necessary manifestations of states. Let us consider the example reported in figure 8.5. Suppose "m" is a necessary manifestation of state "C" and suppose we are reasoning in a possible world W_1 created from a world W when the transition between "A" and "B" was considered (again let's call "α" the assumption introduced in W_1). In such a situation the confirmation of W_1 depends on the observation of "m" (i.e. more generally on the observation of necessary manifestations of a state in the possible world). If "m" can be observed in the particular case under examination, the world W_1 is confirmed (i.e. "α" is confirmed) and reasoning is continued in W_1, analyzing the consequences of "C". This is correct because we introduce into our model an important non-monotonic assumption: the *"uniqueness of paths"* assumption. In other words, given the observation of a finding m, we can confirm the presence of a state S having m as a manifestation if and only if S is the only state which can explain, in the case under examination, the presence of m. Similarly, given a CAUSAL arc connecting two states A and B, the confirmation of the caused state B can lead to the confirmation of the causing state A if and only if A is the only state consistent with the case under examination which can cause B.

It is interesting to notice that the logical correspondent of the intuitive "uniqueness of paths" assumption, has been given using the *"circumscription principle"* [McCarthy 80][McCarthy 86]. This suggests that reasoning on a

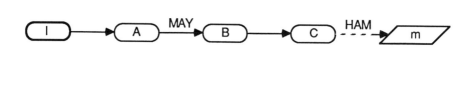

Figure 8.5 - A simple example of a causal path involving a MAY relationship.

causal network has been logically formalized using non monotonic logic.

Conversely if "¬ m" is observed in the case under examination, we can conclude that W_1 is not consistent (since it allows the deduction of "m"), so the assumption "α" must be removed, W_1 is rejected and reasoning is continued in the previous world W.

More specifically, we have extended the classical resolution principles [Robinson 65] (to deal with multiple worlds and different classes of predicative symbols) in such a way that, when the "extended resolution principle" is applied to an inconsistent world, it is able to trace back the inconsistency to the responsible assumption (when such an assumption exists)[2]. Such an "extended resolution principle" is applied to a world each time a necessary manifestation of a state (corresponding to a literal in the world) is discovered to be absent in the case under examination.

The example of figure 8.5 is a very simple one, so that, when reasoning on such a network, it is very easy to trace back an inconsistency to the responsible assumption or to discover which assumptions have to be confirmed when a manifestation of a hypothetical state (i.e. state derived in a hypothetical world) is observed. This is not always the case. In other cases, in fact, the assumption to be confirmed (or removed) cannot be deduced in a definite and unambiguous way. Consider, for example, the situation of figure 8.6 (this is a pathological case, which is not treated by many modal reasoning systems, which imposes restrictions on how assumptions can be made - in particular, the nesting of assumptions is requested [Warren 84][Gabbay 85]) and suppose that only the conjunction of "B" and "D" could cause "C".

When we observe "¬ m" in the case under examination, we can conclude that the world in which we are reasoning is inconsistent, but we cannot simply trace this inconsistency back to one of the assumptions "α" and "β" introduced when the transitions between "A" and "B" and "E" and "D" were respectively considered. In fact, we can only derive that the combination of the two assumptions make the world inconsistent and we must start reasoning again in the preceding worlds to analyze their consistency.

On the other hand, if "m" is observed, both assumptions "α" and "β" have to be confirmed (notice that in this case the "uniqueness of paths" restriction rule on "C" imposes that it is caused only by the conjunction of "B"

---

[2] As we shall outline in the following, in some cases the assumption responsible for an inconsistency cannot be discovered uniquely. In such a case the extended resolution principle is able to discover the logical combination of assumption literals which are responsible for the inconsistency - see next example.

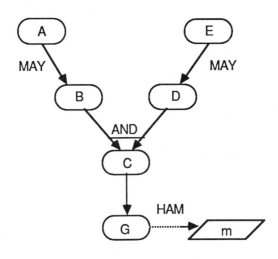

Figure 8.6 - A more complex example of causal path
involving a MAY relationship.

and "D"). Note that this situation is intrinsically ambiguous, so it is right that
the system could not discover which assumption was actually responsible.
There are other complex cases, apart from the simple case of adding nested
assumptions, in which the reasoning system is able to discover the single
assumption which is responsible for an inconsistency (see [Molino et al.
86][Torasso & Console 87][Console & Torasso 88e] for examples of more
complex cases in which hypothetical reasoning is needed).

To conclude this section it is worth making a few comments on the logical formalization of CHECK's deep reasoning. The idea is that a causal network can be modelled using a set of logical formulae and that reasoning on
the network can be modelled through logical reasoning. In particular, a form
of non monotonic logic (reasoning) is needed to deal with hypothetical
assumptions and possible worlds. The actual formalization we have given is
based on an extended form of the resolution principle [Robinson 65] we have
defined and on a particular use of McCarthy's "circumscription principle" that

we have designed, which are then combined in a complex reasoning scheme (for a detailed description see [Console & Torasso 89]).

It is interesting to point out that such a logical framework allowed us to give formal definitions of the concepts of "diagnostic problem" and of "solution to a diagnostic problem". From an intuitive point of view a solution to a diagnostic problem is a set $\Theta = \{H_1, H_2,...,H_n\}$ such that Θ accounts for all the findings observed in a specific case (diagnostic problem). This can be formalized by defining when a world W of the hypothetical reasoning system covers a set of manifestations (findings) and associating with W a set Θ of diagnostic hypotheses (by considering which are the hypotheses defined by the states deduced in W). It is worth noting that such an approach allows us to distinguish between different types of diagnoses and solutions of a diagnostic problem (e.g. "definite" and "plausible" diagnoses) and to introduce some preference and parsimony criteria to determine the 'best' solution (or set of solutions) of a diagnostic problem.

9

MAN-MACHINE INTERFACES

In this chapter we will discuss the problem of interfacing a diagnostic expert system and its users. In particular, two different aspects of the problem will be considered:

- Designing an interface between the system and its final users for the "Consultation phase". The aim of such an interface is to provide facilities for the phases of data acquisition and explanation. Concerning the former, a set of facilities for easy introduction of data by the user has to be provided by the system; concerning the latter, a set of facilities to provide the user with precise and clear explanations has to be designed.

- Designing an interface between the domain expert (or knowledge engineer) and the system for the phase of "Knowledge Acquisition". The aim of such an interface is to make the transfer of expertise (knowledge) from the knowledge engineer to the system as easy and natural as possible.

The chapter is divided into two parts: in the first one, the problems concerning the design of interfaces between the system and its final users will be discussed and the interface designed for CHECK will be presented; in the second part, the problem of "Knowledge Acquisition" will be addressed and the knowledge acquisition module of CHECK (graphical network editor NEED) will be outlined.

9.1 CONSULTATION INTERFACE

The design of the man-machine interface is one of the critical points in the development of diagnostic expert systems. In fact, the acceptability of the system strongly depends on the way it interacts with users. Although there are a number of different forms of interaction, depending on the actual use of the system (consultation, tutoring, etc.) and the type of users (casual users, trained people, etc.), the need for a sophisticated interface is apparent in most cases.

With the term "man-machine interface", one generally intends to enumerate several different forms of interaction, e.g. data acquisition or explanation (some authors use the term 'knowledge acquisition' for the phase of acquisition of data from the user in an expert system consultation; we prefer to reserve this term for the design of a knowledge base by a knowledge engineer). The need for flexible and friendly interfaces was perceived as a problem immediately after the development of the first prototype systems (e.g. one of the prerequisites established at the beginning of the MYCIN project was the ability of the system to "understand questions, acquire new knowledge, explain its advice" [Shortliffe 76]). In all the successive diagnostic expert systems, much attention has been directed towards the design of interfaces and, in particular, to the construction of powerful explanation modules.

Researchers have studied the possibility of building natural language interfaces for expert systems with the aim of allowing the user to introduce data and receive explanations in an easily understandable way. Currently, natural language interfaces are being developed as research prototypes (for example see [Carbonell et al. 83]), but the problem of building a cooperative and flexible natural language interface is still a major challenge. Moreover, in some studies the usefulness of a natural language interface has been questioned.

An alternative that has been widely adopted in many recent systems is the construction of graphical interfaces, which are argued to be the most natural and easy to use for people without programming experience. In particular, different types of graphical interfaces have been proposed. OPAL [Fagan et al. 85] provides the user of ONCOCIN [Langlotz & Shortliffe 83], an expert system for assistance in cancer treatment, with forms to fill in with the chosen therapy; GUIDON-WATCH [Richer & Clancey 85] provides a multi-window interface for both a consultation system (HERACLES [Clancey 85]) and a tutoring system (GUIDON2, based on NEOMYCIN [Clancey & Letsinger 81]); in ESDAT [Horn et al. 84] an interaction system based on a touch-sensitive screen has been developed. An interesting example of a graphical interface especially designed for taking into account the needs of the end-user has been developed within the DELTA-CATS1 project [Bonissone & Johnson 84]

In the classical approach to developing an interface, it is often assumed that the primary source of information about the particular case to be investigated (i.e. diagnosed) is the user of the diagnostic expert system. This is usually true, but in some cases we have to take into consideration that data about the case under examination are already present in a computerized form (for example in a data base) and additional data are provided by instruments rather than the end-user. Let us consider, for example, the problem of diagnosing circuits. In many cases, a lot of information about the structure and the behavior of the circuit is already present, so a diagnostic expert system should exploit this kind of information rather than trust the user (see [Genesereth 84]).

It is worth noting that in diagnostic systems both the problems of which pieces of information should be asked for or presented to the user, and how these tasks should be performed, have been considered [Richer & Clancey 85]. In particular, the most critical problem is the first one - i.e. deciding which pieces of information should be asked for (explained) and when.

In this section we will present the man-machine interface modules of CHECK [Console et al. 87b]. In particular, we shall address the problem of the design of the man-machine interface between the system and the final user, which is constituted by two main modules: the data acquisition module and the explanation one. The presentation of the particular approach we have taken in CHECK (design of a graphical interface for both data acquisition and explanation) is preceded by an analysis of the requirements that a man-machine interface should meet in order to be well accepted by its final users. The definition of such requirements derives from a study of the behavior of human experts when they are presented with a case to be solved (in particular, we have analyzed the behavior of physicians and electronic engineers, observing many similarities in their approaches and we believe that these similarities can be generalized to apply to most diagnostic tasks).

9.1.1 REQUIREMENTS FOR AN EFFECTIVE MAN-MACHINE INTERFACE

In this section we will briefly describe which are the points to be considered when designing a man-machine interface for a diagnostic expert system and we will present a general scheme of architecture that addresses such problems. The architecture is not bound to a particular implementation or to particular facilities, i.e. it can be practically built in different forms. As noted above, the ideas on which the design of such an architecture is based, derive from an analysis of the behavior of human experts (physicians and electronic engineers in particular) when they are presented with a particular case to be solved.

It is worth making a few comments before starting the discussion. Traditionally, a distinction is made between interfaces for data acquisition and for explanation; we will partially follow this distinction even if, actually, there is a strict correlation between the two phases, as will be clearer later.

When considering the phase of data acquisition, the typical problems to be solved are:

- Should the system ask for data or should the user introduce them voluntarily?
- When and how should data be introduced by the user?
- When and how should data be asked for by the system?
- How is the request for data connected to the "reasoning phase" of the system?

Consider, for example, the case of medical diagnosis (as noted before, the considerations made in such a case can generally be extended to other kinds of diagnostic problems). A possible way to answer the questions above is to analyze the behavior of a physician when he/she visits a patient and then to try to simulate it. At first, the attitude of the physician is mainly *receptive* - that is, initial data are provided by the patient (anamnestic phase guided by the patient). The acquisition of initial data may suggest some "*ideas*" about the status of the patient, which in turn may lead the physician to put some more specific questions to the patient to confirm or reject such ideas (anamnestic phase guided by the physician or *evocative phase*). Initial (general) diagnostic hypotheses are then built up through processes of unification and/or differentiation between "ideas". New (more specific) data (physical examination, laboratory data) are requested to confirm, discriminate and, possibly, specialize such hypotheses *(exploratory phase).*

This brief analysis suggests the outline of the design of a data acquisition module. The module should be characterized by two different phases (similar considerations about the design of a man-machine interaction module in a medical diagnostic system can be found in [Gorry & Barnett 68]):

- a *passive* phase;
- an *active* phase.

The first one corresponds to the initial data acquisition from the external world, the second to the phases in which the system asks for data, and it is, therefore, strictly connected and interrelated with the "reasoning process" of the system in the sense that data acquisition both guides and is guided by the reasoning process (the evocative and exploratory phases are discussed above). It should be clear that such a general scheme can be put into practice in different ways: for example, in the passive phase data could be introduced by the user in natural language or through a graphical interface. What it is worth noting is that the design of the data acquisition module cannot take place independently of the design of the problem solving architecture of the system, since they are strictly correlated.

A second problem to be considered concerns the explanation components of the system. The ability to produce precise explanations, in terms that are familiar to the user, is mandatory in order for a system to be accepted in the application context. Such explanations have to be adjusted to the specific use of the system (e.g. the explanations that are generated when the system is used for tutoring must be different from those that are generated when the system is used in an application context). As we have noted in the introduction (section 1.3), the inability to provide good explanations to the user is one of the major weaknesses of heuristic based systems and has suggested that systems based on deep knowledge should be introduced. We believe that the adoption of deep models is mandatory in order to be able to generate good explanations, i.e. explanations that can be accepted by the user.

9.1.2 STRATEGIES FOR DATA ACQUISITION

The major part of the effort for data acquisition is charged to the heuristic module of CHECK. In the deep one, questions about very specific data may be asked by the system during the process of instantiation of the causal network, but such questions are isolated, so there is not a problem of massive data acquisition.

The data acquisition interface of CHECK is based on the use of graphical menus which have to be filled in by the user with proper data (findings and their linguistic values, see figure 9.1, in which the initial menu presented by our liver disease diagnostic application is reported). We have recognized, following the scheme discussed above, two distinct phases of data acquisition: an initial one in which the system is passive and one in which the system actively requests data. The passive phase starts just at the beginning of a consultation, i.e. is the first operation performed by the heuristic module. A graphical menu, which has to be filled in by the user with initial data, is displayed by the system.

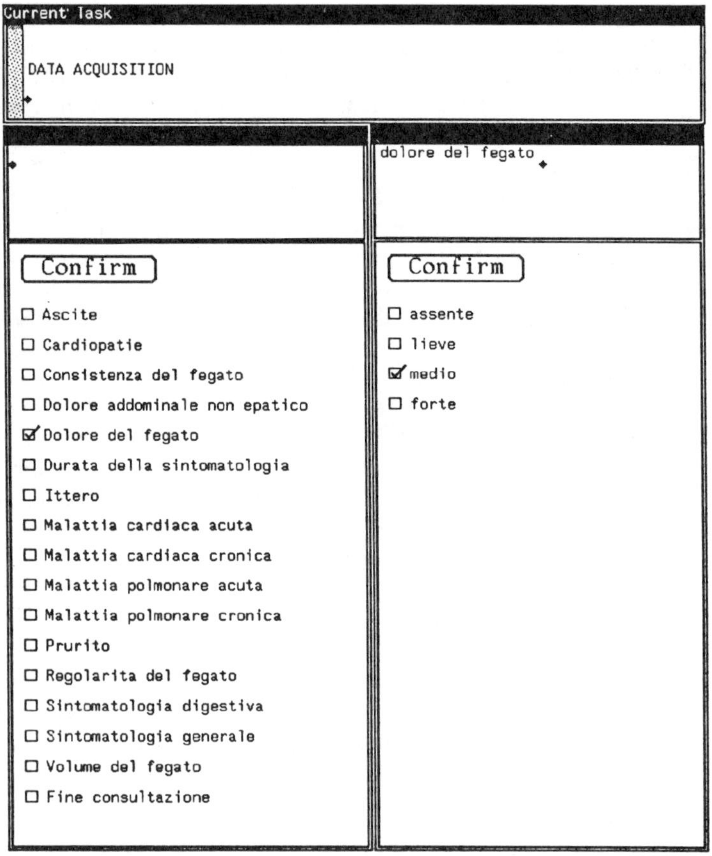

Current Task

DATA ACQUISITION

dolore del fegato

[Confirm]   [Confirm]

☐ Ascite   ☐ assente
☐ Cardiopatie   ☐ lieve
☐ Consistenza del fegato   ☑ medio
☐ Dolore addominale non epatico   ☐ forte
☑ Dolore del fegato
☐ Durata della sintomatologia
☐ Ittero
☐ Malattia cardiaca acuta
☐ Malattia cardiaca cronica
☐ Malattia polmonare acuta
☐ Malattia polmonare cronica
☐ Prurito
☐ Regolarita del fegato
☐ Sintomatologia digestiva
☐ Sintomatologia generale
☐ Volume del fegato
☐ Fine consultazione

Figure 9.1 - Graphical interface for data acquisition.

In order to avoid the introduction of unknown findings the menu contains a list of items (findings) which have to be selected by the user. Only very general findings are inserted into such a menu - that is, only the findings needed to verify the triggering conditions of the higher level diagnostic hypotheses. When the user selects a finding in the menu a second pop-up menu is displayed by the system containing the possible linguistic characterizations of the finding itself, which have to be selected by the user (see figure 9.1). It is worth noting that the system automatically associates default (normal) values with all the findings which have not been selected by the user from the main menu.

An alternative solution for this phase of data acquisition would be a direct introduction of data by the user, in which he/she could introduce the information he/she knows - for example, using natural language. This approach creates some problems, particularly because the user does not necessarily know which data the system really needs, so data the system is not able to deal with may be introduced and data needed by the system not provided (so it has to ask for them, perhaps when verifying a triggering condition). Moreover, an agreement between the system and all its potential users is needed on the terms used to identify findings (and their attributes).

The initial data introduced by the user are sufficient to evoke (trigger) initial (coarse) diagnostic hypotheses. During the process of instantiation of the frames corresponding to such hypotheses more specific data (those contained in the NECESSARY FINDINGS slots and then, if the evidence degree of the match between NECESSARY FINDINGS and actual data is strong enough, those in the SUPPLEMENTARY FINDINGS slot) are requested from the user via graphical menus (active phase). It is worth noting that only very general data are requested in this phase. Moreover, only data relative to relevant hypotheses (i.e. those evoked by initial data) are requested. During the refinement and specialization processes of the initial hypotheses, other more specific data (often related to physical tests or examinations on the system to be diagnosed) may be asked for by the system in the same way. During the entire data acquisition process the user can ask for information (explanations) about data, which is displayed on a window on the screen ("explanation" window in figure 9.2). Moreover, the system displays in a separate window ("clinical_record" window in figure 9.2), during the whole consultation, the record of all data introduced by the user. In particular, the hierarchical data structure is displayed in the window by selecting the name of a datum the user can inspect its current instantiation. For example, in medical applications the clinical record of the patient is displayed and can be accessed by the user at any time during the consultation.

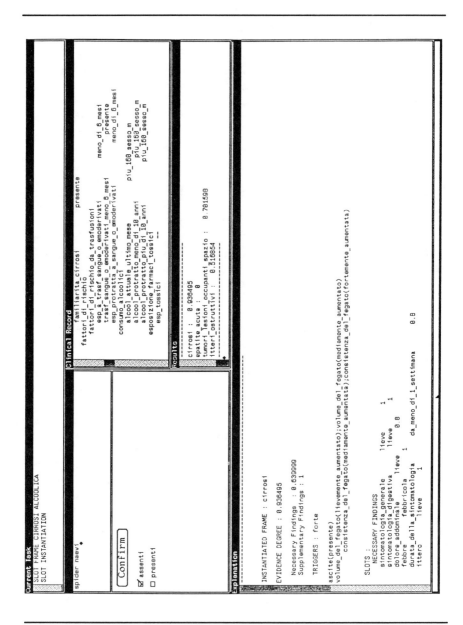

Figure 9.2 - Graphical display of the windows used during the heuristic phase.

It is worth noting that this scheme for data acquisition matches the ideal scenario described above.

9.1.3 EXPLANATION FACILITIES AT THE HEURISTIC LEVEL

We have noticed above that one of the most important reasons for the introduction of deep knowledge is to provide appropriate explanations to the user. This does not mean that at the heuristic level no explanation component is needed. In fact, it may be interesting, in particular for a non-expert user, to have both the deep precise explanation (i.e. a description of the initial perturbations and causal evolutions which have led to a malfunction arising) and the heuristic explanation of how experience can be used to diagnose such a malfunction. This could be particularly useful for tutorial purposes, in order that a student could understand the precise deep processes which explain the presence of a malfunction and at the same time learn how the simple observation of some findings can be used to produce the same diagnosis. In a certain sense, the combination of the two explanations can help the learner to understand the connection between the observation of data and the underlying causal processes in the modelled system.

Moreover, other, even if very simple, kinds of explanations are needed at the heuristic level - in particular, explanations about data and the data hierarchy. Specifically, this means that the user can ask for information about data organization and about the meaning of data asked for by the system (or about their attributes).

For these reasons we have developed some facilities for explanation at the heuristic level. In particular, as we have noticed in the previous section, data (or, more generally the data hierarchy) can be accessed at any time by the user in a special window which is always active in the system ("clinical_record" window in the medical example reported in figure 9.2). As far as diagnostic hypotheses are concerned, the system provides the user with the possibility of displaying instantiated frames. More specifically, during the heuristic consultation the system provides a menu through which the user can select whether he/she wants some instantiated frames to be displayed by the system. In this case, a specific "explanation" window is opened by the system and the selected frame displayed in such a window (see figure 9.2).

9.1.4 GRAPHICAL INTERFACES

In this section we will analyze the graphical interfaces developed for the causal level of CHECK. In particular, we will describe the explanation module, i.e. the module which produces graphical deep explanations for the user. The module is used to display both prototypical networks (in correspondence to general questions from the user about causal knowledge) and instantiated ones (i.e. networks used to confirm the presence of a diagnostic hypothesis in a particular case). From the graphical point of view the two problems are very similar, so in the following we shall discuss them together.

It is worth noting that there are in CHECK two very different modalities for the visualization of a causal network: the *normal* modality and the *trace* one. In the first case the network is displayed at the end of the reasoning process - that is, for example, when a complete portion of the network that can explain the presence of a malfunction has been found and instantiated. In the trace modality, on the other hand, the nodes of the network are displayed as long as the reasoning process of the system proceeds. In this way, the entire reasoning process of the system can be followed (obviously, since the reasoning scheme is hypothetical, it is generally the case that paths of the network are first displayed and then canceled by the system). We believe that both kinds of explanations can be very useful (especially the trace one when reasoning on a particular case).

9.1.4.1 DISPLAY OF THE CAUSAL NETWORK

Let us describe in detail how a causal network is graphically displayed by the system. The first point is to introduce the notation we use to distinguish between the different types of nodes and arcs:

-    STATES are represented by elliptical boxes; only the name of the STATE is shown in the box to make the description more readable; further information can be obtained by selecting the state with the "mouse" and pressing the left button. A new window is popped up by the system which contains a detailed description of the state (the window on the upper right of the screen in the example of figure 9.3). In particular, when an instantiated network is displayed, the attributes (state variables) of the state and their values are shown by the system in such a window. Otherwise the prototypical description of the state is displayed.

-    ACTIONS are represented by rectangular boxes.

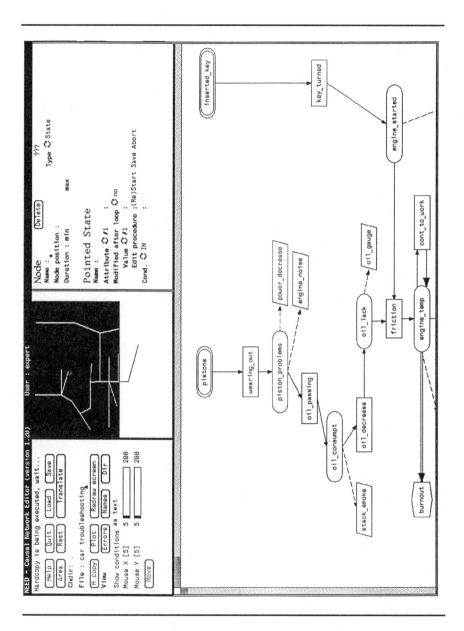

Figure 9.3 - Visualization of an instantiated portion of the causal network which accounts for the diagnostic hypothesis "burnout".

- FINDINGS are represented by rhomboidal boxes. Again only the name of the finding is usually displayed by the system: its precise description (attributes and values) can be obtained by the user selecting the node with the "mouse" (in the same way as for states nodes). There is an exception: when a finding has only one attribute (whose name can be omitted) the pair <finding, value> is directly displayed by the system in the case of an instantiated network. It is worth noting that in order to graphically distinguish between the "histological" manifestations and the other ones, double-line boxes are used to represent FINDING nodes corresponding to histological manifestations.

- INITIAL CAUSES are represented by double-line elliptical boxes.

- HYPOTHESIS nodes are represented by hexagonal boxes.

As far as arcs are concerned, the following notation has been made:

- CAUSAL ARCS or, better, STATE-ACTION and ACTION-STATE arcs (see chapter 7) are represented by simple continuous lines.

- HAM arcs are represented by simple discontinuous lines.

- DEFINED_AS arcs are represented by double continuous lines.

- SUGGEST arcs are represented by dotted-dashed lines.

- LOOP arcs are represented by continuous lines with which a label "Loop" is associated. It is worth noting that the same graphical notation used for CAUSAL arcs has been adopted (on account that the semantic of the two types of arcs is similar).

Moreover, we use the convention that arcs entering a node are ORed if nothing different is explicitly indicated (so that, for example, if two CAUSAL arcs enter a STATE and nothing different is indicated, the two arcs are ORed, so the establishing of one of the causes is sufficient to confirm the STATE itself). To represent the fact that two arcs entering a STATE are ANDed (or XORed, for example) a line with the appropriate label ("AND" or "XOR") is drawn to connect the two arcs.

Some final remarks concern how conditions on arcs can be represented and how MUST and MAY arcs (relationships) are distinguished. For the display of conditions the graphical facility provides two different modalities:

- *text mode:* the text of the condition is directly displayed on the arc. In particular, the general condition or its instantiated version is displayed, depending on whether a general or an instantiated network is being visualized by the system.

- *mark mode:* two different types of markings are used for unconditioned and conditioned arcs; if a conditioned arc is selected with the "mouse", the condition itself is displayed. This mode of visualization is particularly useful when many (and/or long) conditions are associated with arcs, in which cases a text visualization could be very hard to read.

To distinguish between MUST and MAY relationships in a particular model, we simply use the label "MAY" which is associated with "possible" (MAY) arcs. On the contrary, in the visualization of an instantiated network the distinction is no longer made, but a further explanation is associated with confirmed MAY relationships that consists of the description of which findings (manifestations) have been used to confirm the presence of the relationship in the hypothetical reasoning process.

In figure 7.19 an example of visualization of a prototypical network (in the mechanical domain of car troubleshooting) has been reported, whilst in figure 9.3 an instantiated part of the same network used to confirm the presence of the diagnostic hypothesis "burnout" is displayed.

9.1.4.2 ABSTRACT NETWORKS

A major problem in the visualization process of a causal network is connected with the size of the network itself, which usually cannot be displayed on a screen. This can make it very difficult for a user to understand the global causal evolution of a system. This means that explanations constituted by very large and detailed networks are difficult to read and lose most of their expressive power. To solve this problem we have developed two techniques for generating more compact and abstract descriptions.

The first technique is very simple and it is based on a "zoom" facility. More specifically when a large network has to be displayed the system visualizes the whole network in a window on a reduced scale (the scale factor is arranged at run time in order always to display the whole network in the reduced scale window). By selecting a point in this compact visualization with a "mouse", the user can zoom in on part of the network, which is displayed in a detailed form on a separate window (see figure 9.3, the reduced scale window is the central window in the upper part of the screen). By using this "zooming" technique, the user can look at local detailed descriptions without completely losing context information about the global causal network.

More interesting is the second technique we have developed for generating more readable and easy-to-understand explanations, which is based on the definition of "abstract networks". As we have noted above, one of the most critical points in the design of a causal network is the choice of the level of abstraction at which knowledge is represented and manipulated. We have suggested in the last sections that the definition of the lower limit of representation deserves a great deal of attention in order to avoid unexpected behavior and errors in the use of a model. In this section we will discuss the possibility of representing causal knowledge at different levels of abstraction and we will introduce, in particular, the concept of *"abstract network"* (the necessity of representing and manipulating deep knowledge at different levels of detail has been realized by many researchers in recent years; particularly interesting is the ABEL system [Patil 81] in which three levels of representation for causal knowledge, namely "clinical", "intermediate" and "pathophysiological", and operations for abstracting and elaborating description have been designed).

This corresponds to introducing a further level of causal knowledge representation at which the behavior of the modelled system is described in a very abstract way (that is to say, introducing only a few abstract states, the cause-effect relationships among them and their major manifestations).

In the preceding sections we have shown how causal networks can be defined in CHECK, discussing what kind of knowledge they are intended to represent. It should be apparent from the examples of section 7.3 that very complex networks are needed to model practical (real-world) domains (see, for example, the networks of figure 7.20 and consider that alcoholic cirrhosis is only one kind of cirrhosis, and that cirrhosis is only one of the general classes of liver diseases). This can create problems when such networks have to be displayed: a user, in fact, can be taken aback if a very detailed and complex network is directly presented to him/her. He/she will have been unable to follow the general evolution of the modelled system - that is, the causes and consequences of a disorder. An interesting solution to the problem of providing easy-to-understand visualizations of causal knowledge is to first present the user with an abstract description of (parts of) a network (instantiated or not), which can then be refined to obtain more detailed descriptions.

A first very simple way to produce more abstract representations in a causal network derives from the simplification of CAUSAL arcs: as we have noted before, it is possible to give precise descriptions of such relationships involving ACTION nodes and STATE-ACTION and ACTION-STATES arcs, or to give more abstract cause-effect relationships considering only STATES.

A more interesting way of giving abstract descriptions is to collect groups of nodes (STATES and ACTIONS in particular) of a detailed description in more abstract states which represent the abstract behavior of the modelled system. We believe that the possibility of using such types of abstract networks can be very interesting, but that some constraints on their form have to be imposed in order to make the correspondence between abstract and detailed representation clearer. In particular, abstract networks can be defined in CHECK which have to satisfy the following conditions:

-   all the INITIAL CAUSE nodes of the detailed network must be present in the abstract one, i.e. these nodes cannot be eliminated while abstracting a description.

-   HYPOTHESES nodes and the STATES defining the presence of a hypothesis (that is, connected to a "HYPOTHESES" node by a "DEFINED_AS" arc) must be present in an abstract network.

-   STATE and ACTION nodes (and also FINDING nodes, see next condition) can be grouped in AB_STATE (ABstract STATE) nodes. Each loop eventually present in the detailed network must be completely enclosed in an abstract state.

-   FINDING nodes can be maintained in an abstract description or they can be included in abstract states. In particular, CHECK assumes by default that FINDING nodes corresponding to "histological" manifestations cannot appear in an abstract description. For other findings the choice is left to the designer of a particular network, i.e. to the knowledge engineer, who has to mark which findings have to be maintained in an abstract description (i.e. which are the most relevant ones).

-   Two AB_STATES "S_1" and "S_2" are connected by an "AB_CAUSAL" arc (from "S_1" to "S_2") if there is a pair of STATE nodes "$State_1$" and "$State_2$" such that "$State_1$" is included in "S_1", "$State_2$" is included in "S_2" and there is a CAUSAL arc from "$State_1$" and "$State_2$". This condition can be formally expressed as follows:

$$\exists \ (State_1 \ in \ S_1) \wedge \exists \ (State_2 \ in \ S_2)$$
$$\wedge \exists \ x \ (causal\_arc(x) \wedge source(x, State_1) \wedge destination(x, State_2))$$
$$\Rightarrow \exists \ y \ (AB\_causal\_arc(y) \wedge source(y, S_1) \wedge destination(y, S_2))$$

The meaning of AB_CAUSAL arc is to represent cause-effect relationships.

-   An AB_SUGGEST arc connects an abstract state "S_1" to a HYPOTHESIS node "H" if "H" can be suggested by a state in "S_1" (i.e. there is a SUGGEST arc from a STATE "State" included in "S_1" to "H" in the detailed network. Formally, this can be expressed as follows:

$$\exists \ (State \ in \ S_1) \wedge \exists \ H$$
$$\wedge \exists \ x \ (suggest\_arc(x) \wedge source(x, State) \wedge destination(x, H))$$

$$\Rightarrow \exists\, y\ (\text{AB\_suggest\_arc}(y) \wedge \text{source}(y,\, S_1) \wedge$$
$$\text{destination}(y,\, H))$$

The meaning of AB_SUGGEST relationships is similar to the corresponding SUGGEST ones.

- An abstract state "S_1" is connected to a FINDING node "F" by an AB_HAM arc if any one of the STATES included in "S_1" can have "F" as a manifestation. This can be formally expressed as follows:

$$\exists\, (\text{State in } S_1) \wedge \exists\, F$$
$$\wedge\, \exists\, x\ (\text{ham\_arc}(x) \wedge \text{source}(x,\, \text{State}) \wedge \text{destination}(x,\, F))$$
$$\Rightarrow \exists\, y\ (\text{AB\_ham\_arc}(y) \wedge \text{source}(y,\, S_1) \wedge \text{destination}(y,\, F))$$

- DEFINED_AS arcs are identically maintained in abstract networks.
- FORM_OF arcs are identically maintained in abstract networks.
- Abstract relationships can be labelled as necessary (MUST) and possible (MAY) just like detailed ones. In particular: an AB_CAUSAL relationship between the abstract states "S_1" and "S_2" is labelled as a MUST one if at least one of the CAUSAL arcs connecting one state of "S_1" to a state of "S_2" is labelled as a MUST one, i.e. if the following logical relationship holds:

$$\exists\, (x_1 \text{ in } S_1) \wedge \exists\, (x_2 \text{ in } S_2)$$
$$\wedge\, \exists\, x_3\ (\text{causal\_arc}(x_3) \wedge \text{source}(x_3,\, x_1) \wedge \text{destination}(x_3,\, x_2) \wedge$$
$$\text{MUST}(x_3))$$
$$\Rightarrow \exists\, y\ (\text{AB\_causal\_arc}(y) \wedge \text{source}(y,\, S_1) \wedge$$
$$\text{destination}(y,\, S_2) \wedge \text{MUST}(y))$$

On the contrary an AB_CAUSAL arc is labelled as a MAY one only in case the condition reported above fails, that is when all the cause-effect relationships between states in "S_1" and "S_2" are possible; an AB_SUGGEST arc from an AB_STATE "S" to a HYPOTHESIS "H" is labelled as MUST if at least one of the SUGGEST arcs from a state in "S" to "H" is labelled as MUST; finally, an AB_HAM arc from "S" to "F" is labelled as MUST when at least one of the HAM ARCS from a state in "S" to "F" is labelled as MUST.

It is worth noting that abstract networks that satisfy such conditions can be automatically generated by the knowledge acquisition module of CHECK (see section 9.5); the only thing the knowledge engineer has to specify is which nodes (STATES, FINDINGS and ACTION) have to be grouped in each one of the AB_STATES of the abstract network. It is important to point out once again that abstract networks constitute a further level of representation, so their design is not a purely syntactic operation; this prevents an AB_STATE from being just a collection of nodes strictly connected in the graph that represents the causal network.

In figure 9.4 a simple example of the construction of an abstract model from a detailed one is reported: the relationships between the two models have been clearly pointed out. As a more significant example, in figure 9.5 a simple abstract pathophysiological model of the liver disease "alcoholic cirrhosis" is reported, derived from the detailed descriptions that have been partially presented in figure 7.20. Note how in this network AB_STATES have been defined in such a way that one of the states they group is in a prominent position, so it gives its name to the abstract state itself. This is common in the construction of abstract networks and it could be taken to be a general rule.

9.2 KNOWLEDGE ACQUISITION

One of the major problems in the development of Knowledge Based Systems is that of acquiring knowledge from domain experts and coding it in a particular representation formalism. The knowledge representation formalisms that have been used in the first generation of (diagnostic) expert systems (e.g. production rules, frames or hybrid structures) are often not natural ones for experts to use to represent their knowledge about a specific domain, since they are far from experts' usual way of reasoning.

To solve this problem, several knowledge acquisition systems have been developed since the late 70's. The aim of these systems is twofold: on the one hand, they allow domain experts to describe knowledge in a easy and, possibly, natural way; on the other hand, they are able to guide this knowledge elicitation process according to the needs of a particular representation and problem solving strategy, so that they can suitably and easily code the acquired knowledge in the format needed by a particular knowledge representation formalism.

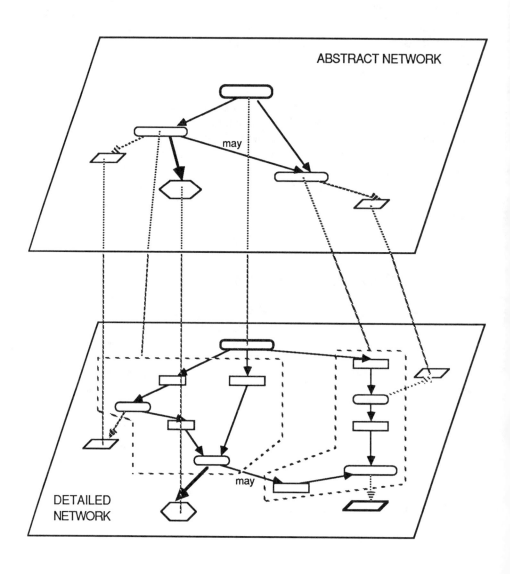

Figure 9.4 - The correspondence between abstract and detailed networks.

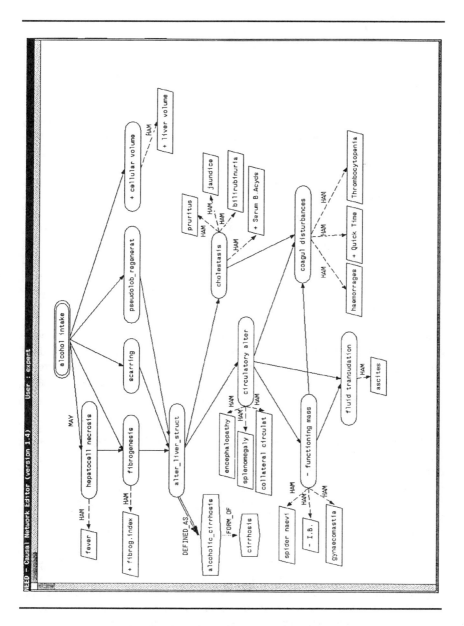

Figure 9.5 - An abstract pathophysiological model in the domain of liver diseases (for the sake of clarity only some finding nodes have been displayed).

Starting from the seminal work of TEIRESIAS [Davis 79], other systems have been developed which are able to guide the operation of knowledge elicitation from experts: ROGET [Bennet 85] and MORE [Kahn et al. 85] are able to acquire sets of heuristic rules through an interaction with a domain expert. Moreover, recently structured tools for acquiring different forms of knowledge have been designed (e.g. KADS [Wielinga & Breuker 84]).

A major step forwards in the simplification of the knowledge acquisition phase is marked again by the development of systems based on deep knowledge. In actual fact this kind of knowledge is closer to the traditional reasoning background of domain experts than heuristic relationships (to be coded in production rules or prototypical representations). Consider, for example, the case of medical domains: deep causal (pathophysiological) knowledge is very close to the "core" knowledge studied by physicians, so it is more natural to formalize it than to formalize heuristic relationships (at least in those domains in which causal models are known). There is, moreover, a further very important advantage in acquiring deep knowledge instead of the heuristic type: greater independence from the individual domain expert from which knowledge has been elicited. In a certain sense, in fact, deep models are "objective" ones, that is they are models of the *actual* behavior of the system to be diagnosed, whilst heuristic knowledge depends on the specific experiences of a particular domain expert. This means that a much lower degree of "subjective interpretation" by the domain expert is present in deep knowledge than in that of the heuristic type. In this way, furthermore, a major agreement between different experts on a model can be obtained and, consequently, the represented knowledge is more widely understandable.

The adoption of graphical interfaces for the design of deep models can further simplify the problem of knowledge acquisition. In fact, a pictorial representation of the relationships between the different objects in a specific domain is very clear and easy to understand, so it is simpler for an expert to represent domain knowledge correctly (the possibility of errors in the initial model is greatly reduced). Moreover, such graphical representations can be easily understood by people other than the designer, so they can be maintained or modified more easily during the lifetime of a particular system.

A problem arising in systems combining deep and heuristic knowledge is that two different representations of a domain have to be given. Apparently two different phases of knowledge acquisition are necessary to build such systems and this could create serious problems (for example, problems of inconsistency between the two levels can arise if they are acquired separately). The consequence is that, in order for a system to be actually realized, only one phase of knowledge acquisition must be present.

Some proposals have been made in recent years for the automatic derivation of heuristic knowledge (heuristic relationships, or experience knowledge)
from deep causal ones; Van de Velde [Van de Velde 86][Steels & Van de
Velde 85] proposed an approach to derive and refine production rules from
deep models; similarly, Fink [Fink et al. 85] suggested that each time deep
knowledge is used to solve a particular problem a heuristic rule can be
abstracted (to be used when the same problem has to be solved again in the
future); in [Sembugamoorthy & Chandrasekaran 86] "deep" knowledge is
compiled in a heuristic problem solving strategy (it is worth noting that
among these systems, only Fink's combines, in an easy way, deep and heuristic reasoning in the problem solving strategy).

For these reasons, in CHECK we have decided to design a module to
acquire only deep causal knowledge. We are currently studying how to derive
effectively the heuristic level from the deep one (we are, in particular, devis-
ing some "derivation rules" for the automatic generation of a prototypical
description of malfunctioning from a description of its causes, evolutions and
manifestations). We shall briefly return to this subject at the end of the book,
when we shall discuss some advanced topics on which we are currently working.

In this section we will concentrate on NEED (NEtwork EDitor), a
graphical editor for the design of deep models based on CHECK's knowledge
representation formalism [Console et al. 87a].

9.2.1 THE GRAPHICAL NETWORK EDITOR NEED

The causal knowledge in CHECK can be introduced and formalized
using NEED, a graphical NEtwork EDitor which solves many of the problems
the knowledge engineer has to deal with in gathering knowledge information
and in maintaining it during the life-cycle of a specific system. This
represents a significant advance with respect to the previous approach which
required the domain expert to provide knowledge directly in a high level
linguistic formalism with a text editor. NEED is formed by a two-level structure: the lower level is the graphic manager which interfaces requests for
drawing shapes and lines to the operating system and to the firmware; the
higher level manages objects (nodes and arcs) directly. In this way it achieves
the full advantages offered by a graphic tool but it is also capable of managing all the information necessary to a reasoning system.

In order to make these aims concrete we could not use any of the graphical editors available because these deal with objects merely from the graphical point of view, namely as a set of pixels arranged somewhere on a screen.

One of the most important and interesting characteristics of NEED is that it is strongly coupled to CHECK's knowledge representation formalism (this means that NEED is not a generic graphic-oriented editor, but a specialized editor for designing CHECK's causal networks). In fact, editing in NEED is guided by the semantics of CHECK's deep modelling formalism in such a way that only "correct" models can be designed by the user (that is, models that can be dealt with by the inference strategy).

With NEED the knowledge engineer is supplied with a tool able to perform the following:

-   *Editing of nodes:* Creating, moving, deleting nodes and modifying their attributes.

-   *Editing of arcs:* Creating, moving, deleting oriented arcs between two nodes and modifying the associated attributes; creation of arcs is made by selecting the source node and the destination node in sequence. In particular, the editor allows the creation of an arc only if, having considered the source and destination nodes (let us say of type T_1 and T_2 respectively), there exists a type of arc that can connect a node of type T_1 to a node of type T_2. This means that, after the two nodes have been selected, a menu is popped up by the system in which the only legal types of arcs (relationships) that can be used to connect the two nodes are listed. For example, if the user selects a STATE and a FINDING node in this order, the only type of arc in the pop-up menu is the "HAM" one; otherwise, if a STATE and a HYPOTHESIS node are selected, the system allows the user to choose between a "SUGGEST" and a "DEFINED_AS" arc. On the contrary, if the user selects two STATE nodes, an error message (together with an explanation of the type of error) is printed by the system.

-   *Zooming facilities:* The fact that in many cases networks are very large and cannot be contained in a screen of the graphic workstation creates problems during the editing phase (as well as during the explanation phase). A zooming facility is provided by NEED: a compacted (reduced scale) description of the global edited network is maintained in a window, whilst more detailed parts can be zoomed and edited in a different window (central window in upper central of the screen in figure 9.6). In the reduced scale window we use the convention that the portion of the causal network which is currently displayed in the main window is visualized in reverse mode (see figure 9.6). To zoom in on part of a network it is sufficient to select a point in the global reduced scale network and automatically the network around that point is zoomed on.

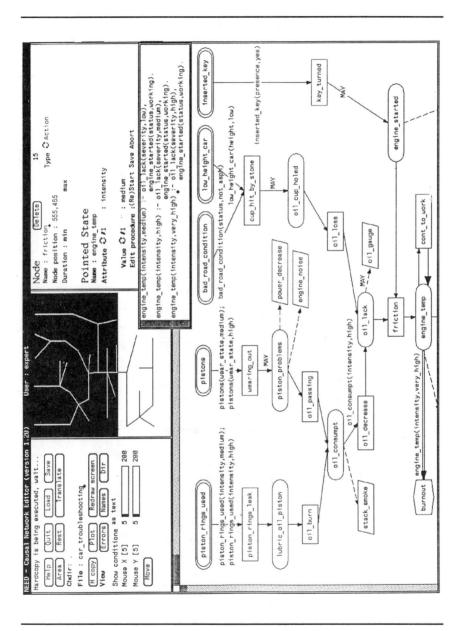

Figure 9.6 - The NEED editor.

- *Defining abstract networks.* As noticed above, to define an abstract network it is sufficient to define AB_STATES nodes: this can be done very easily just by selecting the set of nodes of the detailed network which are part of the abstract state.

- *Making a hardcopy of the screen on a printer:* Useful for documentation or for teaching.

- *Drawing the network on a plotter:* This is perhaps the easiest way to archive a network with all the associated information.

- *Generating the linguistic description of a network:* Such description is used to generate the actual implementation of a system and can be used for documentation.

- *Loading and saving network images into the file system.*

- The last, but perhaps the most important, function we inserted into NEED is an *on-line help window* which (if selected by the user) provides him/her with detailed information about the available functions and the rules which the editor obeys.

Node description	
Field name	Content
Name	node name
Attributes Name Value Value	(for STATES, FINDINGS and INITIAL_CAUSES) name of the attributes of the node, admissible linguistic values for each attribute
Functional Transformation Scheme	(for ACTIONS) Functional transformation describing the attributes of the caused state in terms of those of the causing one
Node posn.	position (cartesian coordinates) of the node shape on the screen
Cond.posn.	position of the instantiation condition on the screen
Cond	logical condition on entering arcs

Table 9.1

Arc description	
Field name	Content
Type	either MUST or MAY
Arc	one of CAUSAL, SUGGEST, HAM, DEFINED_AS, FORM_OF, LOOP
Condition	condition on the arc
Explanation	information about the arc to be displayed to the user
Type posn.	position (cartesian coordinates) of the "MUST"/"MAY" clause
Cond.posn.	position of the condition
Expl.posn.	position of the explanation

Table 9.2

In order to get nodes and arcs displayed and to change information about them, one must accordingly select a node or an arc and the relative field will appear in one of the windows of the editor, ready to be changed at one's ease. The attributes of nodes and arcs currently managed by the editor are shown below (tables 9.1 and 9.2). In particular, in table 9.1 the fields associated with the description of each node, with a simple explanation of the pieces of information they contain, is reported. Similarly, in table 9.2 the fields associated with the description of each arc are listed.

As stated above, NEED is strictly coupled to CHECK's knowledge representation formalism. In the definition of the functionalities of NEED we have noticed that the editor guides the definition of relationships between nodes in such a way that the constraints imposed by CHECK's formalism are satisfied (i.e. the rules listed in Table 7.1). Moreover, other semantic checks are performed by the editor; the following are among the most interesting ones:

-   *Loop analysis.* NEED is able to detect the presence of loops and to verify how structured they are. Each time a loop is introduced by the user in an implicit way (that is to say, not labelling an arc explicitly as a LOOP one), the editor warns the user about the presence of the loop and is able to infer automatically which arc has to be labelled as a LOOP one (this is possible due to the simple form loops can have in CHECK).

- *Uniqueness of names.* Names of nodes must be unique in CHECK, that is, two nodes cannot have the same name.

- *Reachability of nodes.* NEED is able to warn the user about the presence of unreachable nodes. This analysis is performed only when an attempt is made to save the network.

- *Non specified nodes.* In the same way, the editor can warn the user if the internal description of some node (e.g. STATE or FINDING) has not been specified.

- *Absence of INITIAL CAUSE and HYPOTHESIS nodes.* The user is warned if no INITIAL CAUSE or HYPOTHESIS node is present when a network is saved.

- *Syntactic analysis of conditions.* Conditions associated with arcs and in the instantiation part of a node must be correct logical expressions (or better Prolog clauses).

Figure 9.6 shows what the different windows of NEED look like during the design of a causal network: the figure has been made using NEED's hardcopy facility.

9.2.2 FROM GRAPHICAL TO LINGUISTIC DESCRIPTIONS

Another interesting peculiarity of NEED is that it is able to generate two different descriptions of a causal network:

- an internal graphical description, which is used by the editor itself each time a network is loaded and by the explanation module (see section 9.1.4);

- an external linguistic description.

The linguistic description is based on an "*object-oriented language*" (embedded in Prolog) we have designed to describe and implement causal networks. The language has been used in the implementation of CHECK and will be described in more detail in chapter 11. In figure 9.7 we have reported part of the linguistic description generated by NEED in correspondence to the network of figure 7.19. In such a linguistic description each node is represented by a set of clauses, each one of which contains part of the information concerning the node itself. More specifically, almost all the clauses have the following structure:

- the name of the predicate which is the head of a clause corresponds to the name of the node of which the clause itself is a partial description;

- the first argument of the head of a clause defines which part of the node is described by the clause (e.g. list of its causing states, list of its attributes, etc);

- the second argument of the head of a clause contains part of the description of the node (correspondent to the subject listed in the first argument).

It is worth noticing that the linguistic description generated by NEED is directly used by the reasoning component of the system. Moreover, such a description is used by other modules (e.g. it is the input of the heuristic knowledge derivation module we are studying).

```
piston_rings_used(caused_states,
                [ [ [ state,lubric_oil_in_piston ],
                  [ action,piston_rings_leak ],
                  [condition,must,
                  (piston_rings_used(intensity,medium);
                  pistons_rings_used(intensity,high))] ] ]).
piston_rings_used(has_attributes,[intensity]).
piston_rings_used(attribute_admissible_values,
                intensity,[low,medium,high]).

piston_rings_leak(causing_state, [initial_cause,piston_rings_used]).
piston_rings_leak(caused_state,lubric_oil_in_piston).

lubric_oil_in_piston(causing_states,
                [ [ [ initial_cause,piston_rings_used ],
                  [ action,piston_rings_leak ],
                  [condition,must,
                  (piston_rings_used(intensity,medium);
                  pistons_rings_used(intensity,high))] ] ]).
lubric_oil_in_piston(caused_states,
                [ [ [ state,oil_consumpt ],
                  [ action,oil_burn ],
                  [ condition,must,true ] ] ]).
lubric_oil_in_piston(ham,[]).
lubric_oil_in_piston(attributes,[quantity]).
lubric_oil_in_piston(attribute_admissible_values,
                quantity,[low,high]).
lubric_oil_in_piston(calculate_attribute,quantity,low) :-
```

```
                    piston_rings_used(intensity,medium).
lubric_oil_in_piston(calculate_attribute,quantity,high) :-
                    piston_rings_used(intensity,high).

oil_burn(causing_state,[state,lubric_oil_in_piston]).
oil_burn(caused_state,oil_consumpt).

pistons(caused_states,
                    [ [ [ state,piston_problems ],
                      [ action,wearing_out ],
                      [condition,may,
                        (pistons(wear_state,medium);
                         pistons(wear_state,high))] ] ]).
pistons(has_attributes,[wear_state]).
pistons(attribute_admissible_values,
                    wear_state,[low,medium,high]).

wearing_out(causing_state,[initial_cause,pistons]).
wearing_out(caused_state,piston_problems).

piston_problems(causing_states,
                    [ [ [ initial_cause,pistons ],
                      [ action,wearing_out ],
                      [ condition,may,
                        (pistons(wear_state,medium);
                         pistons(wear_state,high))] ] ]).
piston_problems(caused_states,
                    [ [ [ state,oil_consumpt ],
                      [ action,oil_passing ],
                      [ condition,must,true ] ] ]).
piston_problems(ham,
                    [ [ power_decrease,must,true ] and
                      [ engine_noise,must,true ] ]).
piston_problems(has_attributes,[severity]).
piston_problems(attribute_admissible_values,
                    severity,[low,high]).
piston_problems(calculate_attribute,severity,low) :-
                    pistons(wear_state,medium).
piston_problems(calculate_attribute,severity,high) :-
                    pistons(wear_state,high).

power_decrease(manif_of,[[piston_problems,must,true]]).
power_decrease(has_attributes,[intensity]).
power_decrease(attribute_admissible_values,
```

intensity,[low,high]).
power_decrease(attribute_compatibility,intensity,X) :-
          piston_problems(severity,X).

engine_noise(manif_of,[[piston_problems,must,true]]).
engine_noise(has_attributes,[intensity]).
engine_noise(attribute_admissible_values,
                    intensity,[low,high]).
engine_noise(attribute_compatibility,intensity,X) :-
          piston_problems(severity,X).

oil_passing(causing_state,[state,piston_problems]).
oil_passing(caused_state,oil_consumpt).

oil_consumpt(causing_states,
                    [[[state,piston_problems],
                      [action,oil_passing],
                      [condition,must,true]] or
                      [[state,lubric_oil_in_piston],
                      [action,oil_burn],
                      [condition,must,true]]]).
oil_consumpt(caused_states,
                    [[[state,oil_lack],
                      [action,oil_decrease],
                      [condition,must
                        oil_consumpt(intensity,high)]]]).
oil_consumpt(ham,[[stack_smoke,must,true]]).
oil_consumpt(has_attributes,[intensity]).
oil_consumpt(attribute_admissible_values,
                    intensity,[low,high]).
oil_consumpt(calculate_attribute,intensity,X) :-
          lubric_oil_in_pistons(quantity,X).
oil_consumpt(calculate_attribute,intensity,X) :-
          piston_problems(severity,X).

stack_smoke(manif_of,[[oil_consumpt,must,true]]).
stack_smoke(has_attributes,[colour]).
stack_smoke(attribute_admissible_values,
                    colour,[grey,black]).
stack_smoke(attribute_compatibility,colour,grey) :-
          oil_consumpt(intensity,low).
stack_smoke(attribute_compatibility,colour,black) :-
          oil_consumpt(intensity,high).

```
oil_decrease(causing_state,[state,oil_consumpt]).
oil_decrease(caused_state,oil_lack).

.....
oil_lack(causing_states,
                       [ [ [ state,oil_cup_holed ],
                           [ action,oil_loss ],
                           [ condition,must,true ] ] or
                         [ state,oil_consumpt ],
                           [ action,oil_decrease ],
                           [ condition,must,
                             oil_consumpt(intensity,high) ] ] ]).
oil_lack(caused_states,
                       [ [ [ state,engine_temp ],
                           [ action,friction ],
                           [ condition,must,true ] ] ]).
oil_lack(ham, [ [ oil_gauge,may,true ] ]).
oil_lack(has_attributes,[intensity]).
oil_lack(attribute_admissible_values,
                       severity,[low,medium,high]).
oil_lack(calculate_attribute,severity,medium) :-
               oil_consumpt(intensity,high).
oil_lack(calculate_attribute,severity,low) :-
               oil_cup_holed(hole,small).
oil_lack(calculate_attribute,severity,medium) :-
               oil_cup_holed(hole,medium).
oil_lack(calculate_attribute,severity,high) :-
               oil_cup_holed(hole,large).

oil_gauge(manif_of,[[oil_lack,may,true]]).
oil_gauge(has_attributes,[colour]).
oil_gauge(attribute_admissible_values,
                       colour,[normal,yellow,red]).
oil_gauge(attribute_compatibility,colour,normal) :-
               oil_lack(severity,low).
oil_gauge(attribute_compatibility,colour,yellow) :-
               oil_lack(severity,medium).
oil_gauge(attribute_compatibility,colour,red) :-
               oil_lack(severity,high).
.....
inserted_key(has_attributes,[presence]).
inserted_key(attribute_admissible_values,
                       presence,[yes,no]).
.....
engine_started(has_attributes,[status]).
```

engine_started(attribute_admissible_values,
                       status,[non_working,working]).
engine_started(calculate_attribute,status,non_working) :-
               inserted_key(presence,no).
engine_started(calculate_attribute,status,working) :-
               inserted_key(presence,yes).

engine(manif_of,[[engine_started,may,true]]).
engine(has_attributes,[status]).
engine(attribute_admissible_values,
                       status,[off,on]).
engine(attribute_compatibility,status,off) :-
               engine_started(status,non_working).
engine(attribute_compatibility,status,on) :-
               engine_started(status,working).
   .....
engine_temp(has_attributes,[intensity]).
engine_temp(attribute_admissible_values,
                       intensity,[medium,high,very_high]).
engine_temp(calculate_attribute,intensity,medium) :-
               oil_lack(severity,low),
               engine_started(status,working).
engine_temp(calculate_attribute,intensity,high) :-
               oil_lack(severity,medium),
               engine_started(status,working).
engine_temp(calculate_attribute,intensity,very_high) :-
               oil_lack(severity,high),
               engine_started(status,working).
engine_temp(calculate_attribute,intensity,high) :-
               engine_temp(intensity,medium),
engine_temp(calculate_attribute,intensity,very_high) :-
               engine_temp(intensity,high),

temp_indicator(manif_of,[[engine_temp,must,true]]).
temp_indicator(has_attributes,[level]).
temp_indicator(attribute_admissible_values,
                       level,[yellow,red]).
temp_indicator(attribute_compatibility,level,yellow) :-
               engine_temp(intensity,medium).
temp_indicator(attribute_compatibility,level,red) :-
               engine_temp(intensity,high).
temp_indicator(attribute_compatibility,level,red) :-
               engine_temp(intensity,very_high).
   .....

ext_temperature(has_attributes,[value]).
inserted_key(attribute_admissible_values,
                          presence,[normal,high]).
.....
incr_coolant_temp(has_attributes,[intensity]).
incr_coolant_temp(attribute_admissible_values,
                          intensity,[normal,medium,high,very_high]).
incr_coolant_temp(calculate_attribute,intensity,normal) :-
            engine_temp(intensity,medium),
            ext_temperature(value,normal).
incr_coolant_temp(calculate_attribute,intensity,medium) :-
            engine_temp(intensity,medium),
            ext_temperature(value,high).
incr_coolant_temp(calculate_attribute,intensity,medium) :-
            engine_temp(intensity,high),
            ext_temperature(value,normal).
incr_coolant_temp(calculate_attribute,intensity,high) :-
            engine_temp(intensity,high),
            ext_temperature(value,high).
incr_coolant_temp(calculate_attribute,intensity,high) :-
            engine_temp(intensity,very_high),
            ext_temperature(value,normal).
incr_coolant_temp(calculate_attribute,intensity,very_high) :-
            engine_temp(intensity,very_high),
            ext_temperature(value,high).

vapour(manif_of,[[incr_coolant_temp,must,true]]).
vapour(has_attributes,[quantity]).
vapour(attribute_admissible_values,
                          quantity,[absent,present]).
vapour(attribute_compatibility,quantity,absent) :-
            incr_coolant_temp(intensity,normal).
vapour(attribute_compatibility,quantity,absent) :-
            incr_coolant_temp(intensity,medium).
vapour(attribute_compatibility,quantity,present) :-
            incr_coolant_temp(intensity,high).
vapour(attribute_compatibility,quantity,present) :-
            incr_coolant_temp(intensity,very_high).

.....

Figure 9.7 - Part of the linguistic description of the network of figure 7.19.

10

IMPLEMENTATION OF THE HEURISTIC LEVEL

In the next two chapters of the book, we will turn to describing how the CHECK diagnostic architecture has been practically implemented. In particular, in this chapter we will concentrate on how Knowledge Based Systems (Expert Systems) can be successfully implemented in Prolog and we will give some details of how the heuristic level of CHECK has been implemented using FROG (FRames in ProlOG), a Prolog based environment for the design of Knowledge Based Systems which we have recently developed ([Console & Rossi 87] [Console & Rossi 88]). In the next chapter we shall outline how the deep level of CHECK can be implemented and we shall give an overview of the global implementation of the CHECK environment (CHECK + NEED + graphical interfaces).

10.1 EXPERT SYSTEMS IN PROLOG

In the last few years interest in the use of Prolog to build Knowledge Based Systems has grown considerably (for an interesting survey, see [Rossi 86]). In particular, the approaches that have been proposed can be classified into three major classes:

- *Direct implementation.* In this case Prolog itself is used as the Knowledge Representation Language, often relying on its similarity with production systems [Clark & McCabe 82].

-   *Meta interpretation.* Prolog can be successfully used to build meta-interpreters for different knowledge representation formalisms [Sterling 84][Bowen 85]. This approach has several advantages and has been very successful in recent years, but it has a major problem: meta interpreters are often very inefficient since they introduce an extra level of interpretation on to that of Prolog. Recently, in response to such inefficiency problems, it has been proposed that meta-interpretation should be combined with partial evaluation techniques [Takeuchi & Furukawa 86] [Safra & Shapiro 86].

-   *Extensions to Prolog.* This approach is certainly the more general and complex one, and is based on the introduction of extensions to Prolog in order to make it more suitable for representing and reasoning on knowledge. Extensions can be introduced at different levels, modifying the language (and its interpreter) by introducing new features into it (as, for example, in [Ait-Kaci & Nasr 86] in which an extension for taxonomic reasoning has been introduced, or in [Ishizuka & Kanai 85] in which an extension for approximate reasoning has been introduced); or combining Prolog with other programming paradigms or knowledge representation languages (formalisms). With respect to the latter case, some interesting extensions to Prolog have been made by combining it with object oriented paradigms - as, for example, in Orient84/K [Tokoro & Ishikawa 86], Mandala [Furukawa et al. 84] and KRINE [Ogawa et al. 84].

None of these three approaches seems to be completely satisfactory (see [Console & Rossi 88] for an accurate discussion): a direct implementation approach is either very limited (e.g. implementation of rule based systems) or the code to be generated is very complex, so building and maintaining a system can be very difficult (for an example it is sufficient just to have a look at the code generated by Clark and McCabe [Clark & McCabe 82] to implement approximate reasoning in a production rules system coded in Prolog); meta-interpreters are generally very inefficient and complex to build and partial evaluation only partially solves the problem; extensions to Prolog can lead to very complex systems which are very difficult to implement and whose semantics are, in many cases, not completely satisfactory and clear.

For these reasons we have recently proposed a different approach, based on preprocessing techniques, which allows us to solve many of the problems discussed above [Console et al. 86] [Console & Rossi 86]. The general idea of the method is as follows: given a generic knowledge representation formalism and an inference strategy on it, complex Prolog code to implement it in such a way that the Prolog interpreter itself simulates the desired inference strategy can be generated. This can be done by introducing complex predicates and clauses to structure knowledge in which suitable "control predicates" which guide the Prolog interpreter making it simulate the desired scheme of reasoning are inserted. This code is usually very complex and cannot definitely be directly produced by the user who wants to implement a specific Knowledge Based System. The interesting observation is that this code can be sufficiently structured, so it can be automatically generated starting from a high level description of a specific knowledge base. For this reason, given a knowledge representation formalism (e.g. frames, production rules or semantic networks), a high level language for representing both domain knowledge (according to the formalism) and the desired inference strategy to be adopted in a specific case, can be defined. A high level description given in such a language can then be automatically translated by a suitable "preprocessing" tool into the actual implementation of the system. Schematically the approach is described in figure 10.1.

The approach presents several advantages:

-       It is flexible. Given a knowledge representation formalism, it is possible
        to define a high level language in which not only the domain

The high level description of the domain knowledge
and of the control strategy of a specific system

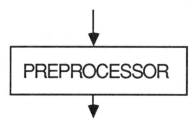

Prolog code to implement the system

Figure 10.1 - The preprocessing approach (scheme).

knowledge of a specific system but also the scheme of reasoning to be adopted can be defined, and it is possible to build a preprocessor which is able to deal with such complex descriptions to generate suitable code in any situation.

- The resulting systems are efficient, since the executed code is standard Prolog. Neither an extra level of interpretation is required nor any overhead is introduced in the Prolog interpreter. Furthermore, this approach is well suited to compilation.

- The generated programs and the preprocessor itself are easily portable and modifiable since they are written in Prolog.

- The preprocessor can be easily implemented in Prolog, provided that suitable syntactical definitions of the high level language are given [Console & Rossi 88].

- The approach allows a natural and easy combination of different knowledge representation formalisms, since it permits each one of them to be embedded in the same environment: Prolog. Different schemes can be obtained by structuring the predicates containing the domain knowledge differently and by inserting different 'control predicates' in different positions so that it is very easy to mix them together to produce a hybrid or composite representation formalism. Moreover, it is possible to combine different forms of reasoning and inference strategies within the same formalism.

A problem that arises as a side-effect of using a preprocessor is the loss of interactivity in the development of systems. We have recently developed various techniques for "flexible preprocessing" to solve these problems (for example, we have developed an "incremental preprocessor" to translate partially specified knowledge bases; a "knowledge base editor" to modify interactively a system - see [Console & Rossi 87] for discussion).

Using this approach we have implemented FROG (FRames in ProlOG), a hybrid environment for the development of expert systems (knowledge based systems more generally).

10.2 THE FROG SYSTEM

FROG [Console & Rossi 87][Console & Rossi 88] is a hybrid environment for the development of knowledge based systems which combines, at various levels, different programming paradigms. In particular, the system allows frames (object-oriented schemes), production rules and logic programming to be combined in the description of a knowledge base. FROG's environment provides the user with a high level language which allows the user to describe, in a very declarative way, both the domain knowledge (in terms of frames, production rules and Prolog clauses) of a particular expert system and the control strategy to be used in the system itself. A translation program (FROG's preprocessor) is then able to translate such high level descriptions in the actual Prolog implementation of the expert system.

Let us analyze in more detail which are the facilities FROG's language provides the user with for the design of an expert system. As noticed above, one of the features of FROG is that it allows both domain and control knowledge of a particular system to be designed, to be represented in a declarative way.

Domain knowledge can be represented by combining, at various levels, the "frame", "production rules" and "logic programming" paradigms provided by the system. At the higher level of abstraction a knowledge base is formed by a group of frame-like structures which can be organized into hierarchies. In particular, different types of frames can be defined:

- *Passive frames* that are used to represent the data on which the system operates. Data hierarchies can be defined and inheritance of descriptions is allowed. It is worth noting that production rules and Prolog programs can be inserted in the slots of such "data frames" (they can be used, for example, as "methods" for evaluating the values of the attributes of the datum or to implement the "interpretation rules", as discussed in chapter 3).

- *Active frames* which are activated during the reasoning process and are characterized by a set of "methods" that describe the control strategy to be adopted in such activation. Active frames can be used to give prototypical descriptions (through a set of slots) or can embed local production systems.

As noticed above, in the high level language of FROG the control strategy to be used in a specific system can be defined by the knowledge engineer. In particular, he/she can define the overall search strategy in the frame system, the criteria of frame activation (triggering rules) and the "activities" to be performed when a frame is activated - that is the control strategy within each frame can be defined (different activation phases of a frame can be defined, in each one of which different "activities" can be performed).

An interesting feature of FROG is that both domain and control descriptions can be given together in a unique Prolog-based language (for more details see [Console & Rossi 88]). The syntax of the language is based on the introduction of a number of Prolog's operators, which allow the user to give more structured definitions (a precise semantic definition is associated with each operator). The definition of a knowledge base is formed by assertions and complex clauses: the possibility of building complex clauses allows us to exploit Prolog's control strategy (or better, Prolog's procedural semantics) to express the control strategy to be used in the system (for example, alternatives in the control strategy can be expressed as Prolog alternatives and so on).

One point is worth making before considering the examples: it is better to interpret FROG's high level descriptions in a "procedural" way (i.e. bearing in mind Prolog's procedural semantics [van Emden & Kowalski 76]); in this way, in fact, the control strategy of the defined systems should appear quite clearly. The operator "frame_control" is used to build clauses which define activities to be performed in a frame. In the example of figure 10.2 an "instantiation" activity is defined on the frame "electrical_problems", which consists either of the activation of the "triggers" followed by the one of the "body" components of the frame, or (in case of failure) of the activation of the "alternative_frames" component.

```
instantiation frame_control electrical_problems :-
        triggers electrical_problems,
        body electrical_problems.

instantiation frame_control electrical_problems :-
        alternative_frames electrical_problems.

triggers electrical_problems :- ignition(status,impossible).
triggers electrical_problems :- ignition(status,faulty),
        lights(intensity,abnormal).


body electrical_problem :- slot lights
                           slot ignition.

alternative_frames electrical_problems :-
        <suggest alternative frames to be considered>.
```

Figure 10.2 - An example definition of an "activity" in a frame.

More particularly, using procedural semantics, the meaning of the description is the following: when the "electrical_problems" frame is considered for instantiation, first the triggers of the frame are activated, then (if the triggers' activation succeeds) the "body" of the frame is activated. In turn, the activation of the body consists of the activation of the two slots, "lights" and "ignition" (whose definition is not reported in figure 10.2). If the activation fails (i.e. the activation of either the triggers or the body of the frame fails), the second clause for the activity is selected and other frames are suggested for further consideration (the definition of the alternative frames to be considered has not been reported in the figure).

Note how alternatives are expressed through Prolog's alternatives and sequencing is expressed through Prolog conjunction. Another simple example of definition in FROG's language is reported in figure 10.3. In this case a "slot" of a prototypical description has been defined.

---

slot lights **has_admissible_values**
            [normal, low_intensity, not_burning]

slot lights :- **conditions** lights.
                    prolog_proc lights.
slot lights :- **rules** lights.

Figure 10.3 - Scheme of definition of a slot in FROG (a simplified description is given - in particular, the definitions of the "conditions", "prolog_proc" and "rules" have been omitted).

The first assertion is used to list the possible values the slot can assume (each slot of a prototypical description frame gives the prototypical representations of a feature of the object represented by the frame). The clauses that follow the prototypical description define the control strategy to be adopted when the slot is activated - that is, some instantiation *conditions* are activated first, followed (if they succeed) by the activation of a Prolog program (which could be intended, in this case, as the definition of a "when filled" facet); otherwise a local production system is activated (which, in turn, could be intended as the definition of an "if needed" facet).

Using a similar approach, all the components of a frame (and, more

generally, of a knowledge base) can be defined together with the control strategy to be adopted in the reasoning process. Through the definition of the
"activities" to be performed when a frame is activated and of "global activities" (or better, activities to be performed when a global frame, called "superframe", is activated), which allow us to define the search strategy in the frame
system (i.e. the strategy to be followed in organizing the different phases of
activation of the frames), the overall control strategy of the system can be
defined.

In the following section we shall give some examples of definitions in
FROG, when describing how FROG itself has been used to implement the
surface level of CHECK. For more detailed descriptions and discussion on
FROG the interested reader is referred to [Console & Rossi 88].

It is worth noting, to conclude this section, that FROG provides a set of
built-in facilities for man-machine interaction through the use of graphical
(window and menu oriented) interfaces. Moreover, to simplify the use of
FROG we are actually developing an editor to help the user to define both
domain knowledge and the inference strategies in a more abstract way.

10.3 USING FROG TO IMPLEMENT
THE SURFACE LEVEL

As it should appear from the (brief) discussion in the previous section,
FROG is particularly suited to the design of diagnostic expert systems (but it
can also be successfully used for other tasks). Many of the choices made in
the design of FROG derive from the experiences of our group in the design of
diagnostic expert systems. For these reasons the design of the surface level of
CHECK using FROG resulted very naturally and did not create particular
problems.

In this section we shall give some details of how some aspects of
CHECK's surface level can be defined using the high level language of
FROG: in particular, a (simplified) definition of the overall control strategy in
the frame system and the definition of a frame are given.

Let us start by giving the high level description of a frame using
FROG's language. In figure 10.4 we give (part of) the definition of the frame
"electrical problems", used as an example in chapter 4, whose abstract
description is reported in figure 4.4. It is worth saying a few words on this
definition. A first important consideration is the fact that in order to describe
the control strategy the description has been subdivided into many clauses (in

the case of a pure static description, just a declaration in an assertion would
have been sufficient).

---

frame electrical_problem **is_a**
      specialization_of [car_wont_start]
      generalization_of [battery_problems, ignition_problems].

activation **frame_control** electrical_problems :-
      triggers electrical_problems,
      body electrical_problems.

activation **frame_control** electrical_problems :-
      alternative_frames electrical_problems.

body electrical_problems :-
      necessary_findings electrical_problems $+_u$
      supplementary_findings electrical_problems.

necessary_findings electrical_problems :-
      slot ignition,
      slot lights.

supplementary_findings electrical_problems :-
      slot battery_water_level;
      slot sparking_plug_change.

slot lights **has_admissible_values**
      [normal, low_intensity, not_burning]

slot lights :-
      conditions lights.

conditions lights :-
      lights(X),
      set_slot_value (X),
      evaluate_slot_evidence (X,[[normal,0.1],
                               [low_intensity,0.7],
                               [not_burning,0.9]],
                               relevance (0.5)).

Figure 10.4 - Definition of the frame "electrical_problems" in FROG.

The definition of only one slot has been given for the sake of brevity: notice that the finding "lights" is referred to in the slot "lights" of the frame and that the value of the attribute of the finding is used to instantiate the slot. The two built-in predicates *set_slot_value* and *evaluate_slot_evidence* are used to associate the instantiation value and evidence value with a slot. The second one, in particular, can be modified by the knowledge engineer according to his/her particular needs. Notice also the use of the two operators $+_f$ and $+_{lo}$ whose semantic has been defined in chapter 6.

Consider now how the general control (and search) strategy of CHECK's heuristic level can be defined. A peculiarity of FROG is that it introduces a "system frame" called "superframe" which is used as the supervisor of the overall control strategy in a designed system (this roughly corresponds to the "consultation" frame used in CENTAUR [Aikins 83]). This means that the control strategy in the system is defined through the definition of the "activities" of the "superframe". Moreover, in order to simplify the definition of the global strategy, FROG provides the user with an abstract data type called "agenda". Agendas can be used as a scheduling data structure to store (in a ranked way) names of frames to be activated. A limited set of operations ("insert", "select_first", "select_last" and "sort(sorting_strategy), where different sorting strategies can be used) is provided by the system. A simplified description of the main steps of CHECK's heuristic level control strategy is reported in figure 10.5. In particular, the steps of inference of the system are defined as the sequence of operations corresponding to the activity "consultation" of the superframe.

---

consultation **frame_control** superframe :-
       data_acquisition,
       activation initial_agenda,
       validation activated_frames_agenda,
       specialization validated_frames_agenda,
       explanation.

Figure 10.5 - Definition of the various phases of CHECK's heuristic level control strategy in FROG.

Notice that three different agendas are used (namely the "initial_agenda", "activated_frames_agenda" and "validated_frames_agenda"), which are built during the phases of reasoning of the system.

11

IMPLEMENTATION OF THE CAUSAL LEVEL

In this chapter we will discuss how the causal level of CHECK is implemented using an object-oriented approach in Prolog. Moreover, at the end of the chapter we shall give a summary of the whole implementation of the CHECK environment, outlining how the various facilities provided by the system (e.g. for man-machine interfaces and knowledge acquisition) are implemented and linked together.

11.1 AN OBJECT-ORIENTED APPROACH TO IMPLEMENT THE CAUSAL LEVEL

In this section we will discuss, from an abstract point of view, the choices we have made to implement the causal level of CHECK. The characteristic of such an implementation is that we have chosen to adopt an *object-oriented* approach [Stefik & Bobrow 86]. The general idea of this approach is the following: each node in the network is represented as an *object* and it belongs to a particular *class* of objects, depending on its type (e.g. STATE or HYPOTHESIS). More specifically, a different class of objects has been defined for each type of nodes in the causal network; each class is characterized by particular properties.

Each object is characterized by two different parts:

-       A set of *local variables*, which are used to store information specific to
        the object itself; some of these contain "read-only" information (as, for
        example, in a STATE the list of its causing states), others can be
        modified during the reasoning process (for example, the variables
        corresponding to the instantiated values of the attributes of a STATE).

-       A set of *methods*. Each method specifies a reasoning step that can be
        performed on a node. For example, in a STATE there are methods
        whose roles are to test the confirmation of causing states, or to test the
        presence of the manifestations of the state, or to instantiate the state
        itself. Each method is a reasoning scheme: obviously methods are asso-
        ciated with the classes of nodes and are inherited by each specific
        object of the class.

    More specifically a class is characterized by a set of methods, whilst
each object is characterized by a set of local variables and inherits the
methods of the class to which it belongs.

    Reasoning on the causal network is performed through *message sending*
between nodes (objects). A message is constituted of three parts and has the
following general form:

                <destination> *identifier* <argument list>

The "destination" is the name of the object to which the message is directed;
the "identifier" is used to distinguish the different types of messages (i.e. it is
the name of the message or the "message selector" in the terminology of
object-oriented programming languages) and allows the receiver to recognize
it; optionally a message can also have a list of arguments.

    Each object can recognize only a limited set of messages, most particu-
larly those for which the name ("identifier") corresponds to the name of a
method of the object itself. When a message is received, the corresponding
method is activated.

    The body of each method, which is executed when the corresponding
message is received, can be formed by different types of operations:

-       access to local variables, for reading their values or for setting new
        values;

-       sending of a message to another object (including itself);

-       invocation of a Prolog procedure. This is an extension we have intro-
        duced. Prolog procedures can be used to verify conditions or to invoke

built-in predicates provided by the system. They are needed mainly because of the fact that we need deductive power in the methods of our object. Moreover, since we do not use a complete object-oriented environment (or programming language), we use Prolog as a substitute for part of the environment itself.

Schematically, all the reasoning on a causal model is performed through message passing between the objects corresponding to the various nodes (the trace of the reasoning process to confirm the diagnostic hypothesis "burnout", reported in figure 12.13, has been obtained visualizing some of the messages passed among the nodes of the network of figure 7.19).

To understand how this scheme is used with the help of an example, let us consider the case of the use of the network in a particular case, i.e. to confirm a diagnostic hypothesis. The deep level is invoked by the surface one by sending a "confirm" message to a hypothesis node. The task to be performed by the HYPOTHESIS node is to search for INITIAL CAUSES and causal paths from such INITIAL CAUSES, that explain the presence of the malfunction corresponding to the hypothesis itself. In response to the "confirm" message, the hypothesis node sends "establish_backward" messages to the states defining the presence of the malfunction corresponding to the hypothesis itself and then waits for their answers. When a state receives an "establish_backward" message it performs the following sequence of operations: first it sends "establish_backward" messages to the states that can cause it (if they are not instantiated yet), then, after it has received an answer from these states, it tests whether the conditions on the entering arcs are satisfied and tries to instantiate itself (this is accomplished through *self* messages). If the instantiation succeeds the state reports a positive answer to the invoking node. When a hypothesis node has received answers from all its defining states it sends them an "establish_forward" message in order to search for the consequences of the malfunction corresponding to the hypothesis itself. A different kind of "establish" message is needed because a different function is requested for those nodes - in fact, backward search of causes is no longer necessary, but forward search of the consequences of the states is requested.
It should be noted that in this case the network is traversed with a combination of backward and forward messages; in particular, in order to gain efficiency, possible causes are searched backward from a hypothesis whilst reasoning on the paths selected through backward messages is obviously (considering the nature of the causal network) performed through forward flow of response messages (containing information to be used in the instantiation phase).

Before analyzing in more detail the organization of each class of objects and the methods which are associated with them, let us briefly discuss why we have chosen this scheme of implementation.

The most obvious advantage of the scheme we have chosen is its great modularity. The introduction of the concept of "class" of nodes allows us to isolate and to describe in a very flexible way, the functions of each type of node. Moreover, the definition of methods and the fact that the whole reasoning process is defined in a uniform way in the body of the methods, with a precise separation of the different steps, makes the description very easy to read and understand. Also the modification of the system (or of its control strategy) is not very difficult and can be done in a very high level way. The modification of a specific causal network (e.g. in the debugging phase of a system) can be done in a very local way: the introduction (or the removal) of a node does not influence the other nodes very much (or better, influence them in a very explicit way) and, especially, does not have any consequence at all on the reasoning (control) strategy. Moreover, the scheme allows us to implement reasoning on a network in a very efficient way.

Let us now describe in more detail the structure of the different types of objects and their methods. The description we shall give is an abstract and simplified one in which a very general outline of the different methods of the objects is given (for example, the detail about the treatment of "possible" (MAY) relationships has been omitted). Moreover, for the sake of clarity in the presentation, instead of describing the general form of the methods associated with the classes of objects, we will start by giving more specialized descriptions of the methods, tailored to the specific objects we shall use in the examples (that is to say, ignoring the presence of "classes" and "inheritance"). At the end of this section we shall present a brief example of how a class (the "STATE" class) and its methods can be defined (and inherited by all the objects that are instances of the class, i.e. in the example by all the STATE nodes in a specific causal network).

Let us start by considering STATE nodes, and, more particularly, the state "oil_lack" in figure 11.1. The abstract description of the object corresponding to this STATE is reported in figure 11.2. In the description of the methods we have used an object-oriented notation, in which the symbols have the following meaning:

-       "←" is the "assign" operator; it can be used to assign values to local variables;

-       "^" is the "return" operator; its argument is the value returned to the sender of the message which has activated the method;

-       "self" is an object name denoting the object itself, so that it is used by an object to send messages to itself;

- ";" is used as a separator of messages to be sent in sequence;

- conditions (such as, for example, "oil_consumpt(intensity,high)" in figure 11.2 are considered as messages, which are sent to a "Boolean" object, as is usual in object oriented programming;

- auxiliary variables can be used in the body of a method (such as, for example, the variable PATH1 in figure 11.2)

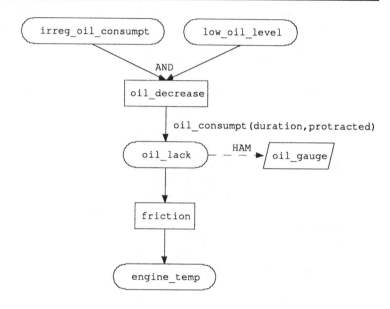

attributes of the state "oil_lack":
intensity = {low, medium, high}

Figure 11.1 - Example of the STATE "oil_lack" derived
from the network reported in figure 7.19.

It is worth making a few comments on the description in figure 11.2. Notice that some of the local variables are "read_only", i.e. they contain static information (such as, for example, the variable "causing_states" which contains the list of STATES, together with ACTIONS and conditions on the CAUSAL arcs, which are causes of the STATE described by the object itself), or prototypical information (e.g. the admissible instantiation values of each   attribute   of   the   STATE,   such   as   the   variable "intensity(admissible_values)"; other variables are to be filled in during the reasoning process (such as, for example, the variable "PATH", which is intended to be filled in with the causal path that justifies the presence of the STATE, or the variable "intensity" to be filled with the specific value of the attribute of the STATE). Actually the use of "read_only" variables is not clear in the example of figure 11.2, since we have given a specialized description of the methods of the object itself. In the real implementation, methods are associated with classes (to the STATE class in the case of the example) so they have a general form and information about the context in which they have to be executed is needed (as it will be discussed in the following). Such contextual information is provided by the "read-only" variables (for example, in the case of the method for the selector "caused_by" the contextual information is provided by the variable "causing_states", see figure 11.4).

---

state oil_lack

<u>local variables</u>

causing_states: [[[state,oil_consumpt] and
                          [state,low_oil_level]],
                        [action, oil_decrease],
                        [condition,must,oil_consumpt(intensity,high)]]
caused_states: [[[state,engine_temp],
                        [action, friction],
                        [condition,must,true]]]
ham: [[oil_gauge,must,true]]
suggest: nil
define: nil
PATH: nil
PATH_CONSEQUENCES: nil
EXPLANATION: nil
ALREADY_INSTANTIATED: false
intensity(admissible_values): [low, medium, high]
intensity(actual_value): nil

<u>methods</u>

instantiate_attribute ATTRIBUTE_NAME:
        ATTRIBUTE_NAME = 'intensity'
            IfTrue (<instantiation procedure>);

caused_by:
        ALREADY_INSTANTIATED ≠ nil

IfTrue ^PATH
IfFalse
    (PATH1 ← oil_consumpt *establish_backward;*
    oil_consumpt(intensity,high);
    PATH2 ← low_oil_level *establish_backward;*
    oil_decrease *act_action;*
    ALREADY_INSTANTIATED ← true;
    ^ PATH ← [oil_lack, [and [oil_decrease, PATH1, PATH2]]].

establish_backward:
    ^ self *caused_by;*
    self *has_manifestations;*
    self *instantiate.*

has_manifestations:
    ALREADY_INSTANTIATED
      IfTrue ^
      IfFalse oil_gauge *is_present.*

instantiate:
    ALREADY_INSTANTIATED
      IfTrue ^
      IfFalse self *instantiate_attribute* intensity;

establish_forward:
    PATH_CONSEQUENCES ≠ nil
      IfTrue
      ^ PATH_CONSEQUENCES
      IfFalse
        (self *caused_by;*
        self *has_manifestations;*
        self *instantiate;*
        PATH3 ← self *causes;*
        ^ PATH_CONSEQUENCES ← [oil_lack, [friction, PATH3]]).

causes: friction *act_action;*
    ^ engine_temp *establish_forward.*

Figure 11.2 - Abstract description corresponding to the STATE "oil_lack" of figure 11.1.

As an example, let us analyze in more detail one of the methods of figure 11.2, the "caused_by" one. As a first operation in the body of the method a message is sent to the "Boolean" object. The pattern of a such message is the following:

<Condition> *IfTrue* <*Block$_1$*> *IfFalse* <*Block$_2$*>

When the "Boolean" object receives such a message, at first a message to evaluate the condition is sent; if the answer to this message is "true" then the block of operations "*Block$_1$*" is considered (i.e. the operations are performed in sequence), otherwise the block "*Block$_2$*" is considered. In the specific case of the method "caused_by" the meaning is the following: if the variable "ALREADY_INSTANTIATED" is already true (i.e. the causes of the STATE have already been established) then the value of the variable "PATH" is returned as the answer; otherwise messages to establish the causing STATES and to verify the activation of the ACTIONS and conditions on the entering arcs are sent, then the variable "PATH" is set with the path causally justifying the presence of the STATE and its value is returned.

The methods described in figure 11.2 (in a simplified and abstract way) are only those concerning the reasoning in a particular case; other methods exist which are used to traverse the network and generate explanations when the causal knowledge is used independently from the data of a particular consultation ("general use" of the network in the terminology of chapter 8).

Let us discuss now another simple example of object-like description of a node in CHECK's networks. Consider in particular the HYPOTHESIS node "burnout" of figure 7.19. The diagnostic hypothesis "burnout" is defined as the presence of the value "very_high" for the attribute "intensity" in the STATE "engine_temp". The object oriented description of the HYPOTHESIS "burnout" is reported in figure 11.3 (here also, for the sake of simplicity, we have decided not to describe the methods of the class "HYPOTHESIS", but to concentrate on defining the specific HYPOTHESIS "burnout", so that again the use of read-only variables is not apparent). Also in this case only a one method has been considered - more specifically, only the one that is considered when a request to confirm the diagnostic hypothesis on a particular case is sent to the object (e.g. by the heuristic level).

The scheme of the "confirm" method is very simple: first messages to establish the causes of the STATES defining the presence of the malfunction corresponding to the diagnostic hypothesis are sent; then, in a similar way, messages to establish the consequences of the same STATES are sent. Likewise, all the other methods of the object "burnout" can be defined.

The examples discussed in this section are very simple ones. In particular, as we noticed, the descriptions are tailored to the specific examples we have used. An important aspect of our implementation is the introduction of the concept of "class": methods are associated with classes and inherited by each instance of the class. To complete the discussion let us outline briefly how a class can be implemented. In figure 11.4 we have reported a simplified description of part of the class "STATE" (more specifically, the method "caused_by" has been reported). The instances of the class STATE are simply described by a set of local variables (e.g. see figure 9.7, in which the description of some objects is reported, as it is produced by the editor NEED).

---

hypothesis: burnout

local variables

DEFINING_STATES: [[engine_temp]
                        [condition,engine_temp(intensity,very_high]]
PATH_CAUSES: nil
PATH_CONSEQUENCES: nil
EXPLANATION: nil

methods

confirm:
        PATH1 ← engine_temp *establish_backward;*
        engine_temp(intensity,very_high);
        PATH_CAUSES ← [[PATH1]];
        PATH_CONSEQUENCES ←
            engine_temp *establish_forward;*
        ^ self *build_explanation.*

Figure 11.3 - The HYPOTHESIS node "burnout" (partial description).

Notice that the definition of the local variables of the objects is linked to the class. In particular, such variables are defined as "instance variables" - that is, their type is defined in the class and a copy of the variables is created for each instance of the class itself, exactly as happens in "object oriented programming" [Stefik & Bobrow 86].

---

class: STATE

<u>instance variables</u>

causing_states: <list of causing states, actions and conditions> (read only)
caused_states: <list of caused states, actions and conditions> (read only)
ham: <list of manifestations and conditions on HAM arcs> (read only)
suggest: <list of suggested hypotheses> (read only)
define: <list of defined hypotheses> (read only)
PATH: <justifying path (causes)> (to be filled in)
PATH_CONSEQUENCES: <justifying path (consequences)> (to be filled in)
EXPLANATION: <explanation> (to be filled in)
ALREADY_INSTANTIATED: <boolean value> (to be filled in)

<u>methods</u>

caused_by:
     ALREADY_INSTANTIATED ≠ nil
       IfTrue
       ^ PATH
       IfFalse
       (CONN ← self *get_connective_causing_states*
       CONN=and
         IfTrue
         ^self *and_caused_by*
         IfFalse
         ^self *or_caused_by*)

and_caused_by:
     STATES ← self *get_causing_states;*
     ACTION ← self *get_entering_action;*
     CONDITION ← self *get_entering_condition;*
     ($\forall$ *STATE$_i$* ∈ STATES *do*
     PATH$_i$ ← *STATE$_i$ establish_backward*);
     ACTION *act_action;*
     CONDITION;
     ^PATH ← [ACTION,[and [*PATH$_1$*, ..., *PATH$_n$*]]]

Figure 11.4 - Partial description of the class "STATE".

The messages "get_connective_causing_states", "get_causing_states", "get_entering_action" and "get_conditions" are used to access the local variable "causing_states" (they have not been specified for the sake of simplicity).

11.2 IMPLEMENTATION IN PROLOG

An interesting point to discuss now is how the scheme discussed above can be practically implemented. A first obvious possibility could be that of using an object-oriented programming language, like, for example, Smalltalk [Goldberg & Robson 83], or one of the recent object-oriented tools for the development of expert systems, like, for example, KEE [Fikes & Kehler 85]. Certainly the use of such tools has several advantages for the implementation of an architecture such as the one discussed above, since they are very close to the (general) design philosophy we have followed. On the other hand, some important differences between our scheme and pure object-oriented ones should be apparent: we need sophisticated deduction capabilities and logical capabilities that are not provided and are often difficult to introduce in such languages (consider, in particular, the fact that we need non-monotonic deduction facilities for our form of hypothetical reasoning); on the other hand, we do not need all the features of object-oriented programming. There is, moreover, another very important reason why the use of an object-oriented language would create problems in the implementation of the causal level of CHECK: the integration with the heuristic level. As we have discussed in the preceding chapters, the two levels are strictly connected: they share common data, they communicate data and control is frequently exchanged between them. It should be clear, therefore, that the use of an environment different from the Prolog one (or, in any case, difficult to integrate with the Prolog one) used in the implementation of the surface level, could create serious problems.

For these reasons we have decided to implement the causal level of CHECK in Prolog: particular techniques have been used in Prolog to obtain the desired features of object-oriented programming (for a very interesting description of a different approach from the one we have followed to implement object-oriented programming in Prolog, see [Zaniolo 84]).

Let us discuss the very general ideas of such an implementation. Each object is represented by means of a set of Prolog clauses, which are characterized by the fact that the name of the predicate (functor) of their left-hand side is the same and it is the name of the object. More particularly, local variables are represented by means of assertions and methods by means of complex clauses.

A simple example can clarify the matter. Consider the (simple) object (a window in a computer graphic system) reported in figure 11.5. The general scheme of the Prolog implementation is reported in figure 11.6.

---

object: *window*$_1$
    local variables:
        width: 5
        length: 8
    methods:
        open: <body of the method>
        resize NewWidth NewLength: <body of the method>

Figure 11.5 - a simple object (window in a graphic system).

---

window1(width, 5).
window1(length, 8).

window1(open) :- <body of the method>.
window1(resize, NewWidth, NewLength) :- <body of the method>.

Figure 11.6 - Scheme of Prolog implementation of the object of figure 11.5.

Let us now consider in more detail how the methods can be implemented. We have noticed that in a method three different types of operations can be performed: access to local variables (for reading or for modifying their values), sending of other messages and invocation of Prolog procedures. All these operation can be implemented very easily in our scheme, in fact:

-    Local variables can be read simply through unification. To modify their values a built-in predicate *set_value* is provided by the system.

-    Sending a message to another object can be implemented using a predicate with the following form:

        destination_object(message_selector, <arguments>)

where "destination_object" is the name of the object to which the message has to be sent and "message_selector" is the name of the selector of the message.

- Prolog procedures can be directly invoked.

- If answers have to be returned, a specific answer argument can be added to the predicates corresponding to the head of a method and to message invocation - that is, using a predicate with the following form:

destination_object(message_selector, <arguments>, answer_argument)

As an example in figure 11.7, the implementation of the "resize" method of the "$window_1$" object of figure 11.5 is reported. In particular, in this example we suppose that each time an attempt is made to modify the dimensions of the window, a check is carried out to verify whether the new dimensions are legal (calling the Prolog predicate "is_legal"); then the values of the local variables "width" and "length" are updated and finally the window itself is opened (through a self "open" message).

```
window1(resize, NewWidth, NewLength) :-
        is_legal(NewWidth, NewLength),
        set_value(width, NewWidth),
        set_value(length, NewLength),
        window1(open).
```

Figure 11.7 - Implementation of the "resize" method of "window1".

The interesting point now is to discuss how the object-oriented *inheritance* can be implemented. We have decided to adopt a very simple approach which allows us to avoid the introduction of a meta-level control.

An immediate possibility, in fact, to obtain inheritance is to introduce it at meta-level, adding to the description of objects and classes an assertion of the type:

is_a(window1, window)
subclass(window, graphical_facility)

to represent respectively that the object "$window_1$" is a member of the class "window", which is in turn a subclass of the class "graphical_facilities". Meta-level control is needed in the execution phase to select which method has to be executed, and this can result in great inefficiency.

Since our idea is to adopt in this case "preprocessing" techniques (see section 10.1 for discussion) to build the Prolog implementation of a specific "object-oriented" system, we have decided to implement inheritance in a very different (and more efficient) way, which is very suitable to a translation approach.

Consider again the "window" system discussed above and let us introduce a class "window" with which the methods "open" and "resize" are associated, so that they are inherited by each member of the class. The description of the class and of two objects ("$window_1$" and "$window_2$") are reported in figure 11.8; in particular, in 11.8(a) the abstract description of the class is reported, whilst in figure 11.8(b) the Prolog implementation of the class and of the two objects is reported. Notice that the body of the method is associated with the class and methods are only called from the instance objects. However, note that a new parameter to store the context of execution of the method has been added (it is worth remembering that object-oriented programming methods are always executed in the environment of the object to which the message is sent, so they operate specifically on the local variables of the object itself). It is important to note that it is thus very easy to redefine a method in an object (or in a class) in such a way that the new definition covers the inherited one (as in object oriented languages).

Using this technique, all the features of object-oriented programming we need to implement causal networks (and causal reasoning) can be embedded within the logic programming framework. More specifically, the clauses describing the nodes (objects) of a network are generated by the graphical network editor NEED (i.e. they correspond to the linguistic description generated by the editor, see section 9.5), whilst those associated with classes (e.g. STATES or HYPOTHESES) are built-in ones (they define the possible reasoning processes that can be performed on the causal network).

11.3 THE CHECK ENVIRONMENT: IMPLEMENTATION

To conclude this chapter let us give a summary of how the CHECK environment is implemented. CHECK is constituted of two main sub-systems:

-       the *knowledge acquisition* sub-system (figure 11.9), which is formed by
        the graphical causal networks editor NEED, the module for deriving the

surface (heuristic) level from the deep one (currently under development) and the preprocessor for generating the heuristic level implementation;

- the *consultation* sub-system (figure 11.10), which is formed by the CHECK diagnostic expert system, the data acquisition and heuristic explanation module and the deep level explanation module.

---

class: window
methods:
    open: <body of the method>
    resize NewWidth NewLength:
        is_legal(NewWidth, NewLength);
        width ← NewWidth;
        length ← NewLength;
        self *open.*

(a)

window(open, CALLER) :- <body of the method>.
window(resize, CALLER, NewWidth, NewLength) :-
        is_legal(NewWidth, NewLength),
        set_value(CALLER, width, NewWidth),
        set_value(CALLER, length, NewLength),
        window(open, CALLER).

window1(open) :- window(open, window1).
window1(resize, NewWidth, NewLength) :-
        window(resize, window1, NewWidth, NewLength).

window2(open) :- window(open, window2).
window2(resize, NewWidth, NewLength) :-
        window(resize, window2, NewWidth, NewLength).

(b)

Figure 11.8 - Implementation of inheritance.

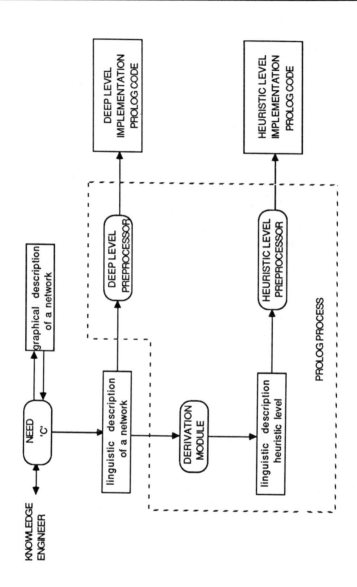

Figure 11.9 - The Knowledge Acquisition subsystem.

The whole system is implemented on SUN-3 workstations under the Unix[1] operating system and is coded partly in Prolog+ (a graphical extension of C-Prolog 1.5 that we have designed) and partly in 'C' language. More specifically, the main facility we have introduced in Prolog+ is that we have introduced built-in predicates for creating and managing processes from the Prolog environment and for communicating, in a synchronous or asynchronous way, with them (a set of library functions to communicate with Prolog from other languages, such as 'C' or 'Pascal' or 'Lisp' has been designed). Moreover, we have designed a graphic managing process and a group of special input-output built-in predicates to communicate with it.

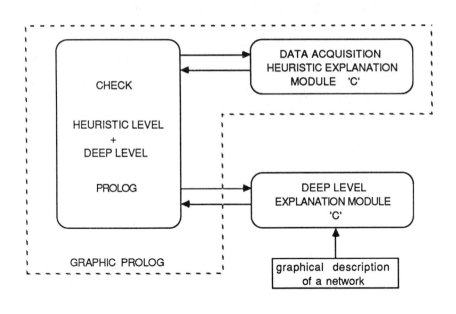

Figure 11.10 - The Consultation subsystem.

[1] Unix is a Trade-mark of Bell Laboratories.

More specifically, the knowledge acquisition sub-system is constituted of two (Unix) processes:

-    "NEED", which is implemented in 'C' language;

-    "translation process", which is a Prolog process which includes the two modules for the derivation of the heuristic level and the heuristic-level preprocessing.

The consultation sub-system is formed by two processes:

-    The "Graphic Prolog", which is in turn constituted of two Unix processes: the Prolog+ interpreter and the "window manager" process, whose code is written in 'C' language and which manages the windows for data acquisition and for the heuristic level explanations. The two processes are strictly connected (for this reason they can be logically considered a unique process) - the "window manager" is "forked" by the Prolog+ interpreter and they communicate through pipelines.

-    The "deep explanation" process, whose code is written in 'C' language and which is responsible for the display of deep level explanations (portions of the causal network). It uses the graphical description of a causal network produced by NEED and is connected to the "graphic Prolog" process (more specifically, Prolog+ interpreter) on which the expert system runs by a bidirectional communication link.

12

DISCUSSION

In this final chapter of the book we shall summarize the main features of CHECK's architecture. More specifically, in section 12.1 we shall present a complete example of an application of CHECK; in section 12.2 we shall discuss some of the research projects, correlated to the CHECK one, on which we are currently working; finally in section 12.3 we shall summarize the main goals and achievements of the CHECK project.

12.1 A COMPLETE EXAMPLE

In this section we shall consider a very simple application of CHECK in the area of mechanical diagnosis (car troubleshooting): first we shall present (part of) the knowledge base used in the example, then we shall present in detail how the system operates, analyzing how the system behaves in the solution of a specific case (in other words, we will show a sample consultation).

12.1.1 THE CAR TROUBLESHOOTING
KNOWLEDGE BASE

The first step regarding our sample application is to present the knowledge base we have used in the example itself. It is worth noting before discussing the example in detail that the application we shall present aims only at summarizing and clarifying the function of CHECK. This means, in particular, that the specific knowledge bases we shall use are incomplete and imprecise descriptions of the domain of application (in other words, we are not interested in the "correctness" and "completeness" of the knowledge base that has been used to describe the car troubleshooting domain).

HEURISTIC LEVEL. Let us first describe the knowledge base at the heuristic level. As we noticed, a heuristic level knowledge base is formed by a hierarchy of diagnostic hypotheses, each one of which is described by a frame-like structure.

The frame-system hierarchy used in the car troubleshooting example is shown in figure 12.1. Notice that the frames "hard_engine_problems" and "electrical_problems" describe diagnostic classes, whilst all the other frames describe specific diagnoses. As far as the description of the frames is concerned, in figure 12.2 we have reported the frame "hard_engine_problems", in figure 12.3 the frame "burnout" and in figure 12.4 the frame "melting". Moreover, a description of the frame "electrical_problems" has been given in figure 6.2.

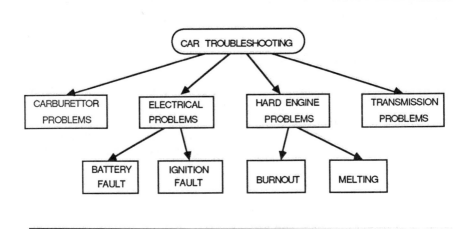

Figure 12.1 - The frame-system hierarchy.

FRAME: hard_engine_problems

TRIGGERS
oil_gauge(colour,red) <u>and</u> temp_indicator(level,red)
relevance 1
oil_gauge(colour,yellow) <u>and</u> temp_indicator(level,red)
relevance 0.8
oil_gauge(colour,red) <u>and</u> temp_indicator(level,yellow)
relevance 0.6

NECESSARY FINDINGS
oil_gauge colour: <red,1> <yellow,0.8>
relevance: 0.8
temp_indicator level: <red,1> <yellow,0.8>
relevance: 1

SUPPLEMENTARY FINDINGS
stack_smoke colour: <black,1> <grey,0.7>
relevance: 0.6
pistons wear_state: <medium,0.8> <high,1>
relevance: 0.9

VALIDATION RULES
confirm <u>if</u> vapour(quantity,present)
<u>in-context</u> -
relevance 1

Figure 12.2 - The frame "hard_engine_problems" (prototypical and control knowledge parts).

FRAME: burnout

TRIGGERS
temp_indicator(level,red) <u>and</u> vapour(quantity,present)
relevance 1
temp_indicator(level,red)
relevance 0.8

NECESSARY FINDINGS
temp_indicator level: <red,1> <yellow,0.7>
relevance: 1
oil_gauge colour: <red,1> <yellow,0.75>
relevance: 0.7
engine status: <on,1>
relevance: 1

SUPPLEMENTARY FINDINGS
vapour quantity: <present,1>
relevance: 1
stack_smoke colour: <black,1> <grey,0.6>
relevance: 0.6

VALIDATION RULES
--

Figure 12.3 - The frame "burnout".

FRAME: melting

TRIGGERS
engine_smoke(quantity,present)   **and**   vapour(quantity,present)   **and**
stack_smoke(colour,black)
relevance 1
temp_indicator(level,red) **and** vapour(quantity,present)
relevance 0.6

NECESSARY FINDINGS
temp_indicator level: <red,1> <yellow,0.3>
relevance: 0.8
oil_gauge colour: <red,1> <yellow,0.4>
relevance: 0.8
engine status: <on,1>
relevance: 1
vapour quantity: <present,1>
relevance: 1

SUPPLEMENTARY FINDINGS
  engine_smoke quantity: <present,1>
    relevance: 1
  ext_temperature value: <high,1>
    relevance: 0.6

VALIDATION RULES
  --

Figure 12.4 - The frame "melting".

Description of the other frames has been omitted for the sake of brevity. However, in figure 12.5 a description of the triggering rules of the frames "carburettor_problems" and "engine_problems" that will be useful in the discussion of the sample consultation is given.

FRAME: carburettor_problems

  TRIGGERS
    fuel(consumption,irregular) <u>and</u> engine(functioning,mumbling)
      relevance 1

FRAME: transmission_problems

  TRIGGERS
    transmission(noise,present)
      relevance 1

Figure 12.5 - Triggering rules for the frames "carburettor_problems" and "transmission_problems".

DEEP LEVEL. Many parts of the causal network concerning the car troubleshooting domain have been used as examples in the preceding chapters of the book. More specifically, the portion of the causal network concerning the "hard_engine_problems" (that is to say, the "burnout" and "melting" diagnostic hypotheses) has been given in figures 7.19 (graphical display) and 9.7 (linguistic description).

The knowledge base discussed above can easily be introduced into the CHECK system. More specifically, the NEED system (section 9.2) can be used to introduce causal knowledge whilst FROG (chapter 10) can be used to define the heuristic level (see, moreover, the discussion in section 12.2.2 on knowledge compilation). NEED and FROG produce runnable Prolog code which can be executed by the CHECK consultation system (which provides all the man-machine interface facilities presented in chapter 9).

12.1.2 USING THE CAR TROUBLESHOOTING CONSULTATION SYSTEM

In this section we shall describe in detail the use of the CHECK consultation subsystem analyzing a simple consultation of the car troubleshooting system. In the meantime, we shall present in one complete example all the man-machine interface facilities described in chapter 9.

During a consultation the heuristic level is first invoked to produce a set of diagnostic hypotheses to be confirmed (discriminated) by the causal level. The first step of the heuristic level control strategy is the data acquisition phase. In particular, as we noticed in section 9.1, a consultation begins with the "passive" data acquisition phase. CHECK provides the user with an initial menu: the user selects from the menu the findings which are present in the specific case under examination and fills in the description of each finding (i.e. of its attributes). We noted that only very general data are needed by CHECK at the beginning of the consultation. In particular, only those findings which are needed to verify the triggering rules of the diagnostic hypotheses which are at the higher level in the hierarchy are inserted in the initial menu to be filled in by the user.

In the specific case of the car troubleshooting application, the initial menu proposed by CHECK is reported in figure 12.6. When the user selects a datum, a new menu is popped up by the system. Using such a menu the user can fill in the description of the attributes of the finding selected in the initial menu. As an example, in figure 12.7 a case is reported where the finding "temp_indicator" is selected from the initial menu (notice that in the specific menu an entry is associated with each admissible value for the attribute "level" of the finding "temp_indicator"). Default values are automatically associated with all the findings that have not been selected by the user from the initial consultation menu.

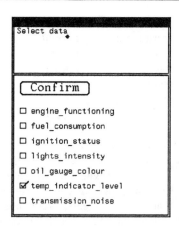

Figure 12.6 - Initial menu for data acquisition.

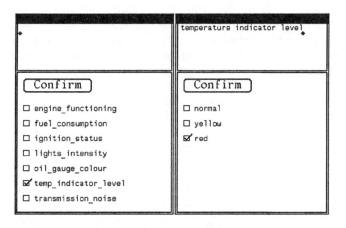

Figure 12.7 - Sub-menu for the description of the finding "temp_indicator".

Let us suppose that in the specific case we are considering the following set of data is provided by the user:

engine	functioning	normal	
fuel	consumption	normal	
ignition	status	normal	
lights	intensity	normal	(1)
oil_gauge	colour	yellow	
temp_indicator	level	red	
transmission	noise	absent	

Given this initial set of data, high level diagnostic hypotheses can be triggered. In the specific case we are considering, only the hypothesis "hard_engine_problems" can be triggered, so all the other diagnostic hypotheses (i.e. "electrical_problems", "carburettor_problems" and "transmission_problems") are not awakened (remember, however, that their activation could be reconsidered during the analysis of associational links, see section 5.3). At this point, the triggered diagnostic hypotheses are considered for activation and the prototypical descriptions of the malfunctions they represent are matched against the data describing the specific case under examination.

In the example, the frame "hard_engine_problems" is activated: NECESSARY_FINDINGS can be successfully matched against the data in (1), whilst in order to verify the SUPPLEMENTARY_FINDINGS, the user is asked some other questions ("active phase" of data acquisition, see section 9.1). More specifically, information about the findings "stack_smoke" and "pistons wear_state" is asked of the user via graphical menus. Let us suppose that the user provides the system with the following answers:

pistons	wear_state	high	
stack_smoke	colour	black	(2)

given the set of data (1) and (2), the evidence value obtained from the activation of the hypothesis "hard_engine_problems" is 0.97, so the hypothesis is considered as a candidate solution and is passed to the validation process.

During the validation process, the "VALIDATION RULES" associated with the frames which have passed the activation phase are considered and the evidence of each hypothesis can be increased (if a CONFIRMATION rule is activated), decreased (if a EXCLUSION rule is activated) or left unchanged. In the specific example we are considering, the only frame to be validated is the "hard_engine_problems" one. In order to activate the CON-FIRMATION rules associated with the frame, the system asks the user to provide information about the finding "vapour". If we assume that the answer of the user is the following:

$$\text{vapour} \qquad \text{quantity} \qquad \text{present} \qquad (3)$$

we have that the CONFIRMATION rule can be fired and the evidence value of the frame increased. The final evidence value for the hypothesis "hard_engine_problems" is the following:

$$e(\text{hard\_engine\_problems}) = 0.999$$

so the frame can be confirmed and considered for refinement.

At the end of this phase the user can ask for explanations of the confirmation/rejection of diagnostic hypotheses. If in our car troubleshooting example the user requests information about how the frame "hard_engine_problems" has been confirmed, the instantiated copy of the frame is displayed by CHECK in a special "explanation" window (see figure 12.8).

```
Explanation
  INSTANTIATED FRAME : hard_engine_problems

  EVIDENCE DEGREE : 0.999

     Necessary Findings   :  0.84
     Supplementary Findings :  0.95

  TRIGGERS
     oil_gauge(colour,yellow)  and  temp_indicator(level,red)  relevance 0.8

  NECESSARY FINDINGS
     temp_indicator     level     red   1
     oil_gauge       colour     yellow   0.84

  SUPPLEMENTARY FINDINGS
     stack_smoke      colour      black   0.6
     pistons       wear_state     high    0.9

  VALIDATION RULES
     confirm:   vapour  quantity  present   1
```

Figure 12.8 - Display of the instantiated frame "hard_engine_problems".

During the refinement phase, the frame "hard_engine_problems" is activated again and its subframes "burnout" and "melting" are taken into consideration. At first the two frames are triggered. In order to verify the first triggering rule of the frame "melting", information about the finding "engine_smoke" is requested from the user. If we assume that the following answer is provided by the user:

  engine_smoke   quantity   absent   (4)

the following results are obtained from the activation of the triggering rules:

  burnout   triggered   relevance: 1
  melting   triggered   relevance: 0.6

Since the hypothesis "burnout" is triggered by a more relevant rule, its activation is considered before the activation of the hypothesis "melting".

During the activation of the frame "burnout" and "melting" further data are required from the user (in order to verify the NECESSARY FINDINGS and the SUPPLEMENTARY FNDINGS contained in the frames). Suppose that, in the specific example we are considering, the following set of data is provided by the user (in particular, the first datum is requested during the activation of the frame "burnout", whilst the second is required during the activation of the frame "melting"):

  engine   status   on
  ext_temperature value   normal   (5)

The final evidence values obtained from the activation and validation (no validation rules are present in the frames "burnout" and "melting") of the frames "burnout" and "melting" are the following:

  e(burnout) = 0.97
  e(melting) = 0.52

As an explanation, the instantiated copies of the frames can be displayed by CHECK in the "explanation" window (see figures 12.9 and 12.10).

Finally, CHECK asks the user whether he/she needs a deep confirmation and explanation of the proposed hypotheses. If the answer of the user is affirmative, the two hypotheses are passed to the causal level for confirmation.

```
Explanation

  INSTANTIATED FRAME : burnout

  EVIDENCE DEGREE : 0.97

      Necessary Findings   :  0.82
      Supplementary Findings :  1

  TRIGGERS
      vapour(quantity,present)  and  temp_indicator(level,red)  relevance 1

  NECESSARY FINDINGS
      temp_indicator      level      red   1
      engine       status      on   1
      oil_gauge       colour      yellow   0.82

  SUPPLEMENTARY FINDINGS
      stack_smoke      colour      black   0.6
      vapour      quantity      present   1

  VALIDATION RULES
      no validation rule is activated
```

Figure 12.9 - Display of the instantiated frame "burnout".

```
Explanation

  INSTANTIATED FRAME : melting

  EVIDENCE DEGREE : 0.52

      Necessary Findings   :  0.52
      Supplementary Findings :  0

  TRIGGERS
      vapour(quantity,present)  and  temp_indicator(level,red)  relevance 0.6

  NECESSARY FINDINGS
      temp_indicator      level      red   1
      engine       status      on   1
      vapour       quantity      present   1
      oil_gauge       colour      yellow   0.52

  SUPPLEMENTARY FINDINGS
      no supplementary finding is present

  VALIDATION RULES
      no validation rule is activated
```

Figure 12.10 - Display of the instantiated frame "melting".

Let us start the analysis of the reasoning at the deep level by considering the problem of the confirmation of the hypothesis "burnout". As stated in chapter 8, the confirmation process is divided into two parts:

- analysis of the causes of the disorder corresponding to the diagnostic hypothesis;

- analysis of the consequences of the disorder corresponding to the diagnostic hypothesis.

In the network of figure 7.19 the hypothesis "burnout" is defined as "very_high intensity of the engine temperature", i.e. as the presence of the state "engine_temp" whose linguistic value for the attribute "intensity" is "very_high".

The first step to establish the presence of the state "engine_temp" is to search backwards for its INITIAL CAUSES, from which forward reasoning to instantiate the network must be started. Since in the two states "oil_lack" and "oil consumption", the causing states are ORed, it is sufficient, in order to confirm the presence of "engine_temp" to find and instantiate a path from any one of the INITIAL CAUSE nodes.

Let us suppose that during the backward search the initial cause "piston_rings_used" is encountered first. Since the presence of such an initial perturbation in unknown to the system, the system asks the user whether the piston rings of the car under examination are used-up or not (we will assume, throughout the example, that information about initial_causes can be requested from the user; otherwise the system should make assumptions about such pieces of information). Let us assume that the answer of the user is the following (the same menu-oriented graphical interface is used both at the heuristic and at the deep level to put questions to the user):

piston_rings_used(intensity,low)

The initial cause node can be instantiated, but, since the condition on the causal arc exiting from the node is not satisfied, the initial perturbation "piston_rings_used(intensity,low)" has no influence in the specific case we are considering.

The next initial cause node encountered in the backward search process is the node "pistons". From the data acquired at the heuristic level it is already known to the system that the "wear_state" of the pistons of the car we are considering is "high", so the initial cause can be instantiated in the following way:

pistons(wear_state,high)

Given such an instantiation for the initial cause "pistons", we have that the condition on the causal arc exiting from the node is satisfied. However, such a causal transition is a MAY one, in the sense that some important condition (or process) has been abstracted in the model. An assumption "α" (see section 8.2.2) is introduced by the system to represent the abstracted condition and a new hypothetical world in which the assumption "α" is assumed to hold is created. In such a world the presence of the state "piston_problems" can be deduced. More specifically, given the functional transformation scheme associated with the action "wearing_out", the following instantiation can be determined for the state "piston_problems" (see figure 9.7 for a linguistic description of the causal network and of the functional transformation schemes to set the attributes of the nodes in the network):

piston_problems(severity,high)

Given the presence of the state "piston_problems", the presence of the findings "power_decrease" and "engine_noise" can be predicted. More specifically, considering the instantiation of the state "piston_problems" and the rules of compatibility between the values of the attributes of a state and that of its manifestations, the following prediction is made by the system:

power_decrease(intensity,high)
engine_noise(intensity,high)

Since in the particular case under examination no information about such findings is known to the system, the system asks the user about their presence (without mentioning the predicted values for the findings themselves). If we assume that the answer of the user coincides with the prediction of the system, the presence of the instantiated state "piston_problems(severity,high)" can be confirmed. This has the important consequence that the hypothetical world in which we are reasoning (and the assumption "α") can then be confirmed. In fact, using the non-monotonic "uniqueness of paths" assumption, the presence of the state "piston problems" can be confirmed at first (in fact the "uniqueness of paths" assumption can be used in this case to assert, non monotonically, that the only state which has "power decrease" as a manifestation is the state "piston problems", so the presence of the state can be deduced from the presence of the finding).

As long as reasoning is performed and the nodes are instantiated, the causal network is displayed by the system ("trace" modality of the causal level explanation interface, see chapter 9). For example, the status of the screen after the state "piston_problems has been instantiated is reported in figure 12.11.

Given the instantiation of the state "piston_problems" and the functional transformation scheme associated with the action "oil_passing", the state "oil_consumpt" is instantiated in the following way:

oil_consumpt(intensity,high)

and the following manifestation is predicted:

stack_smoke(colour,black)

Since such a finding is already known to the system (set (2) of findings), the presence of the instantiated state "oil_consumpt(intensity,high)" is confirmed. In a similar way, since the condition associated with the causal arc exiting from the state "oil_consumpt" is satisfied, the state "oil_lack" can be instantiated in the following way:

oil_lack(severity,medium)

moreover, since the predicted finding

oil_gauge(colour,yellow)

is observed in the specific case under examination, the instantiated state "oil_lack(severity,medium)" is confirmed.

In order to instantiate the state "engine_temp", the presence of the state "oil_lack" is not sufficient since the causal arcs entering the node "engine_temp" are ANDed. A backward search is started which leads the system to the analysis of the initial_cause "inserted_key". Since again no information about such an initial cause is known to the system, a new question is put to the user. Let us suppose that the answer of the user is the following:

inserted_key(presence,yes)

the state "engine_started" can be deduced (in a hypothetical way) and, due to the presence of the predicted manifestation

engine(status,on)

it can be confirmed.

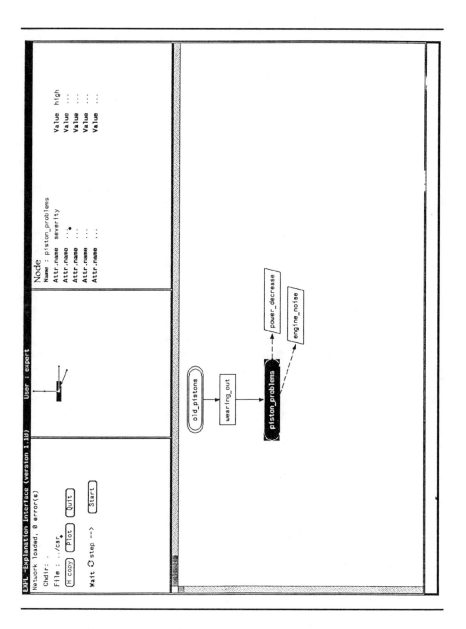

Figure 12.11 - Display of an instantiated portion of causal network. The last node instantiated (or confirmed) by the system is displayed in a reverse way.

The simultaneous presence of the states "oil_lack" and "engine_started" allows the system to deduce the presence of the state "engine_temp", which is instantiated in the following way:

    engine_temp(intensity,high)

Given such an instantiation of the state "engine_temp", the presence of the finding:

    temp_indicator(level,red)

is predicted and since such a predicted value coincides with the observed one, the instantiated state "engine_temp(intensity,high)" can be confirmed.

At this point the loop originating and leading to the state "engine_temp" is considered. The effect of the traversal of the loop (action "cont_to_work") is that the value of the attribute intensity of the state "engine_temp" is increased in the following way:

    engine_temp(intensity,very_high)

This completes the analysis of the causes of the state "engine_temp" which defines the diagnostic hypothesis "burnout". The next step performed by the system is to analyze the consequences of the state "engine_temp". Since the causal arcs entering the state "incr_coolant_temp" are ANDed, the presence of the initial cause "ext_temperature" has to be established in order to instantiate the state "incr_coolant_temp". It is already known to the system that in the case under examination the external temperature is normal (set (5) of data):

    ext_temperature(value,normal)

This allows the system to instantiate the state "incr_coolant_temp"

    incr_coolant_temp(intensity,high)

and to predict the presence of the finding

    vapour(quantity,present)

which has been observed in the specific case under examination. The state "incr_coolant_temp" can be confirmed and, since the condition on the causal arc exiting from the state itself is not satisfied, the analysis of the consequences of the state "engine_temp" is terminated.

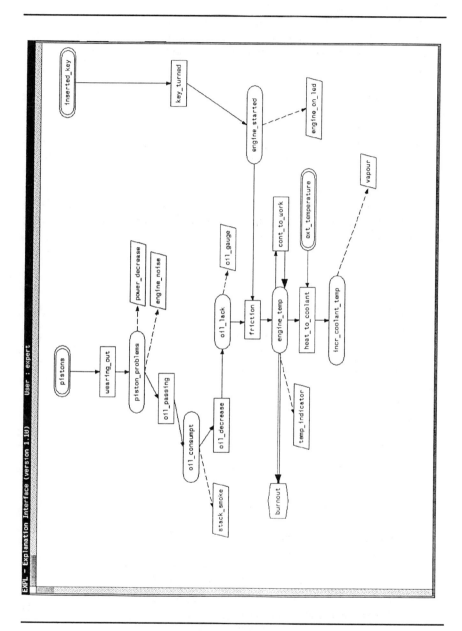

Figure 12.12 - Explanation generated by the system to confirm the hypothesis "burnout".

The causal path which has been instantiated accounts for all the findings observed in the specific case under examination, so the hypothesis "burnout" can be confirmed. The instantiated causal path is proposed to the user as the final explanation of the confirmation of the hypothesis "burnout" (see figure 12.12).

It is worth noting that the same reasoning process can be used to reject the hypothesis "melting" in the specific case under examination. However, given a different set of data (i.e. in the analysis of a different case) the hypotheses "burnout" and "melting" could be diagnosed together as a multiple fault, since a causal path connects the two hypotheses.

An example of the reasoning process is reported in the following (figure 12.13). In particular, in this example we have given a description of how nodes are instantiated, i.e. of the specific values assumed by their attributes in the specific case under examination.

DATA KNOWN BEFORE THE ACTIVATION OF THE CAUSAL LEVEL :

engine(status,on)
engine_smoke(quantity,absent)
stack_smoke(colour,black)
pistons(wear_state,high)
ext_temperature(value,normal)
oil_gauge(colour,yellow)
temp_indicator(level,red)
vapour(quantity,present)

HYPOTHESIS_TO_BE_CONFIRMED: burnout

backward activation of: engine_temp
backward activation of: oil_lack
backward activation of: oil_consumpt
backward activation of: lubric_oil_in_piston
asked_to_user initial cause: piston_rings_used
verified initial cause: piston_rings_used
                    [[intensity,low]]
failed_condition action: piston_rings_leak
backward activation of: piston_problems

verified initial cause: pistons
                        [[wear_state, high]]
instantiated state: piston_problems
                        [[severity,high]]
predicted finding: power_decrease
                        [[intensity,high]]
asked_to_user finding power_decrease
observed finding: power_decrease
                        [[intensity,high]]
predicted finding: engine_noise
                        [[intensity,high]]
asked_to_user finding engine_noise
observed finding: engine_noise
                        [[intensity,high]]
confirmed: piston_problems
instantiated state: oil_consumpt
                        [[intensity,high]]
predicted finding: stack_smoke
                        [[colour,black]]
observed finding: stack_smoke
                        [[colour,black]]
confirmed: oil_consumpt
instantiated state: oil_lack
                        [[severity,medium]]
predicted finding: oil_gauge
                        [[colour,yellow]]
observed finding: oil_gauge
                        [[colour,yellow]]
confirmed: oil_lack
backward_activation of: engine_started
backward_activation of: inserted_key
asked_to_user initial_cause: inserted_key
verified initial cause: inserted_key
                        [[presence, yes]]
instantiated state: engine_started
                        [[status,working]]
predicted finding: engine
                        [[status,on]]
observed finding: engine
                        [[status,on]]
instantiated state: engine_temp
                        [[intensity,high]]
predicted finding: temp_indicator
                        [[level,red]]

```
observed finding:  temp_indicator
                         [ [level,red] ]
confirmed:  engine_temp
instantiated after loop state:  engine_temp
                         [ [intensity,very_high] ]
forward activation of:  incr_coolant_temp
backward_activation of: ext_temperature
verified initial cause: ext_temperature
                         [ [value, normal] ]
instantiated state:  incr_coolant_temp
                         [ [intensity,high] ]
predicted finding:  vapour
                         [ [quantity,present] ]
observed finding:  vapour
                         [ [quantity,present] ]
confirmed:  incr_coolant_temp

CONFIRMED HYPOTHESIS burnout
```

Figure 12.13 - Example of CHECK reasoning process.

12.2 CURRENT AND FUTURE WORKS

In this section we shall briefly overview the main research projects connected to the CHECK one on which we are currently working. More specifically, we shall analyze two main topics:

- extension of the causal reasoning formalism to represent temporal knowledge and introduction of a temporal reasoning component;

- automatic acquisition of heuristic knowledge from the causal one in the knowledge acquisition phase (knowledge compilation).

12.2.1 TEMPORAL REASONING

The notion of causality is strictly dependent on the notion of time, so a discussion about causality in which the notion of time is completely disregarded can be meaningless (see [Sosa 75] for a review of the recent philosophical works on causality and its correlation to the notion of time and [Shoham 87] for an Artificial Intelligence contribution to the field).

The need for the introduction of temporal information and a temporal reasoning component has been felt since the beginning of the CHECK project. It should be clear, in fact, that time plays a very important role in diagnostic reasoning. During the analysis of a specific case, each finding can be observed in a specific period of time: some findings are not observable at the time diagnosis is performed, but they might have been observable in the past or it may be the case that they will be observable in the future. In a timeless approach to diagnosis one has to project the time line onto a unique point: the moment when diagnosis is performed. Moreover, reasoning has to be performed with the implicit assumption that all the manifestations of a malfunction must be present at such a unique time, in order to confirm the malfunction as a solution of the diagnostic problem.

If one analyzes the literature about diagnostic problem solving, it becomes clear that the problem of temporal reasoning has not yet received the attention it deserves (among the few approaches to temporal reasoning within diagnostic problem solving, those proposed by Fagan [Fagan 80], Blum [Blum 82], Long [Long 83a] and Hamlet and Hunter [Hamlet & Hunter 87] are the most interesting ones).

In order to deal with the notion of time at the causal level of CHECK (we believe that dealing with time at the heuristic level is, generally, much more complicated and not helpful to our approach, since the heuristic level is used only as a focusing component), we have started to extend the causal modelling formalism described in chapter 7 and we have introduced a temporal reasoning component. The role of such a reasoning component is that of verifying the temporal consistency of a causal explanation.

More specifically, the causal modelling formalism has been augmented by the introduction of two different types of information (for detailed discussion, see [Console et al. 88b]):

-    a time interval representing the temporal extension of the node has been associated with each STATE, FINDING and INITIAL_CAUSE node;

-    with each CAUSAL and HAM arc is associated information about the temporal delay induced by the transition represented by the arc (e.g. in a CAUSAL arc the delay between the causing state and the caused one arising). Such a delay can be represented as an interval of admissible delays (that is we admit the presence of some fuzziness in the representation).

The temporal reasoning process we have designed to verify the temporal consistency of a causal explanation is based on the following idea: given the the temporal extension of the FINDING node observed in the specific case under examination (or at least of some of them), one can determine whether it is possible to associate a temporal extension with each node in the network in such a way that (1) the constraints imposed by the known temporal extensions and time delays are satisfied and (2) some general consistency rules (e.g. "causes must precede their effects", ..) are fulfilled. The reasoning scheme has been designed in such a way that it is able to deal with incomplete and imprecise temporal information. A complete discussion of the temporal reasoning component (formal definitions and properties) in the causal reasoning framework can be found in [Console et al. 88b].

The temporal reasoning scheme briefly outlined in this section (see [Console et al. 88b] for a complete description) has been implemented, but it has not yet been integrated into the CHECK system. Some aspects of the temporal reasoning components have to be studied further in order to integrate them with CHECK (in particular, the treatment of temporal relationships associated with loops in the causal model has to be studied). Moreover, such an integration requires some changes to the system to enable the causal and temporal reasoning components to co-operate in the solution of a problem. In particular, our idea is that the steps of causal and temporal reasoning must be interleaved: the temporal consistency of an instantiated causal path is verified as long as the path is built by the causal reasoning component.

12.2.2 KNOWLEDGE COMPILATION

We noticed in section 9.2 that one of the major weaknesses of multi-level architectures is the fact that multiple representations of the same domain have to be acquired from the domain expert. Not only is this a problem from the practical point of view (knowledge acquisition is one of the critical phases in the design of a knowledge based system) but also from the theoretical point of view, since consistency among the multiple knowledge levels must be guaranteed.

In order to solve such a problem, we are currently developing in the CHECK system a module for the automatic synthesis of the heuristic knowledge base from the causal knowledge base.

The approach we have used has been (partly) suggested by the recent achievements of "Explanation Based Learning" [Dejong & Mooney 86][Mitchell et al. 86]. However, the main feature of our approach is that we generate a heuristic description of a diagnostic hypothesis (an operational description in the terminology of EBL) from a causal model (domain theory in the terminology of EBL) without the use of examples.

The approach we use in the compilation process is to run a general simulation on a causal model using constraint propagation techniques. Such simulations can be used to detect inconsistencies in the model itself and to derive a heuristic model (if no inconsistencies are detected) during the Knowledge Acquisition phase. The knowledge compilation module is currently under development and will be integrated into the environment in the near future.

12.3 CONCLUSIONS

In this book we have analyzed and described a set of Artificial Intelligence techniques developed for diagnostic problem solving. In particular, we have described in detail CHECK, a two-level diagnostic architecture we have designed and implemented over the past few years.

The choices we have made in the design (and implementation) of the system have been discussed with the use of several examples. Much attention has been devoted to the description of the formalisms adopted to represent both heuristic and causal knowledge and to the description of the reasoning schemes adopted at the two levels of the system.

The choices made at the deep (causal) level deserve some final comment. We believe that an approach to representing deep (causal) knowledge such as the one we have adopted (as well as Patil's and Long's approaches to cite the most relevant ones) has some advantages over ontological approaches (that is, for example, "first principle" or "structure and function" approaches). Although causal models are not "as deep as" ontological representations, they seem to be more suitable to model complex physical and physiological domains and thus to build diagnostic architectures (and systems) able to operate on real-world domains and problems.

The final part of the monograph has been devoted to presenting how CHECK architecture has been implemented and how, given an application domain, a specific system can be obtained. Moreover, we have described some of the current research issues we are presently working on and which will be integrated in the CHECK environment in the near future.

REFERENCES

Adlassnig, K.P. (1982). "A survey on medical diagnosis and fuzzy subsets"; in (M.M.Gupta, E.Sanchez eds.): *Approximate Reasoning in Decision Analysis*, North Holland, 1982: 203-217.

Aikins, J.S. (1983). "Prototypical knowledge for expert systems"; *Artificial Intelligence*, 1983 (20): 163-210.

Ait-Kaci, H., Nasr, R. (1986). "LOGIN: A logic programming language with built-in inheritance"; *Journal of Logic Programming*, 1986 (3): 185-215.

Andreassen, S., Woldbye, M., Falk, B., Andersen, S. (1987). "MUNIN: A causal probabilistic network for interpretation of electromyographic findings"; in *Proc. 10th IJCAI*, Milano, 1987: 366-372.

Barnett, J.A. (1981). "Computational methods for a mathematical theory of evidence"; in *Proc. 7th IJCAI*, Vancouver, 1981: 837-842.

Bennet, J.S. (1985). "ROGET: A knowledge based consultant for acquiring the conceptual structure of a diagnostic expert system"; *Journal of Automated Reasoning*, 1985 (1): 49-74.

Blum, R.L. (1982). "Discovery and representation of causal relationships from a large time-oriented clinical data base", *Lecture Notes in Medical Informatics 19*, Springer Verlag 1982.

Bobrow, D. G. (ed) (1980). "Special issue on non-monotonic reasoning"; *Artificial Intelligence*, 1980 (13).

Bobrow, D. G. (ed) (1984). "Special issue on qualitative reasoning"; *Artificial Intelligence*, 1984 (24).

Bonissone, P.P., Johnson H.E. (1984). "Expert system for diesel electric locomotive repair"; in *Human & Systems Management*, 1984 (4): 255-

262.

Bonissone, P.P., Tong, R.M. (1985). "Editorial: reasoning with uncertainty in expert systems"; *Int. J. of Man-Machine Studies,* 1985 (22): 241-250.

Bowen, K. (1985). "Meta-level programming and knowledge representation"; *New Generation Computing,* 1985 (3): 359-383.

Buchanan, B.G., Shortliffe, E.H. (1984). *Rule-based Expert Systems; The MYCIN Experiments of the Stanford Heuristic Programming Project,* Addison Wesley, 1984.

Bylander, T., Mittal, S. (1986). "CSRL: A language for classification problem solving and uncertainty handling"; *The AI Magazine,* August 1986: 66-77.

Carbonell, J., Boggs, W.M., Mauldin, M.L., Anick, P.G. (1983). "The XCALIBUR project: a natural language interface to Expert Systems"; in *Proc. 8th IJCAI,* Karlsruhe, 1983: 653-656.

Chandrasekaran, B. (1983). "Towards a taxonomy of problem solving types"; *AI magazine,* 4 (1), 1983: 9-17.

Chandrasekaran, B. (1987). "Towards a functional architecture for intelligence based on generic information processing tasks"; in *Proc. 10th IJCAI,* Milano, 1987: 1183-1192.

Chandrasekaran, B., Milne, R. (eds) (1985). "Special section on reasoning about structure, behavior and function"; *Sigart Newsletter,* 1985 (93): 4-55.

Chandrasekaran, B., Mittal, S. (1983a). "Deep versus compiled knowledge approaches to diagnostic problem-solving"; *Int. J. of Man-Machine Studies,* 1983 (19): 425-436.

Chandrasekaran, B., Mittal, S. (1983b). "Conceptual representation of medical knowledge for diagnosis by computer: MDX and related systems"; in: (M.C.Yovits ed.) *Advances in Computers,* vol 22, Academic Press, 1983.

Charniak, E. (1983). "The Bayesian basis of common sense medical diagnosis"; in *Proc. AAAI 83,* Washington, 1983: 70-73.

Cheeseman, P. (1985). "In defense of probability"; in *Proc. 9th IJCAI,* Los Angeles, 1985: 1002-1009.

Clancey, W.J. (1983). "The advantage of abstract control knowledge in expert systems design"; in *Proc. AAAI 83,* Washington, 1983: 74-78.

Clancey, W.J. (1985). "Heuristic classification"; *Artificial Intelligence,* 1985 (25): 289-350.

Clancey W.J., Letsinger R. (1981). "NEOMYCIN: Reconfiguring a rule-based expert system for application to teaching"; in *Proc. 7th IJCAI,* Vancouver, 1981: 829-836.

Clancey, W.J., Shortliffe, E.H. (eds.) (1984). *Readings in Medical Artificial Intelligence: The First Decade*, Addison Wesley, 1984

Clark, K.L., McCabe, F.G. (1982). "PROLOG; A language for implementing expert systems"; in (J.E.Hayes and D.Michie eds.): *Machine Intelligence, 10*, 1982: 455-470.

Cohen, P.R. (1986). *Heuristic Reasoning About Uncertainty: An Artificial Intelligence Approach*, Pitman, 1986.

Console, L., Cravetto, C., Molino, G., Torasso, P. (1988a). "Generating causal explanations on simulated situations", in *Medical Informatics 88*, British Computer Society, 1988: 1-7.

Console, L., Fossa, M., Torasso, P. (1987a). "Knowledge acquisition via a graphical interface"; in (I. Plander ed.) *Artificial Intelligence and Information-Control Systems of Robots 87*, North Holland, 1987: 173-178.

Console, L., Fossa, M., Torasso, P., Molino, G, Cravetto, C. (1987b). "Man-machine interaction in CHECK"; in (J. Fox, M. Fieschi, R. Engelbrecht eds.) *AIME 87*, Lectures Notes in Medical Informatics 33, Springer Verlag, 1987: 205-212.

Console, L., Furno, A., Torasso, P. (1988b). "Dealing with time in diagnostic reasoning based on causal models"; in (Z. Ras, L. Saitta eds.) *Methodologies for Intelligent Systems 3*, North Holland, 1988: 230-239.

Console, L., Martelli, A., Rossi, G. (1986). "A technique for using Prolog in the implementation of Expert Systems"; (in Italian) in *Proc. 1st. Nat. Conf. on Logic Programming*, Genova, 1986: 160-166.

Console, L., Rossi, G. (1986). "Implementing inference strategies in Prolog based Expert Systems"; in (R.Trappl ed.): *Cybernetics and Systems 86*, Reidel Publ. Co., 1986: 767-774.

Console, L., Rossi, G. (1987). "FROG: A Prolog-based system for Prolog-based knowledge representation"; in (I. Plander ed.) *Artificial Intelligence and Information-Control Systems of Robots 87*, North Holland, 1987: 179-184.

Console, L., Rossi, G. (1988). "Using Prolog for building FROG, a hybrid knowledge representation system"; to appear in *New Generation Computing*, 1988.

Console, L., Torasso, P. (1988c). "Heuristic and causal reasoning in medical diagnosis"; in *Proc. AAAI Symposium on Artificial Intelligence in Medicine*, Stanford, 1988: 16-17.

Console, L., Torasso, P. (1988d). "A logical approach to deal with incomplete causal models in diagnostic problem solving"; in (B.Bouchon, L.Saitta, R.Yager eds.) *Uncertainty and Intelligent Systems*, Lecture

Notes in Computer Science 313, Springer Verlag, 1988: 255-264.

Console, L., Torasso, P. (1988e). "A multi-level architecture for diagnostic problem solving"; in (A.Martelli, G. Valle eds.) *Computational Intelligence 88*, North Holland, 1988: 97-108.

Console, L., Torasso, P. (1989). "Hypothetical reasoning in causal models"; to appear in *Int. Journal of Intelligent Systems*, 1989.

Cramp, D.G., Carson, E.R., Leaning, M.S. (1985). "Some design features for a user-friendly computer-aided decision support system incorporating mathematical models"; in (I.De Lotto, M.Stefanelli eds.): *Artificial Intelligence in Medicine*, North-Holland, 1985: 11-20.

Cravetto, C., Lesmo, L., Molino, G., Torasso, P. (1985a). "LITO2: A frame based expert system for medical diagnosis in hepatology"; in (I.De Lotto M.Stefanelli eds.): *Artificial Intelligence in Medicine*, North-Holland, 1985: 107-119.

Cravetto, C., Lesmo, L., Massa Rolandino, R., Molino, G., Torasso, P.: (1985b). "An expert system for liver disease diagnosis (LITO2)"; in *Proc. 9th Annual Symp. on Computer Applications in Medical Care*, Baltimore, 1985, 330-334.

Davis, R. (1979). "Interactive transfer of expertise: acquisition of new inference rules"; *Artificial Intelligence*, 1979 (12): 121-158.

Davis, R. (1983). "Reasoning from first principles in electronic troubleshooting";in *Int. J. of Man-Machine Studies*, 1983 (19): 403-424.

Davis, R. (1984). "Diagnostic reasoning based on structure and behavior"; *Artificial Intelligence*, 1984 (24): 347-410.

Davis, R., King, J.J. (1977). "An overview of production systems"; in (E.Elcock, D. Michie eds.): *Machine Intelligence 8*, Horwood, 1977.

Dejong, G., Mooney R. (1986). "Explanation-based learning: An alternative view", in *Machine Learning*, 1986 (1): 145-176.

de Kleer, J. (1986). "An assumption-based TMS"; *Artificial Intelligence*, 1986 (28): 127-162.

de Kleer, J., Brown, J.S. (1984). "A qualitative physics based on confluences"; *Artificial Intelligence*, 1984 (24): 7-83.

de Kleer, J., Brown, J.S. (1986). "Theories of causal ordering"; *Artificial Intelligence*, 1986 (29): 33-61.

de Kleer, J., Williams, B.C. (1987). "Diagnosing multiple faults"; *Artificial Intelligence*, 1987 (32): 97-130.

Doyle, R. (1979). "A truth maintenance system"; *Artificial Intelligence*, 1979 (12): 231-272.

Duda, R.O. (1980). "The PROSPECTOR system for mineral exploration", Final Rep. SRI Project 8172, SRI Int., 1980.

Duda, R.O., Hart, P.E., Nilsson, N. (1976). "Subjective Bayesian methods for rule-based inference systems", *Proc. AFIPS 47*, 1976: 1075-1082.

Engelman, C., Stanton , W. (1984). "An integrated frame-rule architecture"; in (A. Elithorn, R. Banerji eds.): *Artificial and Human Intelligence*, North Holland 1984.

Erman, L., Hayes-Roth, F., Lesser, V., Reddy, D.R. (1980). "The HEARSAY II speech understanding system: integrating knowledge to resolve uncertainty"; *ACM Computing Surveys,* 1980 (12): 2-56.

Fagan, L. (1980): "VM: representing time-dependent relations in a medical setting", Ph.D. Thesis, Dept. of Computer Science, Stanford University 1980.

Fagan, L., Differding, J., Langlotz, C., Tu, S. (1985). "Knowledge acquisition and strategic therapy planning for cancer clinical trials"; in (I.De Lotto and M.Stefanelli eds.): *Artificial Intelligence in Medicine*, North-Holland, 1985: 75-81.

Fikes, R., Kehler, T. (1985). "The role of frame-based representation in reasoning"; *Communication of the ACM*, 1985 (28,9): 904-920.

Fink, P., Lusth, J., Duran, J. (1985). "A general expert system design for diagnostic problem solving"; *IEEE Trans. on Pattern Analysis and Machine Intelligence*, 1985 (PAMI-7): 553-560.

Forbus, K. (1984). "Qualitative process theory"; *Artificial Intelligence*, 1984 (24): 85-168.

Furukawa, K., Takeuchi, A., Kunifuji, S., Yasukawa, H., Ohki, M., Ueda, K. (1984). "MANDALA: a logic based knowledge programming system"; in *Proc. of the Int. Conf. on Fifth Generation Computer Systems*, Tokyo 1984: 613-622.

Gabbay, D.M., Reyle, U. (1985). "N-PROLOG: an extension of Prolog with hypothetical implications"; *Journal of Logic Programming*, 1985 (1): 319-355.

Geffner, H., Pearl, J. (1987). "A distributed approach to diagnosis"; in *Proc. Third IEEE Conference on Application of Artificial Intelligence*, Orlando, 1987: 156-162.

Genesereth, M.R. (1984). "The use of design descriptions in automated diagnosis"; *Artificial Intelligence*, 1984 (24): 411-436.

Genesereth, M.R., Nilsson, N.J. (1987). *Logical foundations of artificial intelligence;* Morgan Kaufmann, 1987.

Ginsberg, M. (1986). "Counterfactuals"; *Artificial Intelligence,* 1986 (30):

35-79.

Glymour, C. (1985). "Independence assumption and Bayesian updating"; *Artificial Intelligence,* 1985 (25): 95-99.

Goldberg, A., Robson, D. (1983). *SMALLTALK-80: The Language and its Implementation",* Addison-Wesley, 1983.

Gordon, J., Shortliffe, E.H. (1985). "A method for managing evidential reasoning in a hierarchical hypothesis space", *Artificial Intelligence,* 1985 (25): 323-357.

Gorry, G.A., Barnett, G.O. (1968). "Sequential diagnosis by computer"; *JAMA,* 1968 (205,12): 141-146.

Greco, G., Rocha, A.F. (1987). "The fuzzy logic of text understanding"; *Fuzzy Sets and Systems,* 1987 (23,2): 347-360.

Halpern, J., Rabin, M. (1987). "A logic to reason about likelihood"; *Artificial Intelligence,* 1987 (32): 379-405.

Hamlet, I., Hunter, J.: "Representation of time for medical expert systems", in (J. Fox, M. Fieschi, R. Engelbrecht eds.) *AIME 87,* Lectures Notes in Medical Informatics 33, Springer Verlag, 1987: 112-119.

Hart, P.E. (1982). "Directions for AI in the eighties"; *Sigart Newsletter,* 1982 (79).

Hayes, P. (1979). "The naive physics manifesto"; in (D. Michie ed.) *Expert Systems in the Micro-Electronic Age,* Edinburgh University Press, 1979: 242-270.

Hayes, P. (1984). "Entity oriented parsing"; in *Proc. of COLING 84,* Stanford, 1984: 212-217.

Hayes-Roth, F., Waterman, D, Lenat, D. (1984). *Building Expert Systems,* Addison-Wesley, 1984.

Horn, W., Trappl, R., Ulrich, D., Chroust, G. (1984). "A frame-based real-time graphic interaction system"; in (R. Trappl ed.) *Cybernetics and System Research 2,* North Holland, 1984: 825-830.

Hunt, E. (1975). *Artificial Intelligence,* Academic Press, 1975.

Ishizuka, M., Kanai, N. (1985). "Prolog-ELF incorporating fuzzy logic"; *New Generation Computing,* 1985 (3): 479-486.

Iwasaki, Y., Simon, H.A. (1986). "Causality in device behavior"; *Artificial Intelligence,* 1986 (29): 3-32.

Johnson, L., Keravnou, E.T. (1985). *Expert systems technology: A guide,* ABACUS Press, 1985.

Josephson, J., Chandrasekaran, B., Smith, J., Tanner, M. (1987). "A mechanism for forming composite explanatory hypotheses"; *IEEE Trans. on*

Systems, Man and Cybernetics, 1987 (SMC-17): 445-454.

Kahn, G. (1984). "On when diagnostic systems want to do without causal knowledge"; in *Proc. ECAI 84,* Pisa, 1984:21-30.

Kahn, G., Nowlan, S. McDermott, J. (1985). "Strategies for knowledge acquisition"; *IEEE Trans. on Pattern Analysis and Machine Intelligence,* 1985 (PAMI-7): 511-522.

Kassirer, J.P., Gorry, G. (1978). "Clinical problem solving: a behavioral analysis"; *Annals of Internal Medicine,* 1978 (89): 245-255.

Kohout, L.J., Bandler, W. (1986). *Knowledge Representation in Medicine and Clinical Behavioral Science,* ABACUS Press, 1986.

Kolodner, J., Kolodner, R. (1987). "Using experience in clinical problem solving: introduction and framework"; *IEEE Trans. on Systems Man and Cybernetics,* 1987 (SMC-17): 420-430.

Koton, P. (1988). "Integrating causal and case-based reasoning for clinical problem solving"; in *Proc. AAAI Symposium on Artificial Intelligence in Medicine,* Stanford, 1988: 53-54.

Kripke, S. (1959). "A completeness theorem in modal logic"; *Journal of Symbolic Logic,* 1959 (24): 1-14.

Kuipers, B. (1984). "Commonsense reasoning about causality: deriving behavior from structure"; *Artificial Intelligence,* 1984 (24):169-204.

Kuipers, B., Kassirer, J. (1984). "Causal reasoning in medicine: analysis of a protocol"; *Cognitive Science,* 1984 (8): 363-385.

Kunz, J. (1984). "Analysis of physiological behavior using a causal model based on first principles"; in *Proc. AAAI 84,* Austin, 1984: 225-229.

Langlotz, C.P., Shortliffe, E.H. (1983). "Adapting a consultation system to critique user plans"; *Int. J. of Man machine Studies,* 1983 (19): 479-496.

Langlotz, C.P., Shortliffe, E.H., and Fagan, L.M. (1986). "Using decision theory to justify heuristics"; in *Proc. AAAI 86,* Philadelphia, 1986: 215-219.

Lau, J., Pauker, S.G. (1985). "Decision analysis using extended methods"; in *Proc. 9th Annual Symp. on Computer Applications in Medical Care,* Baltimore, 1985: 193-197.

Lesmo, L., Marzuoli, M., Molino, G., Torasso, P. (1984c). "An expert system for the evaluation of liver functional assessment"; *Journal of Medical Systems,* 1984 (8):87-101.

Lesmo, L., Saitta, L., Torasso, P. (1980). "Computer aided evaluation of liver functional assessment"; in *Proc. 4th Annual Symp. on Computer Applications in Medical Care,* Washington, 1980: 181-189.

Lesmo, L., Saitta, L., Torasso, P. (1984a). "An approximate reasoning framework for expert systems"; in *Proc. 6th Int. Cong. of Cybernetics and Systems*, Paris, 1984: 169-174.

Lesmo, L., Saitta, L., Torasso, P. (1984b). "An interpreter of fuzzy production rules"; in (R.Trappl ed.): *Cybernetics and Systems Research 2*, North-Holland, 1984: 793-798.

Lesmo, L., Saitta, L., Torasso, P. (1985). "Evidence combination in expert systems"; *Int. J. of Man-Machine Studies*, 1985 (22): 307-326.

Lesmo, L., Torasso, P. (1987). "Prototypical knowledge for interpreting fuzzy concepts and quantifiers"; *Fuzzy Sets and Systems*, 1987 (23,2): 361-370.

Long, W. (1983a). "Reasoning about state from causation and time in a medical domain". *Proc. AAAI 83*, Washington, 1983: 251-254.

Long, W. (1983b). "A program for the management of heart failure"; Techn. Report NEMCH, MIT; June 1983.

Long, W., Naimi, S., Criscitiello, M.D. (1987). "The development and use of causal models for reasoning about hearth failure"; in *Proc. 11th Annual Symp. on Computer Applications in Medical Care*, Washington, 1987.

McCarthy, J. (1980). "Circumscription: a form of non-monotonic reasoning"; *Artificial Intelligence*, 1980 (13): 27-39.

McCarthy, J. (1986). "Application of circumscription to formalizing common-sense knowledge"; *Artificial Intelligence*, 1986 (28): 89-118.

McDermott, D., Doyle, J. (1980). "Non-monotonic logic I"; *Artificial Intelligence*, 1980 (13): 41-72.

McDermott, D. (1982). "Non-monotonic logic II: non-monotonic modal theories"; *Journal of the ACM*, 1982 (29): 33-57.

Milanese, M, Molino, G., Torasso, P. (1985). "The Torino Liver Project"; in (D.D. Tsiftsis ed.) *Objective Medical Decision Making*, Lectures Notes in Medical Informatics 28, Springer Verlag, 1985: 94-102.

Miller R.A., Pople H.E., Myers J.D. (1982). "INTERNIST-1, an experimental computer-based diagnostic consultant for general internal medicine"; *New England Journal of Medicine*, 1982 (307): 468-476.

Milne, R. (1985). "Fault diagnosis through responsibility"; in *Proc. 9th IJCAI*, Los Angeles, 1985: 425-431.

Minsky, M. (1975). "A framework for representing knowledge"; in (P. Winston ed.) *The Psychology of Computer Vision*, McGraw Hill, 1975.

Mitchell, T., Keller, R., Kedar-Cabelli, S. (1986). "Explanation-based learning: A unifying view"; *Machine Learning*, 1986 (1): 47-80.

Mittal, S., Chandrasekaran, B., Sticklen, J. (1984). "Patrec: A knowledge-directed database for a diagnostic expert system"; *IEEE Computer,* 1984 (16,9): 51-58.

Molino, G.,Cravetto, C., Torasso, P., Console, L. (1986). "CHECK: a diagnostic expert system Combining HEuristic and Causal Knowledge"; *Int. J. of Biomedical Measurement, Informatics and Control,* 1986 (1,4): 182-193.

Moore, R.C. (1985). "Semantical considerations on nonmonotonic logic"; *Artificial Intelligence,* 1985 (25):75-94.

Negoita, C. (1985). *Expert Systems and Fuzzy Systems;* The Benjamin/Cummings Publ. Co., 1985.

Newell, A. (1982). "The knowledge level"; *Artificial Intelligence,* 1982 (18): 87-127.

Newell, A., Shaw, J., Simon, H. (1959). "Report on a general problem solving program"; in *Proc. Int. Conf. on Information Processing,* Paris, 1959: 256-264.

Nilsson, N.J. (1971). *Problem Solving Methods in Artificial Intelligence,* McGraw Hill, 1971.

Nilsson, N.J. (1986). "Probabilistic logic"; *Artificial Intelligence,* 1986 (28): 71-87.

Ogawa, Y., Shima, K., Sugawara, T. and Takagi, S. (1984). "Knowledge representation and inference environment: KRINE, an approach to integration of frame, Prolog and graphics"; in *Proc. of the Int. Conf. on Fifth Generation Computer Systems,* Tokyo, 1984: 643-651.

Partridge, D. (1987). "The scope and limitations of first generation expert systems"; *Future Generation Computing Systems,* 1987 (3): 1-10.

Patil, R. (1981). "Causal representation of patient illness for electrolyte and acid-base diagnosis". Cambridge: MIT, 1981. MIT/LCS/TR-267

Pauker, S.G., Gorry, G.A., Kassirer, J.P., Schwartz, W.B. (1976). "Toward the simulation of clinical cognition: taking a present illness by computer"; *The American Journal of Medicine,* 1976 (60): 981-995.

Pazzani, M. (1987). "Explanation-based learning for knowledge-based systems"; *Int. J. of Man Machine Studies,* 1987 (26): 413-433.

Pearl, J. (1986). "On evidential reasoning in a hierarchy of hypotheses"; *Artificial Intelligence,* 1986 (28): 9-15.

Pearl, J. (1987). "Distributed revision of composite beliefs"; *Artificial Intelligence,* 1987 (33): 173-215.

Peng, Y, Reggia, J. (1987). "A probabilistic causal model for diagnostic problem solving - Part I: Integrating symbolic causal inference with numeric probabilistic inference"; *IEEE Trans. on Systems Man and*

Cybernetics, 1987 (SMC-17): 146-162.

Prade, H. (1985). "A computational approach to approximate and plausible reasoning with applications to expert systems"; *IEEE Trans. on Pattern Analysis and Machine Intelligence,* 1985 (PAMI-7): 260-283.

Reggia, J.A., Nau, D.S., Wang, P.Y. (1983). "Diagnostic expert systems based on a set covering model; *Int. J. of Man Machine Studies,* 1983 (19): 437-460.

Reiter, R. (1980). "A Logic for default reasoning"; *Artificial Intelligence,* 1980 (13): 81-132.

Reiter, R. (1987). "A Theory of diagnosis from first principles"; *Artificial Intelligence,* 1987 (32):57-96.

Rescher, N. (1964). *Hypothetical Reasoning,* North Holland 1964.

Richer, M.H., Clancey, W.J. (1985). "GUIDON-WATCH: A graphic interface for viewing a knowledge-based system"; *IEEE Computer Graphics,* 1985 (5,11): 51-64.

Robinson, J (1965). "A machine oriented logic based on the resolution principle"; *Journal of the ACM,* 1965 (12): 23-41.

Rollinger, C.H. (1983). "How to represent evidence - aspects of uncertain reasoning"; in *Proc. 8th IJCAI* Karlsruhe, 1983: 358-361.

Rossi, G. (1986). "Uses of Prolog in the implementation of expert systems"; *New Generation Computing,* 1986 (4): 321-330.

Ruspini, H. (1987). "Epistemic logics, probabilities and the calculus of evidence"; in *Proc. 10th IJCAI,* Milano, 1987: 924-931.

Safra S., Shapiro, E. (1986). "Meta interpreters for real"; in *Proc. IFIP-86 Congress,* Dublin, 1986: 271-278.

Saitta, L., Torasso, P. (1981). "Fuzzy characterization of coronary disease"; *Fuzzy Sets and Systems,* 1981 (5): 245-258.

Sanchez, E. (1987): "Soft queries in knowledge systems"; in *Proc. Second IFSA congress,* Tokyo, July 1987: 597-599.

Sembugamoorthy, V., Chandrasekaran, B., (1986): "Functional representation of devices and compilation of diagnostic problem solving systems"; in (J.Kolodner, C.Riesbeck eds.): *Experience, Memory and Reasoning,* Lawrence Erlbaum, 1986.

Shafer, G. (1976). *A Mathematical Theory of Evidence,* Princeton Univ. Press, 1976.

Shoen, E., Smith, R.G. (1983). "A display oriented editor for STROBE"; in *Proc. AAAI 83,* Washington, 1983: 356-358.

Shoham, Y. (1987). *Reasoning about Change: Time and Causation from the*

Standpoint of Artificial Intelligence, MIT Press, 1987.

Shortliffe, E.H. (1976). *Computer-Based Medical Consultation: MYCIN*, Elsevier, 1976.

Shortliffe, E.H., Buchanan, B.G. (1975). "A model of inexact reasoning"; *Mathematical Biosciences*, 1975 (23): 351-379.

Simmons, R. (1986). "Commonsense arithmetic reasoning"; in *Proc. AAAI 86*, Philadelphia, 1986: 118-124.

Sosa, E. (1975). "*Causation and Conditionals*", Oxford University Press 1975.

Spiegelhalter, D.J., Knill-Jones, R.P. (1984). "Statistical and knowledge-based approaches to clinical decision-support systems, with an application in gastroenterology"; *J. Royal Statistical Soc*, A 147, Part 1, 1984: 35-77.

Steels, L. (1985). "Second generation expert systems"; *Future Generation Computing Systems*, 1985 (1): 213-221.

Steels L., Van de Velde W. (1985). "Learning in second generation expert systems"; in (R.Kowalik ed.): *Knowledge-based Problem Solving*, Prentice Hall, 1985.

Stefik, M., Aikins, J., Balzer, R., Benoit, J., Birnbaum, L., Hayes-Roth, F., Sacerdoti, E. (1982). "The organization of expert systems, a tutorial"; *Artificial Intelligence*, 1982 (18): 135-173.

Stefik, M., Bobrow, D.G. (1986). "Object-oriented programming: Themes and variations"; *The AI magazine*, Winter 1986: 40-62.

Sterling, L. (1984). "Expert systems = knowledge + meta-interpreter"; Tech. Rept. CS84-17, Weizmann Institute, Tel Aviv, 1984.

Sticklen, J., Chandrasekaran, B., Josephson, J. (1985). "Control issues in classificatory diagnosis"; in *Proc. 9th IJCAI*, Los Angeles, 1985: 300-306.

Sticklen, J., Chandrasekaran, B. (1988). "MDX2: An integrated medical diagnostic system"; in *Proc. AAAI Symposium on Artificial Intelligence in Medicine*, Stanford, 1988: 90-95.

Sussman, G.J., Steele, G.L. (1980). "CONSTRAINTS - A language for expressing almost-hierarchical descriptions"; *Artificial Intelligence*, 1980 (14): 1-39.

Szolovits, P., Pauker, S.G. (1978). "Categorical and probabilistic reasoning in medical diagnosis"; *Artificial Intelligence*, 1978 (11): 115-144.

Szolovits, P. (ed.) (1982). *Artificial Intelligence in Medicine*, Westview Press, 1982.

Szolovits, P. (1985). "Types of knowledge as bases for reasoning in medical

AI programs"; in *Proc. Int. Conf. on Artificial Intelligence in Medicine*, Pavia, 1985.

Takeuchi A. and Furukawa K. (1986). "Partial evaluation of Prolog programs and its application to meta programming"; in *Proc. IFIP-86 Congress*, Dublin, 1986: 415-420.

Thompson, T.F., Clancey, W.J. (1986). "A qualitative modeling shell for process diagnosis"; *IEEE Computer*, 1986 (3): 6-15.

Tokoro, M. and Ishikawa, Y. (1986). "Orient84/K: A language within multiple paradigms in the object framework"; in *Proc. of the 19th. Annual Hawaii Int. Conf. on System Science*, 1986 :198-207.

Torasso, P. (1985). "Knowledge based expert systems for medical diagnosis"; *Statistics in Medicine*, 1985 (4): 317-325.

Torasso, P., Console, L. (1987). "Causal reasoning in diagnostic expert systems"; in *Proc. V Int. Conf. on Applications of Artificial Intelligence*, Orlando, 1987: 598-605.

Torasso, P., Console, L. (1989). "Approximate reasoning and prototypical knowledge"; to appear in *International Journal of Approximate Reasoning*, January 1989; a preliminary version appeared in *Proc. Second IFSA Congress*, Tokyo, 1987: 686-689.

Van de Velde, W. (1985). "Naive causal reasoning for diagnosis"; in *Proc. Int. Conf. on Expert Systems and their Application*, Avignon, 1985.

Van de Velde, W. (1986). "Explainable knowledge production"; in *Proc. ECAI 1986*, Brighton, 1986: 8-21.

van Emden, M.H., Kowalski, R.A. (1976). "The semantics of predicate logic as a programming language"; in *Journal of the ACM*, 1976 (23): 733-742.

Van Melle, W. (1979). "A domain independent production rule system for consultation program"; in *Proc. 6th IJCAI*, Tokyo 1979: 923-925.

Warren, D.S. (1984). "Database updates in pure Prolog"; in *Proc. Int. Conf. on Fifth Generation Computer Systems*, Tokyo, 1984: 244-253.

Weber, S. (1983). "A general concept of fuzzy connectives negations and implications based on t-norms and t-conorms"; *Fuzzy Sets and Systems*, 1983 (11): 115-134.

Weiss, S., Kulikowski, C., Amarel, S., Safir, A. (1978). "A model based method for computer-aided medical decision making"; *Artificial Intelligence*, 1978 (11): 145-172.

Weld, D.S. (1986). "The use of aggregation in causal simulation"; *Artificial Intelligence*, 1986 (30): 1-34.

Wielinga, B.J., Breuker, J.A. (1984). "Interpretation of verbal data for knowledge acquisition"; in *Proc. ECAI 84,* Pisa, 1984: 41-50.

Wielinga, B.J., Breuker, J.A. (1986). "Models of expertise"; in *Proc. ECAI 86,* Brighton, 1986: 306-318.

Yager, R.R. (1983). "Quantified propositions in a linguistic logic"; *Int. J. of Man-Machine Studies,* 1983 (19): 195-227.

Yager, R.R. (1987). "Using approximate reasoning to represent default knowledge"; *Artificial Intelligence,* 1987 (31): 99-112.

Zadeh, L.A. (1978). "Fuzzy sets as a basis for a theory of possibility", *Fuzzy Sets and Systems,* 1978 (1): 3-28.

Zadeh, L.A. (1983). "The role of fuzzy logic in the management of uncertainty in expert systems"; *Fuzzy Sets and Systems,* 1983 (11): 199-227.

Zadeh, L.A. (1986). "A simple view of the Depster-Shafer theory of evidence and its implication for the rule of combination"; *The AI Magazine,* 1986 (7,2): 85-90.

Zaniolo, C. (1984): "Object oriented programming in Prolog"; in *Proc. Int. Symposium on Logic Programming,* 1984: 265-271.

INDEX